Atlas of Military History

Collins

Atlas of Military History

Collins

An Imprint of HarperCollinsPublishers

ISBN-10: 0-00-716639-7
ISBN-13: 978-0-00-716639-8

ISBN-10: 0-06-084997-5 (in the United States)
ISBN-13: 978-0-06-084997-9
FIRST U.S. EDITION Published in 2006

Edited and designed by D & N Publishing, Marlborough, Wiltshire

Editorial Direction: Philip Parker, David Goodfellow, Fiona Hobbins
Cartographic and Design Direction: Martin Brown
Editing: Donald Sommerville
Design: Shane O'Dwyer
Index: Chris Howes

Picture credits
Front cover and page 3 Christopher F. Foss; **8–9** 1990, Photo Scala, Florence – courtesy of the Ministero Beni e Att. Culturali; **30–31** and **44–45** Ancient Art & Architecture Collection Ltd, London; **58–59** akg-images; **72–73** akg-images/Erich Lessing; **88–89** Getty Images/Hulton Archive; **106–107** Getty Images/Hulton Archive; **126–127** Yevgeny Khaldei/CORBIS; **158–159** Hulton- Deutsch Collection/CORBIS

10 09 08 07 06
9 8 7 6 5 4 3 2 1

Printed and bound in Italy by LEGO, Vicenza

The Collins Atlas of Military History takes an entirely new look at the history of warfare through the ages. It takes as its starting points the visual representation of major battles, campaigns, and wars through maps. Covering the entire span of military history, from the earliest recorded battles in the ancient Near East to the recent conflicts in Afghanistan and Iraq, the present volume's scope is vast, but its fundamental premise is very simple. By actually seeing the routes of the Roman legionaries laid down just as they would be in a modern atlas or tracing lines portraying the Soviet offensive on Berlin in 1945, it is relatively simple to understand in graphic form what would otherwise take ten thousand words to describe.

The story of how warfare developed from the chariots of the ancient world to the smart weaponry of the 21st century is a complex one. It is not the intention of this book to cover each and every war and battle in detail. Instead, campaigns and conflicts that exemplify major developments in tactics and the waging of war have been chosen. The text focuses on great military leaders such as Alexander the Great of Macedonia, Frederick the Great of Prussia, Napoleon, and Zhukov, on the tactics they evolved, and on the changes in technology that have shaped the face of warfare through the ages.

A wide historical perspective is vital to understanding the roots of conflicts in the modern world. Without an appreciation of the supremacy of defensive warfare in the First World War, for example, the terrible cost in lives suffered by both sides on the Western Front is difficult to understand. In just 192 pages, the reader can see the battles of the Roman legions visually represented, follow the campaigns of Napoleon, understand the course of the Thirty Years War in Europe, trace the routes of the Crusades, and follow the course of the American Civil War. Although the maps are at the core of this book and its approach, they are supported by comprehensive and analytical text that acts as a companion to their coverage and together with them creates a package of unrivaled breadth and accessibility. **The Collins Atlas of Military History** offers an easy, informed, and pleasurable way into the subject. Particularly suitable for students, but intended to appeal to all lovers of military history, this book truly brings past wars into focus.

CONTENTS

PART I | **THE FIRST MILITARY EMPIRES**

egyptians and hittites

5000 to 2000 BC

c. **2500 BC**
first indications of warfare with large numbers of troops

c. **1500 BC**
first use of the bow and the horse in warfare

1469 BC
first known battle – Megiddo

1275 BC
Battle of Kadesh between Ramses II and Hittites

c. **1200 BC**
introduction of chariot

The first military campaigns for which enough evidence survives took place in the Middle East, involving Egypt, Assyria, the Hittites, and the Persians as the main parties. From Sumerian culture of southern Mesopotamia, around 2500 BC, we have indications of warfare involving large numbers of troops. The Sumerians fielded a clunky forerunner to the war chariot: pulled by what appears to be the Middle East version of today's donkey, these functioned as mobile platforms for archers.

Two major developments occurred around 1500 BC: the first military use of the bow and use of the horse in combat. The combination produced armies with excellent mobility on open ground—and relatively long-range killing capabilities. These two inventions turned Middle Eastern armies towards a mobile, missile-based force (in contrast to the massed, armored infantry that Greece was later to develop). From 1200 BC the chariot became the key weapon system, one that would remain in service for 1,000 years.

1 **kingdoms and empires, c. 1500–1100 BC**

Hittite empire established by Suppiluliuma I, 1344–1322 BC

Mitanni territory at its greatest extent, *c.* 1480–1340 BC

Mitanni after *c.* 1340 BC (under Hittite and Assyrian control)

Assyrian territory gained by Ashur-uballit I, 1353–1318 BC

Babylonia under Burnaburiash II, 1347–1321 BC

Elam under Tepti-ahar, *c.* 1353–1318 BC

Egypt under Amenophis IV and Tutankhamun, 1352–1335 BC

✗ battle

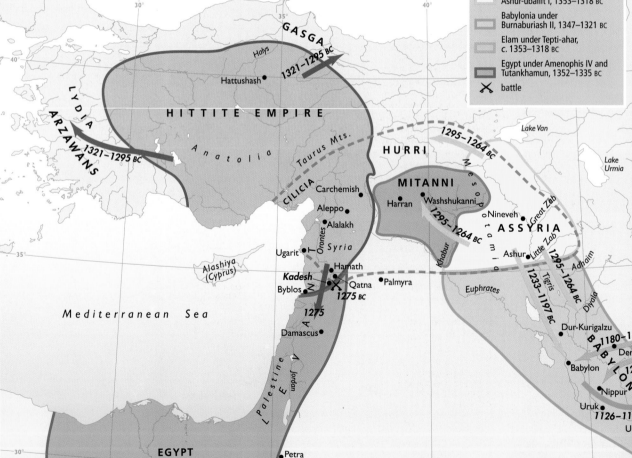

The most prolific users of chariots were the Egyptians who, in the 2nd millennium BC, under such pharaohs as Tuthmosis III and Ramses II, achieved their pinnacle of military power, dominating modern Palestine. The value that the Egyptians placed on the chariot is illustrated by the large numbers of representations of pharaohs driving chariots through piles of enemies. The first known battle—Megiddo—occurred in the mid-15th century BC, when Tuthmosis III shattered a Canaanite coalition. His victory allowed Egypt to extend its borders to their greatest extent in history, as far north as Syria and as far east as the Euphrates. However, Egyptian campaigns into the north aroused the fear of another nation, centered on what is now Anatolia in Turkey: the Hittites.

The Hittite army possessed chariots similar to the Egyptians', but some were heavier, with a crew of three. Advancing into modern Syria, a Hittite army under King Suppiluliumas, marched to confront the Egyptian Pharaoh Akhenaten. Akhenaten died, and his daughter Ankhsenamun (widow of Tutenkhamun) bought off Suppiluliumas with her offer to marry one of his sons. However, two Egyptian ministers had the Hittite prince assassinated at the border, and the war was on again.

Egyptian–Hittite rivalry culminated in the Battle of Kadesh in 1275 BC. Ramses II was intent on stopping Hittite forays into western Syria and sought to destroy the army of the Hittite king, Muwatallis. With Ramses at their head, the Egyptians smashed the Hittite chariots, forcing Muwatallis to take refuge inside Kadesh. Both commanders claimed victory. The result was a non-aggression treaty, but the Hittites remained in control of Syria.

1 The second half of the 2nd millennium saw the growth of a number of competing powers in the Near East. The map (below left) indicates the territorial position circa. 1330 BC. To the west, New Kingdom Egypt fought for control of Syria–Palestine first with Mitanni and then with the Hittites, while to the east the Kassite kings of Babylon were increasingly threatened by the emergent powers of Assyria to the north and Elam to the east. Mitanni archives record the existence of professional troops and militia, the striking force of the Mitanni army being a corps of 200 chariots.

2 The strip of fertile land between the Mediterranean and the Syrian desert was a target for Egyptian imperialism, beginning with the campaigns of the early pharaohs of the Eighteenth Dynasty (map right). By the reign of Tuthmosis, Egypt's power reached north from the Third Cataract in Nubia to the Euphrates. His grandson, Tuthmosis III, fought 17 campaigns in Palestine and Syria, setting up a monument next to his grandfather's on the Euphrates in the region of Carchemish. Boundaries were established by treaties first with the land of Mitanni, later with the Hittites. After much of this empire had crumbled away in the next 130 years, Seti I and Ramses II temporarily recovered some of the region.

2 Egyptian campaigns in Syria and Palestine

—— northern limit of campaigns of Tuthmosis I (1507–1494 BC) and Tuthmosis III (1490–1436 BC)

—— boundary between Egyptian and Mitannian zones of influence at the end of the reign of Amenophis II (1438–1412 BC)

—— boundary between Egyptian and Hittite zones of influence at the end of the reign of Akhenaten, 1347 BC

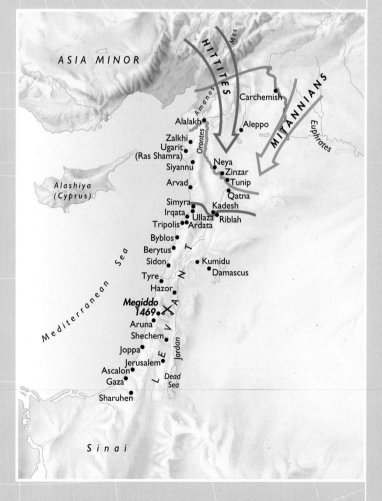

assyrians and persians

853 BC
Battle of Qarqar; Shalmaneser III defeats an alliance of western states, including Ahab of Israel

7th century BC
Assyrians under Ashurbanipal (668–627 BC) control almost the entire Middle East

612 BC
fall of Nineveh to the Babylonians and Medes

559 BC
Cyrus the Great seizes the throne of Media

500 BC
Ionian city-states revolt against their Persian overlords

In about 1200 BC new waves of invaders descended on the eastern Mediterranean. The Sea People, as the Egyptians called them, dramatically reshaped the political landscape of the Middle East: Egypt barely survived the onslaught; the Hittite Kingdom collapsed; the city-states of Syria were overrun; and the Egyptians lost all their lands east of and including the Sinai. The only power to be unaffected was the Kingdom of Assyria in Mesopotamia.

Over the next 500 years Assyrian armies, led by such kings as Shalmaneser III, Sennacherib, and Ashurbanipal, conquered and ruled a great empire. Their campaigns prefigured those of the Mongols in terms of their ruthless treatment of those they defeated. By the 7th century BC, the Assyrians controlled almost the entire Middle East, from Egypt to the Taurus Mountains, from Sidon and Tyre to the capital of the Medes, Susa, just north of the Persian Gulf.

Assyria reached its zenith in the beginning of the 7th century BC, before it imploded, caught between the powers it had previously trampled and new powers from the east: Babylon and the Medes. The fall of Nineveh, in 612 BC, signalled the death knell for this remarkable society. Assyria's disintegration left the field open for four smaller powers to fight over the remains: Babylon, which had some success under Nebuchadnezzar; Egypt, which was in decline; and two mini-powers, Lydia to the west and Media in the east.

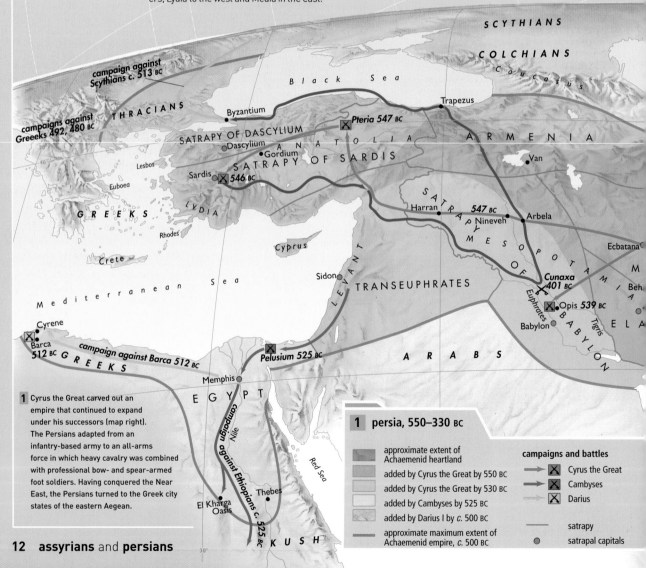

1 Cyrus the Great carved out an empire that continued to expand under his successors (map right). The Persians adapted from an infantry-based army to an all-arms force in which heavy cavalry was combined with professional bow- and spear-armed foot soldiers. Having conquered the Near East, the Persians turned to the Greek city states of the eastern Aegean.

1 persia, 550–330 BC

- approximate extent of Achaemenid heartland
- added by Cyrus the Great by 550 BC
- added by Cyrus the Great by 530 BC
- added by Cambyses by 525 BC
- added by Darius I by c. 500 BC
- approximate maximum extent of Achaemenid empire, c. 500 BC

campaigns and battles

- → ✕ Cyrus the Great
- → ✕ Cambyses
- → ✕ Darius

— satrapy
● satrapal capitals

The power of the Median kings was usurped from within by a Persian faction, led by Cyrus the Great, who seized the throne in 550 BC, conquered Babylon and Lydia, and within a few years had overwhelmed Egypt. By the early 6th century BC Persia was the superpower of the Middle East, the Persian Empire one of the largest in the known world. The élite force in its army was not the chariot wing but "The Immortals," the king's personal guard of 10,000 infantry, so-named because the division was always kept up to strength. The Immortals, however, were not heavy infantry, such as predominated in Greece, but more moderately armored spear and bow men.

By the time King Darius turned his attention to Europe, the Persian cavalry was the best of its time, but the light infantry consisted of levies from usually reluctant allies. In the 5th century BC the Ionian city states revolted against their Persian overlords, supported by several cities on mainland Greece. The result was a confrontation between the Greek citizen armies of hoplite farmers, and Persia, with its light cavalry and infantry. Within 175 years, the Greeks ruled the western world and the Persian Empire had ceased to exist.

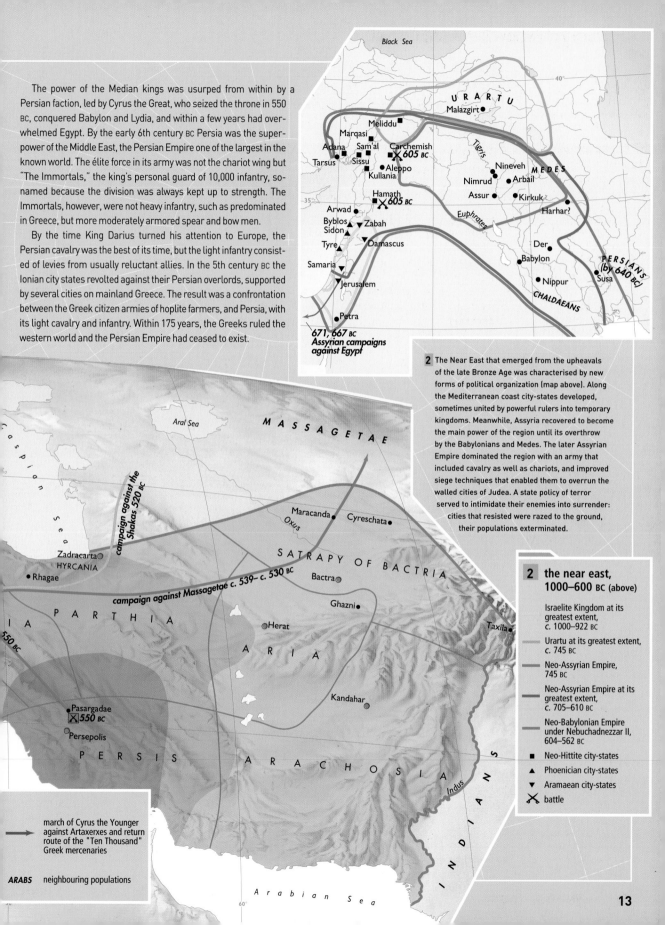

671, 667 BC
Assyrian campaigns against Egypt

2 The Near East that emerged from the upheavals of the late Bronze Age was characterised by new forms of political organization (map above). Along the Mediterranean coast city-states developed, sometimes united by powerful rulers into temporary kingdoms. Meanwhile, Assyria recovered to become the main power of the region until its overthrow by the Babylonians and Medes. The later Assyrian Empire dominated the region with an army that included cavalry as well as chariots, and improved siege techniques that enabled them to overrun the walled cities of Judea. A state policy of terror served to intimidate their enemies into surrender: cities that resisted were razed to the ground, their populations exterminated.

campaign against the Shakas 520 BC

campaign against Massagetae c. 539– c. 530 BC

2 | the near east, 1000–600 BC (above)

Israelite Kingdom at its greatest extent, c. 1000–922 BC

Urartu at its greatest extent, c. 745 BC

Neo-Assyrian Empire, 745 BC

Neo-Assyrian Empire at its greatest extent, c. 705–610 BC

Neo-Babylonian Empire under Nebuchadnezzar II, 604–562 BC

■ Neo-Hittite city-states

▲ Phoenician city-states

▼ Aramaean city-states

⚔ battle

march of Cyrus the Younger against Artaxerxes and return route of the "Ten Thousand" Greek mercenaries

ARABS neighbouring populations

the **greco-persian** wars

500 BC
Ionian Greek city-state colonies revolt against Persian empire of Darius I

494 BC
Battle of Lade: Persian Darius I's navy defeats the Greeks

492 BC
Persians under Mardonius conquer Thrace and Macedon, but their fleet was damaged in a storm

490 BC
Battle of Marathon

480 BC
Persian victory at Thermopylae. Greeks win crushing naval battle at Salamis

479 BC
Greek victory at Plataea

The Greek military system relied principally on the hoplite, an armored infantry spearman so named for his shield, the *hoplon*. The Persian military, in contrast, was better suited to the open spaces of south-west Asia, where speed and maneuverability won battles. Given their training and experience, Persian cavalry were far superior to that of the Greeks, but Persian infantry was ill-equipped to stand toe-to-toe with hoplites.

The Persian empire continued to expand under Darius I, conquering the Greek city-state colonies in Anatolia (modern-day western Turkey). Around 500 BC these cities rose in revolt, appealing to their mother cities in Greece to give them aid. Athens and Eretria sent a small naval contingent. Darius' navy defeated the Greek squadrons at the Battle of Lade (494 BC) and his army put several Ionian cities to the torch. Darius despatched an expeditionary force to punish Athens and Eretria.

The Persian forces captured Eretria, then shipped their army to a beach on the Marathon plain, 19 miles from Athens, near a convenient road that led to the city. Forewarned, the Athenian army arrived just after the Persians had disembarked and occupied a narrow valley, Vrana, that flanked the Persian route of advance to the city. Although victorious, the Athenians managed to capture only seven ships; a rearguard action by the Persian cavalry covered their escape. Internal conflict delayed the Persian riposte until 480 BC, when Xerxes, the new King of Kings, led a fresh expedition to avenge Marathon.

Most of the Greek cities in the north surrendered without a fight. In the south, a Hellenic league, with Sparta as its leader, sent a land and naval force to buy time to prepare fortifications on the isthmus. At Thermopylae, 300 Spartans held off the entire Persian army for several days, while an inconclusive naval battle took place off Artemisium. The Spartan delaying force, under their king, Leonidas, was wiped out to the last man; the galley fleet withdrew when its land flank was uncovered.

The Persians marched into a poorly defended Athens, which they sacked. But their fleet was lured into closed waters near the island of Salamis and destroyed by the Athenian and Corinthian navies. With their logistic support destroyed, the majority of the Persian army withdrew to Asia while some 20,000–25,000 men remained behind near Plataea. In 479 BC a Hellenic army representing most of southern Greece defeated the Persians. The Persian rout was then completed by their defeat at Mycale the same year. With the Persians expelled from Europe the Spartans returned home, while an appeal from the Ionian Greeks to Athens created the Delian League.

MACE
ILLYRIA
THESSALY
Therm

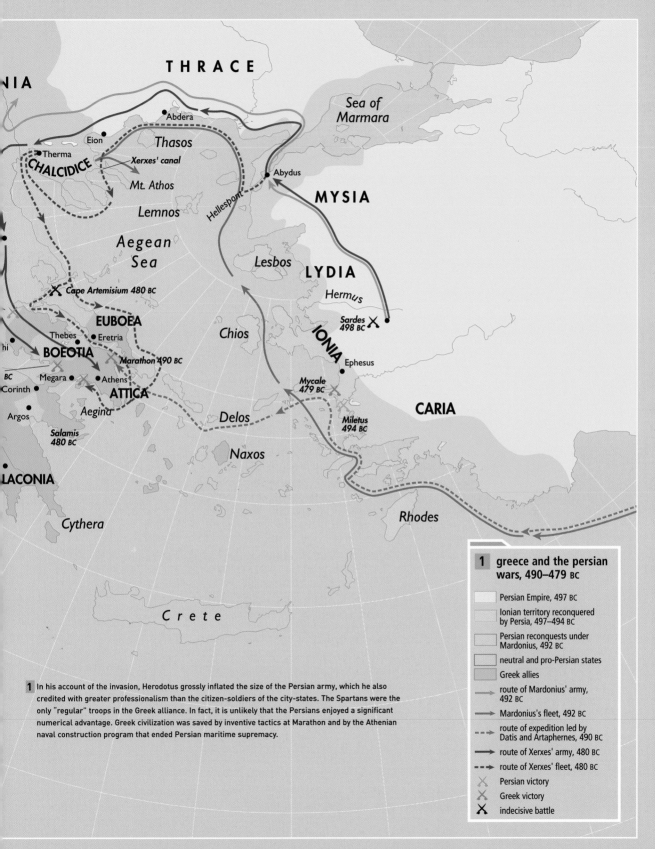

THRACE

• Abdera

Eion

• Therma

CHALCIDICE

Xerxes' canal

Thasos

Mt. Athos

Lemnos

Hellespont

Aegean Sea

Sea of Marmara

Abydus

MYSIA

Lesbos

LYDIA

Hermus

Chios

Sardes 498 BC

✗ Cape Artemisium 480 BC

EUBOEA

Thebes   • Eretria

hi

BOEOTIA

BC   Megara •

Corinth •

Argos •

Ephesus

IONIA

Mycale 479 BC ✗

Marathon 490 BC

✗ Athens

ATTICA

Aegina

Salamis 480 BC

Delos

Miletus 494 BC

CARIA

Naxos

Rhodes

LACONIA

Cythera

Crete

1 **greece and the persian wars, 490–479** BC

Persian Empire, 497 BC

Ionian territory reconquered by Persia, 497–494 BC

Persian reconquests under Mardonius, 492 BC

neutral and pro-Persian states

Greek allies

→ route of Mardonius' army, 492 BC

→ Mardonius's fleet, 492 BC

- - → route of expedition led by Datis and Artaphernes, 490 BC

→ route of Xerxes' army, 480 BC

- - → route of Xerxes' fleet, 480 BC

✗ Persian victory

✗ Greek victory

✗ indecisive battle

1 In his account of the invasion, Herodotus grossly inflated the size of the Persian army, which he also credited with greater professionalism than the citizen-soldiers of the city-states. The Spartans were the only "regular" troops in the Greek alliance. In fact, it is unlikely that the Persians enjoyed a significant numerical advantage. Greek civilization was saved by inventive tactics at Marathon and by the Athenian naval construction program that ended Persian maritime supremacy.

the **peloponnesian** war

431 BC
Peloponnesian War starts

429 BC
Athenian naval victory at Naupactus

425 BC
Athens captures Sphacteria. Spartan peace overtures rebuffed

422 BC
Spartan victory at Amphipolis. Brasidas and Cleon both killed

421 BC
negotiation of Peace of Nicias (new Athenian leader)

418 BC
Battle of Mantinea: Sparta defeats Argive-led army

407 BC
Spartan fleet wins naval battle off Notium

406 BC
Athenians win victory at Arginusae, and again decline offer of peace

405 BC
Athenian fleet destroyed while beached at Hellespont

404 BC
Athens surrenders

The war between the Peloponnesian League, led by Sparta, and the Delian League, led by Athens, pitted a land power against a sea power. The asymmetric nature of the conflict helped prolong hostilities for 27 years. Athens collected tribute from allies who were bound to her by treaty, and their fleet of 300 triremes allowed them to win the majority of the naval battles, even when outnumbered. Although the Peloponnesian League's naval forces were outnumbered, it could muster some 30,000–35,000 hoplites, more than twice as many as Athens. At the league's core was the Spartan army, the only professional fighting force in Greece.

The first phase of the war, the Archidamian War (431–421 BC), saw the Spartan army invade Attica each year, while the Corinthian navy attempted to break out of the Gulf of Corinth. The Athenian admiral, Phormio, operating from Naupactus, defeated a succession of Corinthian sorties and prevented Corinth from maintaining its economic links to colonies in Italy. Athens established a base at Pylos on the western coast of the Peloponnese. Sparta landed a small army on an adjacent island (Sphacteria), but Athenian naval forces isolated them. After a series of failed negotiations, Athenian naval forces were able in 425 BC to land superior Athenian land forces on to the island, destroying the majority of the Spartan force and capturing the survivors.

Negotiations followed, culminating in the Peace of Nicias in 421 BC, but it was no more than an armistice. Many of Sparta's allies became disaffected and formed a new league with Argos. At the Battle of Mantinea (418 BC), Sparta won the one and only large hoplite battle of the Peloponnesian War when it defeated an Argive-led army that included an Athenian contingent. This victory, plus the Athenian invasion of Sicily, prompted a renewal of hostilities.

In 415 BC, Athens launched a pre-emptive attack on Syracuse, a potential Spartan ally. The fact that the Athenians could launch the original expedition and subsequently reinforce it without hindrance from the Peloponnesian League testifies to their control over the western sea routes to Sicily. But the

1 The whole Greek world became involved in the prolonged war between Athens and Sparta from 431 BC (map right). Sparta was stronger on land, but Athens kept firm control of the sea. After 10 years an uneasy peace was made (421 BC), but when Athens lost almost its entire fleet in Sicily, the Spartans pressed home their advantage. Even so, it was only with considerable naval and financial support from the Persians that they were able to overcome the Athenian navy.

Rome

LATIUM

Cumae • Neapolis

T y r r h e n i a n S e a

M A G N A   G R A E C I A

Lipara
Segesta • Messana Lo
Himera Rhegium
Selinus • *S i c i l y*
Catana
Gela ✗ Syracuse 413
Camarina

1   the peloponnesian war, 431–404 BC

▨ Athens and members of the Delian League	● allies of Sparta in Magna Graecia
▢ ally of Athens	→ Athenian campaigns
▢ Sparta and allies	→ Spartan campaigns
▢ neutral states	✗ Athenian victory
● allies of Athens in Magna Graecia	✗ Spartan victory

loss of 160 Athenian and 56 allied triremes in the confined waters of Syracuse harbor equalized the naval forces available to both sides for the first time in 50 years.

Sparta was now able to establish a series of fleets in western Asia Minor that contested Athens' sea lines of communication across the Aegean and the Hellespont. Although Athens had lost naval superiority and had suffered a series of political upheavals at home, its superior tactical prowess still enabled its navy to win a series of naval battles over an eight-year period. Yet these were not enough; Athenian allies rebelled and ceased paying tribute, further weakening the Athenian navy. In 405 BC the Athenian fleet, maintaining its eastern sea lanes in the Hellespont, was destroyed while beached and Athens, faced with imminent starvation, surrendered a year later.

2 At their third attempt, the Syracusan army extended a defensive wall past the Athenian siege lines, preventing the total blockade of the city (map right). The Spartan general Gylippus then trapped the Athenian fleet within the great harbor and the besiegers found themselves cut off. The surrender and enslavement of the expeditionary force was a catastrophe for Athens and its fleet never recovered its qualitative advantage.

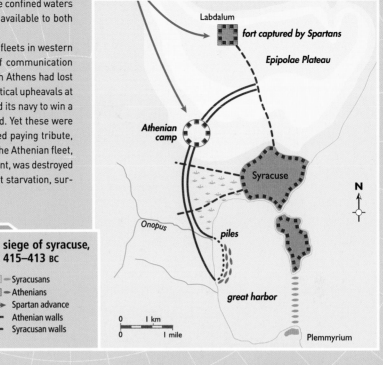

Labdalum

fort captured by Spartans

Epipolae Plateau

Athenian camp

Syracuse

N

Onopus

piles

great harbor

Plemmyrium

2 | **siege of syracuse, 415–413 BC**

☐➝ Syracusans
▨➝ Athenians
➝ Spartan advance
— Athenian walls
--- Syracusan walls

0   1 km
0   1 mile

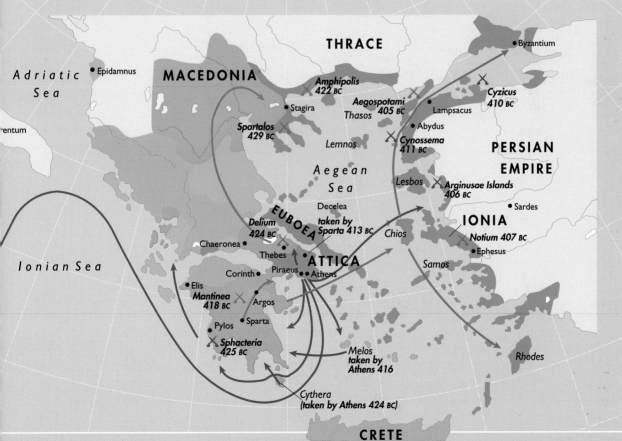

Adriatic Sea

• Epidamnus

THRACE

MACEDONIA

• Byzantium

✕ *Amphipolis* 422 BC

• Stagira

Aegospotami 405 BC

Thasos

• Lampsacus

✕ *Cyzicus* 410 BC

✕ *Spartalos* 429 BC

Lemnos

• Abydus

✕ *Cynossema* 411 BC

PERSIAN EMPIRE

Aegean Sea

Lesbos ✕ *Arginusae Islands* 406 BC

Decelea

• Sardes

-entum

EUBOEA

Chios

IONIA

Ionian Sea

Delium 424 BC

taken by Sparta 413 BC

Notium 407 BC

• Ephesus

Chaeronea •

Thebes •

ATTICA

Samos

Corinth • Piraeus • • Athens

• Elis

Mantinea 418 BC ✕

Argos

Rhodes

Pylos • • Sparta

✕ *Sphacteria* 425 BC

Melos taken by Athens 416

Cythera (taken by Athens 424 BC)

CRETE

alexander the great and the successor wars

338 BC
Battle of Chaeronea: Macedon (under Philip II) overpowers Theban-led coalition

336 BC
Philip assassinated. Son, Alexander III, secures Greece and the Balkan Peninsula

334 BC
Alexander invades Persia

333 BC
Battle of Issus

331 BC
Battle of Gaugamela (or Arbela): Alexander defeats Darius

323 BC
Alexander dies

280 BC
Three main successor states emerge: Macedon, Egypt, and the Seleucid kingdom

217 BC
Battle of Raphia between Antiochus and Egypt

200 BC
Rome declares war on Philip V of Macedon

197 and 168 BC
Macedonians defeated

1 The meteoric career of Alexander brought the Macedonian army to the limits of the known world. In 10 years of unceasing warfare, he led his men to victory over the Persian army, the cities of Phoenicia, mountain tribes, and Scythian horsemen. That his empire would not outlive him was evident before his death: false news of his demise triggered several revolts prior to his fatal sickness at Baghdad.

Wars between the Greek city-states continued after the Peloponnesian War until the northern state of Macedon overwhelmed a Theban-led coalition at the Battle of Chaeronea in 338 BC.

The victorious Macedonian king Philip II was assassinated in 336 BC. Two years later, his son Alexander III led the Macedonian army into Asia, on a one-way journey that won him the reputation of the greatest field commander of the Ancient world. He shattered a Persian army led by local satraps in western Asia Minor, personally leading a headlong cavalry charge that nearly cost him his life. Alexander's communications with Macedon were vulnerable to the Persian fleet, which was also capable of supporting revolts within Greece, so he led the army against the coastal cities of the eastern Mediterranean. King Darius III of Persia arrived in 333 BC, but he was defeated at Issus, and his army disintegrated. The Persian Empire began to fracture. Its provinces included a wide variety of races, subject peoples with no particular allegiance to the ruling Achaemenid dynasty. Egypt's cities surrendered to Alexander. Alexander's general Ptolemy was to found the last dynasty of pharaohs, which ended with Cleopatra VII. In 331 BC Alexander marched into the heartland of Asia for a final confrontation with Darius, who had raised and equipped another army. Darius fled the field at Gaugamela, and was pursued for some months by Alexander until assassinated by Bessus, the satrap of Bactria.

Alexander devoted the next 10 years to conquering the farthest reaches of the Persian Empire. In 323 BC, aged only 33, and having conquered most of the civilized world, he died of fever (or possibly poison).

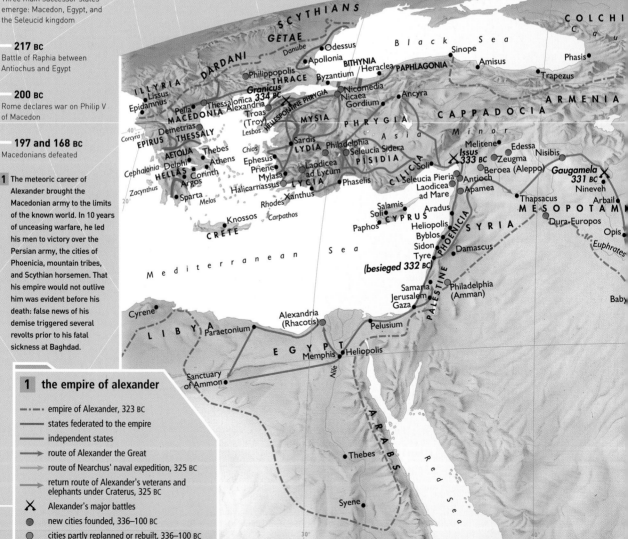

1 the empire of alexander

- –·–·– empire of Alexander, 323 BC
- ——— states federated to the empire
- ——— independent states
- ——→ route of Alexander the Great
- ——→ route of Nearchus' naval expedition, 325 BC
- ——→ return route of Alexander's veterans and elephants under Craterus, 325 BC
- ✕ Alexander's major battles
- ● new cities founded, 336–100 BC
- ● cities partly replanned or rebuilt, 336–100 BC

Alexander's sudden death precipitated a series of wars that ended only with the arrival of Roman power in the region. Alexander's generals (the Diadochoi, or Successors) fought to inherit, if not his throne, at least an empire of their own. By the assassination of Seleucus, the last of Alexander's officers, in 280 BC, three main successor states emerged: Macedon, Egypt. and the Seleucid Kingdom that stretched from the eastern shores of the Mediterranean to Baghdad.

Over a century after Alexander's death, the Egypt of the Ptolemys and the Seleucids in the Middle East/Syria were at war over the ports and cities that were part of Coele-Syria, the modern-day Mediterranean Middle East. In 218 BC, fresh from suppressing a series of eastern rebellions, the Seleucid Kingdom's young ruler, Antiochus III, invaded Coele-Syria and marched against Egypt. The ensuing Battle of Raphia (217 BC) left Palestine in Egyptian hands while Antiochus devoted his considerable energy to further campaigns in Bactria, Arabia, and as far east as the Punjab.

2 Antigonus "One Eye" was killed at the Battle of Ipsus in 301 BC, ending the most serious attempt by one of Alexander's generals to control the entire empire. By the time the last of the original 'successors' was killed in 280BC, Alexander's empire had fractured into many states. The most powerful were based on Egypt, the old Persian heartland, and Macedonia itself. Macedonian intrigues with the Carthaginians during the Second Punic War were not forgotten in Rome, which declared war on Philip V in 200 BC. The Macedonians were defeated in 197BC and again in 168BC. Between the Macedonian wars, Rome intervened in the eastern Aegean where smaller states allied with her against Antiochus III, ruler of the Seleucid empire (map below). Antiochus was defeated at Magnesia in 190BC, the success of cavalry under his own command failing to stop the legions demolishing his phalanx.

2 the hellenistic world, 188 BC

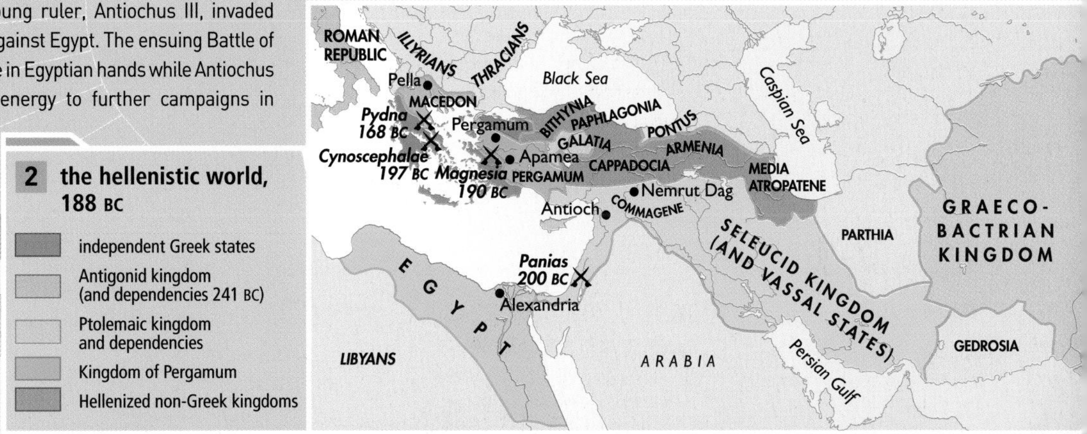

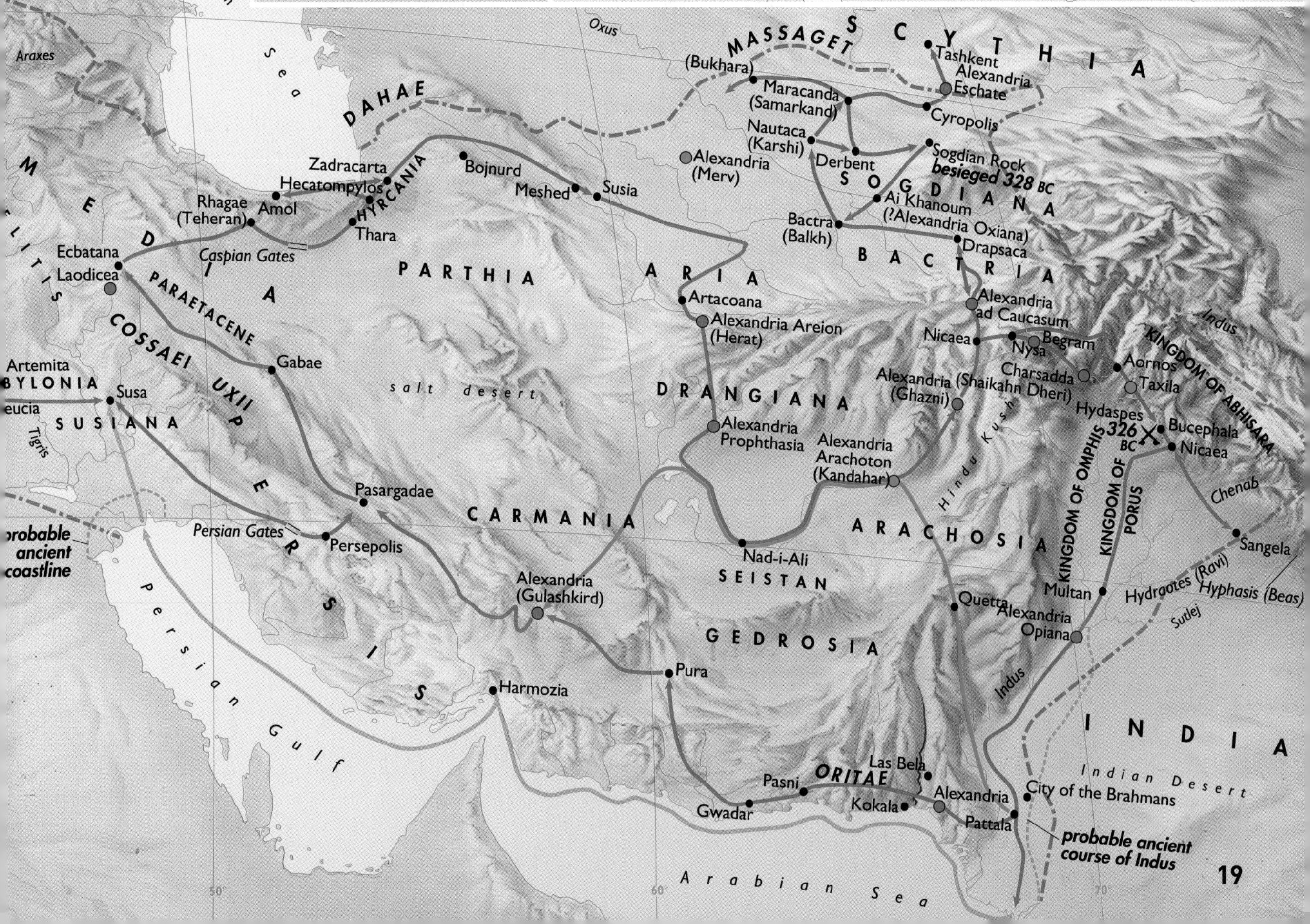

- independent Greek states
- Antigonid kingdom (and dependencies 241 BC)
- Ptolemaic kingdom and dependencies
- Kingdom of Pergamum
- Hellenized non-Greek kingdoms

Map labels (Hellenistic world inset)

ROMAN REPUBLIC
ILLYRIANS
THRACIANS
Black Sea
Pella
MACEDON
Pydna 168 BC
Pergamum
BITHYNIA
PAPHLAGONIA
GALATIA
PONTUS
ARMENIA
Caspian Sea
Cynoscephalae 197 BC
Magnesia 190 BC
Apamea
CAPPADOCIA
MEDIA ATROPATENE
PERGAMUM
Nemrut Dag
COMMAGENE
Antioch
SELEUCID KINGDOM (AND VASSAL STATES)
PARTHIA
GRAECO-BACTRIAN KINGDOM
EGYPT
Panias 200 BC
Alexandria
ARABIA
Persian Gulf
LIBYANS
GEDROSIA

Map labels (main map)

Caspian Sea
Cyrus
Araxes
Oxus
MASSAGET
SCYTHIA
DAHAE
(Bukhara)
Tashkent
Alexandria Eschate
Maracanda (Samarkand)
Cyropolis
Nautaca (Karshi)
Zadracarta
Bojnurd
Alexandria (Merv)
Derbent
SOGDIANA
Sogdian Rock besieged 328 BC
Hecatompylos
HYRCANIA
Meshed
Susia
Ai Khanoum (?Alexandria Oxiana)
Rhagae (Teheran)
Amol
Bactra (Balkh)
Drapsaca
BACTRIA
Thara
Ecbatana
Caspian Gates
PARTHIA
ARIA
Alexandria ad Caucasum
Laodicea
MEDIA
PARAETACENE
Artacoana
Nicaea
Nysa
Begram
KINGDOM OF ABHISARA
Indus
COSSAEI
UXII
Gabae
salt desert
Alexandria Areion (Herat)
Charsadda (Shaikahn Dheri)
Aornos
Taxila
Artemita
BABYLONIA
Susa
SUSIANA
DRANGIANA
Alexandria (Ghazni)
Hydaspes
Bucephala
Nicaea
Seleucia
Tigris
Alexandria Prophthasia
Alexandria Arachoton (Kandahar)
ARACHOSIA
KINGDOM OF OMPHIS
KINGDOM OF PORUS
326 BC
Chenab
Pasargadae
CARMANIA
Hindu Kush
Sangela
Persian Gates
Persepolis
Nad-i-Ali
SEISTAN
Multan
Hydraotes (Ravi)
Hyphasis (Beas)
probable ancient coastline
PERSIS
Alexandria (Gulashkird)
Quetta
Alexandria Opiana
Sutlej
GEDROSIA
INDIA
Persian Gulf
Pura
Indian Desert
Harmozia
Las Bela
ORITAE
Alexandria
City of the Brahmans
Pasni
Kokala
Gwadar
Pattala
probable ancient course of Indus
Arabian Sea

19

the **punic** wars

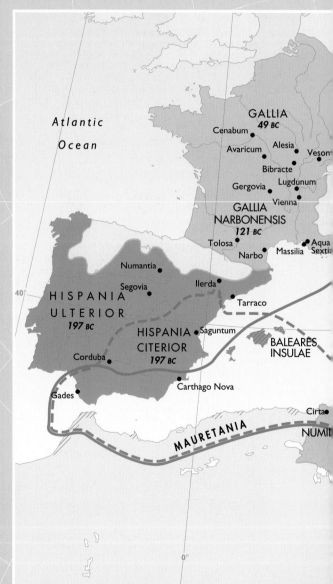

264–242 BC
First Punic War

259 BC
Victory of Roman fleet off Cape Ecnomus; expedition lands in Africa but is defeated

241 BC
Romans destroy the Carthaginian fleet off Lilybaeum; Carthage sues for peace; cession of Carthage's possessions in Sicily to Rome

219 BC
Rome fights Carthaginian general Hannibal for control of Spain

218–201 BC
Second Punic War

217 BC
Battle of Lake Trasimene

216 BC
Battle of Cannae, Rome's worst ever defeat

202 BC
Roman general Scipio Africanus (237–183 BC) defeats Hannibal at Zama

146 BC
Romans take and destroy Carthage, ending the Third Punic War

1 The acquisition of overseas provinces by Rome was seldom by design (map right). Although Roman commanders needed little encouragement to undertake military campaigns, they preferred to make treaties with defeated enemies rather than turn their territories into provinces. However, the wars against the Hellenistic kingdoms of the eastern Mediterranean in the 2nd and 1st centuries BC left the Romans with possessions that could yield substantial tribute.

By the 4th century BC, Rome had extended its power to southern Italy. Rome, Carthage, and the Macedonian successor state of Epirus were vying for control of Sicily. Epirus fought Rome from 281–272 BC when its king, Pyrrhus, died; he defeated Rome's armies, but at such heavy cost the expression "Pyrrhic victory" was coined. Against the Carthaginians Rome fought a series of Punic Wars. The first lasted from 265–241 BC. Rome conquered Sicily, but an invasion of North Africa met with disaster. After a period of uneasy peace, the two powers clashed over control of Spain in 219 BC, while Hannibal led his army towards the Alps.

Hannibal beat the Roman armies at Trebbia and Lake Trasimene (217 BC), leading Rome to adopt a defensive policy championed by Fabius, but a populist consul, Varro, claimed the nobility were prolonging the war for their own profit and that he could end it immediately. This "political general" led 80,000 Roman infantry against 50,000 Carthaginians, of whom half were Gallic auxiliaries. Varro was completely out-generaled by Hannibal at Cannae. Varro concentrated his force against the centre of the Carthaginian line only to find his army encircled by Hannibal's elite infrantry and cavalry. About 60,000 Romans were killed. The Carthaginians lost about 6000.

Rome had the political will to survive 15 years of campaigning in Italy. New legions were raised, the city resorting to the recruitment of freed slaves. Rome's fortifications were formidable; it was impossible for Hannibal to storm the city. The Fabian strategy was tried again, and this time the Romans persisted with it, keeping their army close to Hannibal's but never risking battle. The Romans habitually fortified their camp, nullifying the Carthaginians' cavalry superiority. Isolated detachments of Carthaginians were attacked, the Romans retiring behind their fortifications if pressed. Rome could replace its losses in such skirmishes, but Hannibal could not. The few Italian cities that had deserted Rome came to regret it, the fate of Capua anticipating that of Carthage. The Roman navy prevented reinforcements reaching Hannibal by sea. Hannibal's brother marched an army overland from Spain, but Hannibal learned of the attempted reinforcement only when Hasdrubal's severed head was tossed into his camp.

Rome's superior manpower enabled a second front to be opened; sustained by Roman naval superiority, new armies were deployed to Spain where they drove out the Carthaginians. This "indirect approach" stampeded the Carthaginian senate into negotiations. An armistice was arranged and Hannibal's army sailed home. Its arrival stiffened the Carthaginians' resolve, and a final battle took place near the small town of Zama (202 BC). Publius Cornelius Scipio won the nickname "Africanus" for this, his most famous and important victory.

In 146 BC, the Romans ended 150 years of hostilities with Carthage by storming the city. The survivors were sold as slaves and the city demolished. The Carthaginian language was eventually lost and only the writings of later historians shed any light on Carthage's military institutions and its most famous general, Hannibal.

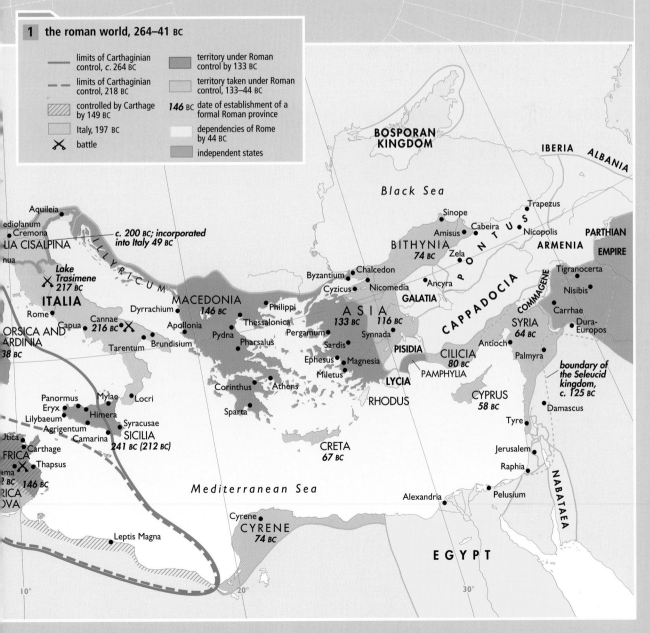

1 the roman world, 264–41 BC

- limits of Carthaginian control, c. 264 BC
- limits of Carthaginian control, 218 BC
- controlled by Carthage by 149 BC
- Italy, 197 BC
- battle
- territory under Roman control by 133 BC
- territory taken under Roman control, 133–44 BC
- *146* BC date of establishment of a formal Roman province
- dependencies of Rome by 44 BC
- independent states

c. 700 BC
Phoenicians have the first dedicated warships

5th century BC
trireme (three banks of oars) replaces bireme (two banks)

4th–3rd centuries BC
warships grow larger: Roman and Carthaginian fleets use quadriremes and quinqueremes

31 BC
naval Battle of Actium. Quinquireme is standard battleship on the Mediterranean

By around 700 BC the Phoenicians had developed the first dedicated warships. Experience soon stimulated the design of oar-propelled warships. Independent of the wind, these narrow-beamed ships had the maneuverability and acceleration to force an action with lumbering sail-driven merchant ships. By the 5th century BC the Phoenician bireme had been largely superseded by the triple-banked trireme.

In 480 BC, 10 years after Marathon, the Persians launched a second invasion of Greece. The Persian soldiers, battle-hardened conquerors of an already vast empire, were accompanied by a large fleet of perhaps 400 warships. It came as a disagreeable surprise to encounter a Greek fleet of similar size off Artemisium. Themistocles, the far-sighted leader of Athens, had persuaded the citizens to spend the profits from their new-found silver mines on a massive program of naval construction. The Athenian navy held off the Persian fleet.

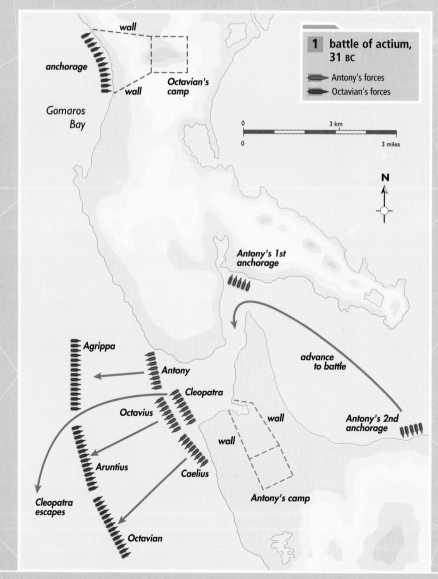

1 The final battle of the civil war following Caesar's murder was fought off the Greek coast at Actium. Cleopatra's squadron broke through the enemy center, but she hoisted sail and escaped to Egypt with the treasury. Mark Antony's flagship was a gigantic warship with multiple banks of oars, but most ships on both sides were quinqueremes, the standard Roman warship since the Second Punic War.

1 battle of actium, 31 BC

Antony's forces
Octavian's forces

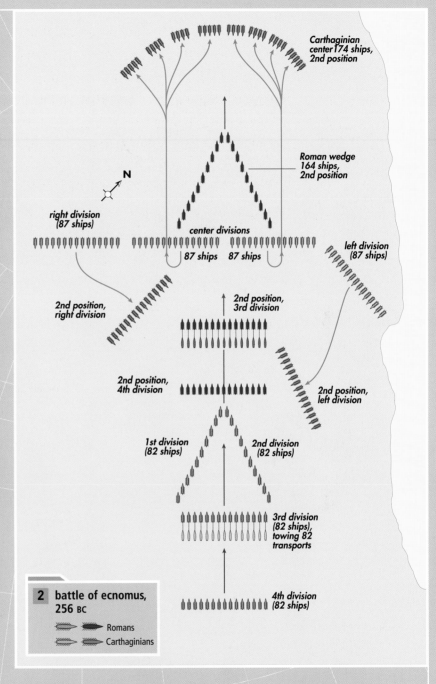

2 A Roman invasion fleet of 330 vessels sailed for Africa but was intercepted off Sicily by 350 Carthaginian ships. The Romans won the battle, capturing 64 enemy ships and sinking 30 for the loss of 24 of their own. Both the Carthaginian admiral and one of the two Roman consuls were later tortured to death by the Carthaginian authorities.

Carthaginian center 174 ships, 2nd position

Roman wedge 164 ships, 2nd position

N

right division (87 ships)

center divisions

87 ships   87 ships

left division (87 ships)

2nd position, right division

2nd position, 3rd division

2nd position, 4th division

2nd position, left division

1st division (82 ships)

2nd division (82 ships)

3rd division (82 ships), towing 82 transports

4th division (82 ships)

2 **battle of ecnomus, 256 BC**

Romans
Carthaginians

Next, by offering battle off Salamis in the Bay of Eleusis, the Athenians lured the Persians to defeat. The Greeks lacked the experience of their opponents, and their triremes were heavier and less maneuverable, but they were able to concentrate on the leading Persian squadrons as they entered the bay. Caught in a bottleneck, the Persians had no room to exploit their superior seamanship. A flanking attack by their Egyptian squadron was similarly defeated by Corinthian triremes on the western side of Salamis, and the Persian warships withdrew in confusion.

All major sea battles in the ancient Mediterranean took place close to the shore. Oar-powered warships demand large crews and because triremes could only carry a few days' provisions the fleets put ashore each night for food and water. This made it difficult to impose a blockade. Fleets were vulnerable when beached for the night, a weakness highlighted during the Peloponnesian War when the Athenian navy was annihilated at Aegospotami in 405 BC. Lysander, the Spartan commander, massacred the Athenian oarsmen. Athens had demonstrated extraordinary powers of economic recovery in nearly 30 years of conflict, but while the city might be able to rebuild ships, trained seamen were irreplaceable. Athens surrendered.

Warships grew larger during the 4th and 3rd centuries BC. Roman and Carthaginian fleets used quadriremes and quinqueremes. The Roman fleet relied on boarding rather than ramming and they achieved naval superiority during the First Punic War, and maintained it during the Second Punic War (218–201 BC).

By 31 BC, when the Battle of Actium decided the Roman Civil War in favor of Octavian (later Augustus), the quinquereme was the standard battleship of the ancient Mediterranean. Larger vessels had been tried, but proved too cumbersome. Lighter warships, some relying as much on their sails as their oars, proved of greater value, and would play a greater role as Roman naval power waned in the absence of organized opposition. During the following centuries of the *Pax Romana*, warships all but vanished from the Mediterranean.

58 to 52 BC

390 BC
Gallic invasion reaches Rome

295 BC
Battle of Sentinum, prompted by Gallic invasion

58 BC
Julius Caesar's first Gallic campaign

57 BC
Caesar pacifies Belgica

55 BC
Caesar goes to the Low Countries to repel a group of invading Germans, and in turn invades German territory

53 BC
Caesar puts down another Belgian revolt and enters Germany again. Winter—all central Gaul raises a revolt. Caesar crosses Alps and suppresses the Gauls

52 BC
siege of Alesia: Caesar forces surrender of Vercingetorix

51 BC
last Gallic resistance put down

Throughout the Early Republic, Rome had been subjected to frequent invasions from the north. The Gauls even sacked the city of Rome in 390 BC and two later major battles, Sentinum (295 BC) and Telamon (225 BC), were fought against them. The Gauls were made up of conglomerations of aggressive tribes, most of which had settled in what is now France and Germany. Some moved as far south as the Po Valley. Warfare was for them a way of life, bravery in battle a sure road to elevation in the tribal hierarchy. As a result, the Gauls could be most impressive and difficult foes, especially with their savage initial charge, which could sweep all before it. The Romans called it *furor*, and they feared its effect mightily. It required all the legion's discipline, as well as superiority in armament, to keep the Roman soldiers in place when confronted by the Gallic *furor*.

The Gauls that Caesar met in the 1st century BC were the same tribes the Romans had encountered in Italy in the 3rd century BC. Their armies employed *furor*, although their weapons and armor had improved. Despite Caesar's efforts to gather votes at home by putting a spin on how fearsome they were, through his famous book *de Bello Gallico*, it is obvious that Caesar had little trouble smashing three large Gallic armies: the Helvetii, at Bibracte (58 BC); the Nervii, at the Sabis (57 BC); and the Germanic tribes under Ariovistus, somewhere west of the Rhine.

Caesar's Gallic campaigns involved several naval ventures. In order to neutralize the Armorican tribes, Caesar built a fleet of Liburnian biremes from scratch and engaged in a full-scale battle

1 Divided among themselves, the Gallic tribes were defeated one after another by the Romans (map right). Caesar exploited their inability to maintain a large army for any length of time. Avoiding battle in the early stages of a campaign, Caesar went over to the offensive as the Gauls began to disperse. He probably outnumbered the tribal armies by the time they met on the battlefield, something he was determined to conceal in his published account of the wars.

2 Vercingetorix, chief of the Arveni tribe in central Gaul, waged a "scorched earth" policy against Gallic tribes that allied themselves to Rome (map left). Caesar besieged him at Gergovia, but had to break off the siege to deal with another revolt. In 52 BC he besieged him at Alesia (Alise-Sainte-Reine) where he defeated another Gallic army that attempted to raise the siege. Vercingetorix led many attempts to break out, but was ultimately obliged to surrender.

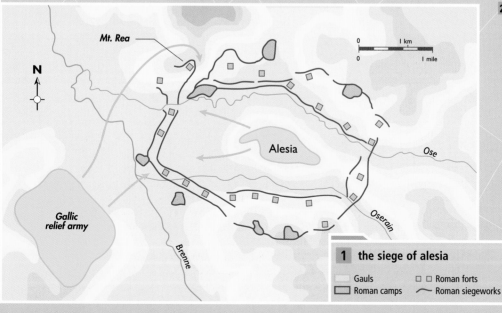

1 the siege of alesia

☐ Gauls	☐ ☐	Roman forts
☐ Roman camps	⌇	Roman siegeworks

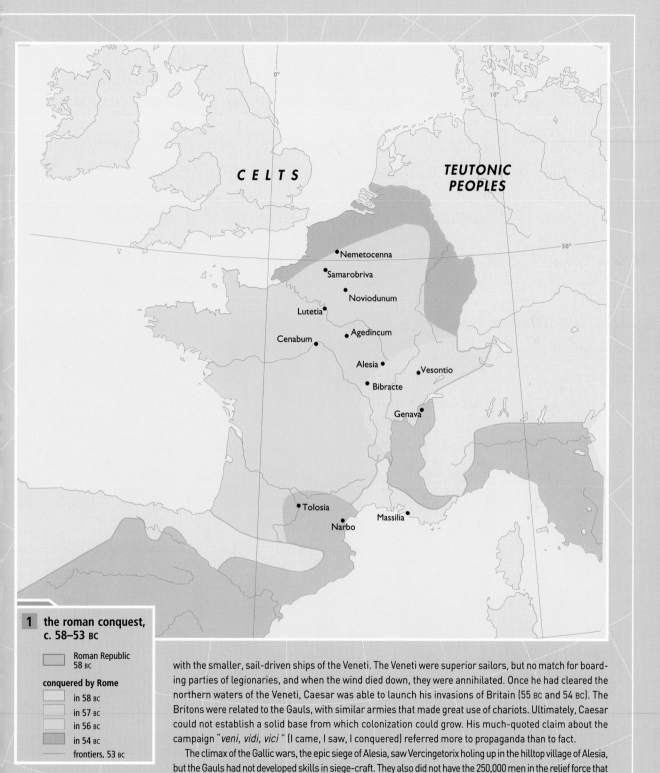

CELTS

TEUTONIC
PEOPLES

Nemetocenna
Samarobriva
Noviodunum
Lutetia
Agedincum
Cenabum
Alesia
Vesontio
Bibracte
Genava
Tolosia
Narbo
Massilia

1 the roman conquest,
c. 58–53 BC

Roman Republic
58 BC

conquered by Rome

in 58 BC

in 57 BC

in 56 BC

in 54 BC

frontiers, 53 BC

with the smaller, sail-driven ships of the Veneti. The Veneti were superior sailors, but no match for boarding parties of legionaries, and when the wind died down, they were annihilated. Once he had cleared the northern waters of the Veneti, Caesar was able to launch his invasions of Britain (55 BC and 54 BC). The Britons were related to the Gauls, with similar armies that made great use of chariots. Ultimately, Caesar could not establish a solid base from which colonization could grow. His much-quoted claim about the campaign "*veni, vidi, vici*" (I came, I saw, I conquered) referred more to propaganda than to fact.

The climax of the Gallic wars, the epic siege of Alesia, saw Vercingetorix holing up in the hilltop village of Alesia, but the Gauls had not developed skills in siege-craft. They also did not have the 250,000 men in the relief force that Caesar claims in his account. The logistics of assembling and feeding such a huge army were far beyond the ability of the Gallic chiefs. The military genius on display at Alesia was, rather, in the Roman preparations for the assault of the relief force. Vercingetorix was forced to surrender and Gallic resistance was effectively ended.

rome, germany, and parthia

109 BC
revolt of Numidian king
Jugurtha (finally defeated and
captured (104 BC)

102 BC
Romans (under Marius) crush
the Teutons at Aquae Sextiae

101 BC
Romans defeat the Cimbri at
Vercellae

53 BC
Battle of Carrhae—Parthian
victory over the invading
Crassus, who is killed

AD 9
Battle of the Teutoburger
Wald—Rome's most famous
defeat in Germany

By the end of the 2nd century BC, Gallic migrations in northern Europe had pushed some of the "Germanic" tribes towards the expanding Roman frontier. The foremost of these were the Teutons and Cimbri, who, in the 15 or so years before 100 BC, pushed west and south towards the Roman frontier. In 113 BC, they came into contact with Rome, winning four victories against small, poorly led Roman armies. When it counted, however, the Romans crushed first the Teutons, at Aquae Sextiae, and then the Cimbri, at Vercellae. Nevertheless, the halt to German aggression was temporary, as Caesar and the emperors were to find out.

The Germans tended to rely more in battle on physical bulk and brute force than the Romans. They had a few swords and virtually no armor. What they did add to the tactical mix was a method of attack Romans called "the wedge". A section of Germans would charge in a solid block with the idea of concentrating effort and energy at one point. Against mediocre troops, or other tribes, this could be a most effective tactic. Against veteran legions, it proved useless. Nowhere was this better demonstrated than at the Battle of Vercellae (101 BC). King Beorix, his Cimbri, and the German wedge could do little against the implacability of Marius' legions.

The Numidians, in Africa, and the Parthians, in the regions east of Syria, were similar in their approach to warfare. Both armies consisted almost entirely of light cavalry, and the Romans had great difficulty countering them. Numidians excelled at a hit-and-run style of warfare. Their cavalry would charge up to an enemy line of infantry, discharging their javelins as they got near, then wheeling and galloping away. If the infantry, stung by too many spears, moved out to challenge them, they swooped in, isolated the rash few and hacked them to pieces. The Romans, lacking cavalry suitable to handle this tactic, usually went on the defensive. The larger and the better the contingent of Roman cavalry, the more able it was to take the offensive.

Against the last king of Numidia, Jugurtha, who had revolted in 109 BC against Roman attempts to turn him into a puppet, the Roman legions came close to being picked apart, but their discipline, just enough cavalry to make a difference, and Marius' leadership provided Rome with two victories—and Jugurtha in chains.

Against the Parthians, they had less success. The Parthians perfected the "Parthian shot," the ability of their cavalry to fire accurately while galloping away. They were so adept at hit-and-run that a large consular army under Marcus Licinius Crassus (triumviral associate of Julius Caesar) was picked to death and destroyed at Carrhae (53 BC). Crassus' fate put Rome off any advance east of Syria for generations.

1 The Parthians overran much of the territory of the Seleucid empire (map right). Their advance westwards brought them into contact with the expanding power of Rome and in 53 BC their mounted archers surrounded and destroyed the legions of the Roman general Crassus. Parthian armies consisted mainly of these horse archers, whose ability to shoot behind them gave rise to the expression "Parthian shot." A core of heavily armored lancers (cataphracts) stood ready to charge, once the arrow storm had depleted the enemy ranks and disordered their formation.

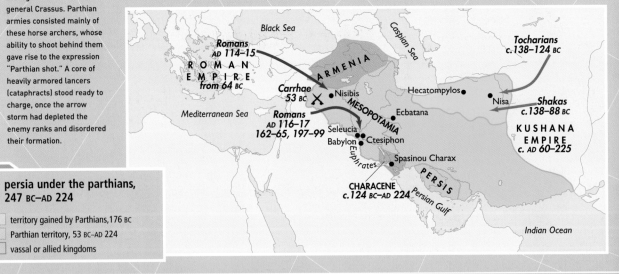

1 persia under the parthians,
247 BC–AD 224

☐ territory gained by Parthians, 176 BC
☐ Parthian territory, 53 BC–AD 224
☐ vassal or allied kingdoms

2 battle of the teutoburger wald, AD 9

areas raided by Romans

N.B. the whole area was forested

2 Rome's most famous defeat in Germany occurred in AD 9 when Varus' three legions were wiped out during their retreat to the fort at Aliso (map right). Roman vengeance followed: Germanicus led a punitive expedition in AD 14 and Drusus launched a two-pronged assault the following year. The Roman frontier seemed set to reach the Elbe, but Tiberius halted the war, afraid that victorious generals might emulate Caesar and return to Rome to seize power.

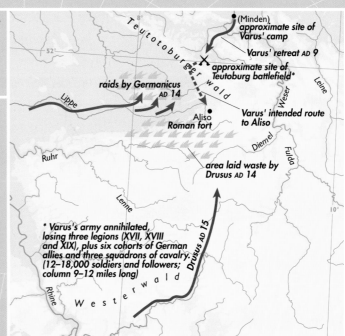

(Minden)
approximate site of Varus' camp

Varus' retreat AD 9

*approximate site of Teutoburg battlefield**

raids by Germanicus AD 14

Aliso
Roman fort

Varus' intended route to Aliso

area laid waste by Drusus AD 14

Drusus AD 15

Varus's army annihilated, losing three legions (XVII, XVIII and XIX), plus six cohorts of German allies and three squadrons of cavalry. (12–18,000 soldiers and followers; column 9–12 miles long)

W e s t e r w a l d

---

3 Unlike the Gallic tribes, the semi-nomadic Germans had no fixed bases for the Romans to attack (map left). Animal herds were their main source of food so there were no grain stores for the Romans to seize. However, by exploiting the rivers and the coast, the Romans were able to launch a series of summer campaigns, their armies sometimes overwintering at a temporary base established at Aliso. Tribes were bribed or bullied into alliance with Rome, but their long-term loyalty could be ensured only by an immediate military presence.

Tiberius' fleet AD 14

BURGUNDIONES

Roman naval expedition

CHAUCI

AD 15

tribes loyal to Rome 11 BC–AD 15

approximate route of Roman expedition

LANGOBARDI

CHERUSCI

line of temporary forts

SUGAMRI

Caecina's expedition AD 15

Noviomagus

Vetera
main Roman garrison town

Aliso
Drusus' depot 11 BC; *Tiberius' winter quarters; besieged by Germans* AD 16

(Arnsburg)

river navigable in summer

CHATTI

Colonia Agrippensis (Cologne)

Drusus AD 15

(Friedburg)
Drusus' fort AD 15
supply route

HERMUNDURI

Mogontiacum (Mainz)

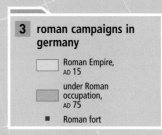

3 roman campaigns in germany

Roman Empire, AD 15

under Roman occupation, AD 75

■ Roman fort

54 to 44 BC

60 BC
first triumvirate divides Roman Empire between Julius Caesar, Marcus Crassus, and Pompey

53 BC
Crassus killed in Parthia

49 BC
Caesar declares war on Pompey, instigating five years of civil war, from which he emerges victorious

44 BC
Caesar murdered on Ides of March

31 BC
Battle of Actium: Caesar's nephew Octavian's victory makes him sole ruler of Rome

27 BC
Octavian granted title "Augustus" by the Senate; Roman Republic becomes an empire

AD 357
Battle of Argentoratum: Emperor Julian defeats the German invaders

AD 378
Roman army defeated by Goths, led by Fridigern, at Adrianople

After Caesar crossed the Rubicon to initiate his bid for supreme power, senatorial limitations on the armies became irrelevant. The numbers of Romans under arms rose to staggering proportions in the ensuing civil wars. For the next 150 or so years, most of the major battles involved legions fighting other legions, with some "time outs" to fight Germans in the north and to subdue rebellions in the east.

In 49 BC Caesar's army faced one loyal to Pompey (Gnaeus Pompeius) in Spain. Caesar outmaneuvered his opponents, cutting them off from their water supply and forcing a surrender. Caesar then shipped his army to the Balkans to attack Pompey at Dyrrhachium (Dubrovnik). The rival armies fought a pitched battle at Pharsalus in August 48 BC. Pompey's legions made little progress against Caesar's veterans and he fled to Egypt where he was murdered.

Caesar was in turn assassinated in 44 BC. His nephew Gaius Julius Caesar Octavianus (Octavian), who with Mark Antony had defeated the assassins, became sole ruler of Rome. In 27 BC, victorious at Actium (the last major naval battle of the ancient world), he was granted the title Augustus by the senate and the republic's transformation into an empire was all but complete.

By the reign of Septimius Severus (AD 193–211), the factors that led to the decline of the Roman military system were in place. By the early 3rd century, social and economic power had devolved to the provinces. Citizenship was extended to most peoples within the empire and the importance of Rome itself diminished. This affected the legions, most of which were not only stationed on the frontiers but were now allowed to settle where they served, raise families, and take jobs. Integration with local communities had a corrosive effect on the legions' military quality. The fearsome discipline of the legion disappeared, and with it the legions' advantage over "barbarian" forces. By the beginning of the 4th century, the legion had effectively disappeared.

Two major battles towards the end of the 4th century illuminate the changes that time and policy had brought. At Argentoratum (or Strasbourg) in 357, Emperor Julian routed an army of German tribes under King Chnodomer, but at Adrianople in 378, an over-eager Roman army under Emperor Valens, seeking to rid Thrace of the Goths for ever, attacked the Gothic camp only to be driven back by Gothic cavalry, enveloped, and then smashed.

But by the end of the 4th century, Rome's "legions" were now no more than a local militia; cavalry dominated the battlefield and both arms of the legion were largely recruited from "barbarian" allies.

1 From 27 BC the emperor himself was responsible for the administration of the imperial provinces (those in which legions were stationed). The others were governed by pro-consuls appointed by the senate (map above). At the start of the imperial period some parts of the empire were ruled by friendly client kings; as they died their lands became Roman provinces. Emperors could gain great glory by extending the empire. Although campaigns in the 1st century AD in Germany had only limited success, the eastern Balkans, North Africa, Arabia, and Britain were all added to Rome in the following century. Trajan added Dacia, Armenia, Assyria, and Mesopotamia, pushing the frontiers to their greatest extent. Hadrian, his successor, abandoned Trajan's conquests, save Arabia and Dacia, to consolidate more defensible frontiers.

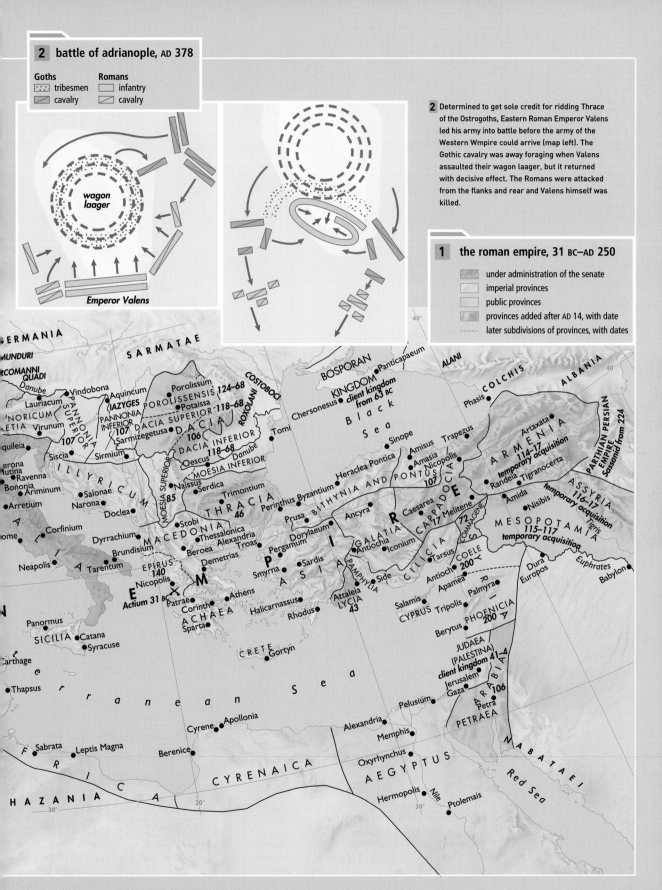

2 battle of adrianople, AD 378

Goths
- ▦ tribesmen
- ▨ cavalry

Romans
- ▢ infantry
- ▨ cavalry

wagon laager

Emperor Valens

2 Determined to get sole credit for ridding Thrace of the Ostrogoths, Eastern Roman Emperor Valens led his army into battle before the army of the Western Wmpire could arrive (map left). The Gothic cavalry was away foraging when Valens assaulted their wagon laager, but it returned with decisive effect. The Romans were attacked from the flanks and rear and Valens himself was killed.

1 the roman empire, 31 BC–AD 250

- ▨ under administration of the senate
- ▢ imperial provinces
- ▢ public provinces
- ▨ provinces added after AD 14, with date
- ▦ later subdivisions of provinces, with dates

GERMANIA
MUNDURI
RCOMANNI
QUADI
SARMATAE
ALANI
COLCHIS
ALBANIA

Danube
Lauriacum
Vindobona
NORICUM
ETIA Virunum
Aquincum
IAZYGES
PANNONIA INFERIOR
PANNONIA SUPERIOR
Potaissa
Porolissum
POROLISSENSIS 124–68
COSTOBOCI
ROXOLANI
107
PORO LISSENSIS 118–68
DACIA SUPERIOR 118–68
DACIA
DACIA INFERIOR 118–68
107
Sarmizegetusa
106
Tomi
BOSPORAN KINGDOM
Panticapaeum
client kingdom from 63 BC
Chersonesus
Phasis
ARMENIA
Artaxata
114–17 temporary acquisition
PARTHIAN PERSIAN EMPIRE Sassanid from 224

quileia
erona
utina
Ravenna
Bononia
Ariminum
Arretium
Rome
Corfinium
Neapolis
Panormus
SICILIA Catana
Syracuse
Carthage
Thapsus
Sabrata
Leptis Magna
F
HAZANIA

Siscia
Sirmium
ILLYRICUM
Salonae
Narona
Doclea
Dyrrachium
Brundisium
Tarentum
EPIRUS 140
Nicopolis
Actium 31 BC
Patrae
Corinth
Sparta
ACHAEA
Athens

MOESIA SUPERIOR
Oescus
MOESIA INFERIOR
Naissus
85
Serdica
Trimontium
Stobi
MACEDONIA
Thessalonica
Beroea
Alexandria
Demetrias
THRACIA
46
Perinthus
Byzantium
Troas
Pergamum
Dorylaeum
Smyrna
Sardis
ASIA
Ephesus
M
Halicarnassus
Rhodus
CRETE
Gortyn

Black Sea

Heraclea Pontica
BITHYNIA AND PONTUS
Prusa
Sinope
Amisus
Amasia
Nicopolis
107
Trapezus
Ancyra
GALATIA
Antiochia
Iconium
Caesarea
CAPPADOCIA
17
Melitene
72
COMMAGENE
Randeia
Tigranocerta
ASSYRIA 116–17 temporary acquisition
Amida
Nisibis
MESOPOTAMIA 115–117 temporary acquisition

CILICIA
Tarsus
COELE 200
Antioch
Apamea
Palmyra
PHOENICIA 200
Berytus
Dura Europos
Euphrates
Babylon

PAMPHYLIA
Side
Attaleia
LYCIA 43
Salamis
CYPRUS
Tripolis

JUDAEA (PALESTINA)
client kingdom 41–4
Jerusalem
Gaza
Pelusium
ARABIA
Petra
106
PETRAEA

Mediterranean Sea

Cyrene
Apollonia
Berenice
CYRENAICA
Alexandria
Memphis
Oxyrhynchus
AEGYPTUS
Hermopolis
Nile
Ptolemais
NABATAEI
Red Sea

40°
20°
30°

the **fall** of the **roman empire**

400 to 500

410
Alaric and Visigoths sack Rome

418
Visigoths found kingdom of Toulouse in Gaul

429
Vandal kingdom founded in North Africa

451
Battle of Catalaunian Fields (Châlons) in Gaul: Romans and Germanic tribes together defeat Attila and his Huns

476
the last emperor in the west, Romulus Augustulus, deposed by Odoacer, the commander-in-chief of the Roman army

from 481
Clovis, the Frankish leader, rules over Gallo–Germans and Franks in northern Gaul

507
Battle of Vouillé: Frankish king Clovis defeats Visigoths

In the course of the 5th century, a flood of Germanic and other tribes brought down the Western Roman Empire. In 407, Britain was abandoned; Gaul and North Africa were lost before the middle of the century. By 489, the heart of the empire, Italy, had been taken over by the Ostrogoths. In many ways, the defeat of the Western Empire was surprising; the Eastern, or Byzantine, Empire survived for another thousand years. In numbers, organization, tactics, and strategy, the "barbarians" were far inferior to the Romans. So why did the Germanic tribes emerge victorious?

With threats all along the imperial frontiers, the invasions had first of all to be resisted locally. Thus the relative weight of forces did not favor the Romans as much as the overall, absolute balance suggested. But, more importantly, the empire proved easy to fragment. Institutionally and ideologically, the empire turned out to be too weak for its citizens to feel forced or obliged to provide the taxes and manpower necessary to defeat the invasions. All too often, regions faced the invaders in isolation and many cities that could have withstood a siege failed to summon the necessary resistance. The invaders, on the other hand, utilized their military potential more efficiently.

After an enormous plundering spree, which left few parts of the empire unaffected, the tribes settled within it. Fascinated and impressed by the empire, the "barbarians" tried hard to become Romans. As they acquired Roman titles and functions from the waning imperial powers, they also fought wars competing for claims of succession to the empire, in whole or in part. Also important was the idea that victory in war was a sign of divine approval. For many chieftains and their followers, conversion to Christianity was clinched by the perception that the Christian god was a "God of hosts" who provided the ultimate aid in their just pursuit of worldly power. Wars

Atlantic Ocean

•Lucus August
SUEVES (SUEBI)
411–585

KINGDOM OF THE SUEVES

VIS
50

Tolet
overrun
Moors 7

•Felicitas Julia

VANDALS ALANS
409–429
•Gades

•Cor

•Tingis

1 Clovis founded the Frankish Kingdom (map left). From modern-day Belgium and northern France, he launched raids against the Visigoths in Aquitaine, the Gallo-Roman remnant of the Roman Empire under Syagrius, the Burgundians, and the Alamans. His plundering and occasional battles created an empire based not on conquest but on the acceptance of overlordship and the payment of tribute. The looseness of the empire is illustrated by the penetration of Germanic words into the local languages. Rule was an ephemeral, constantly contested, superimposition over existing societies.

1 the frankish kingdom, 511

Frankish territory at the beginning of Clovis's rule, 481

controlled by Syagrius before the Frankish conquest

conquered by Clovis by 497

conquered by Clovis, 507

boundaries between the kingdoms of Clovis's sons from 511

frontiers, 511

dates are those of Frankish conquest

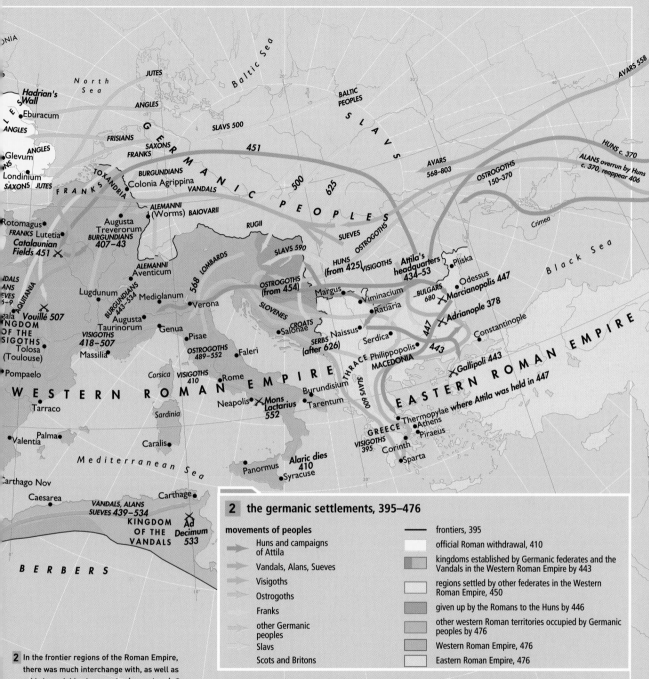

2 the germanic settlements, 395–476

movements of peoples

→ Huns and campaigns of Attila

→ Vandals, Alans, Sueves

→ Visigoths

→ Ostrogoths

→ Franks

→ other Germanic peoples

→ Slavs

→ Scots and Britons

— frontiers, 395

☐ official Roman withdrawal, 410

☐ kingdoms established by Germanic federates and the Vandals in the Western Roman Empire by 443

☐ regions settled by other federates in the Western Roman Empire, 450

☐ given up by the Romans to the Huns by 446

☐ other western Roman territories occupied by Germanic peoples by 476

☐ Western Roman Empire, 476

☐ Eastern Roman Empire, 476

2 In the frontier regions of the Roman Empire, there was much interchange with, as well as raids by, neighboring peoples (map above). On occasion entire peoples were settled as "federates" associated with the army for defense purposes. Other "barbarians" served in the ranks and in the top military posts of the imperial armies. The Huns created a major disruption and pushed groups such as the Goths and Vandals from the frontier regions of the empire. By the early 6th century, especially in the west, a number of successor states of mixed population had emerged on former Roman territory.

were not about the conquest of territory with a view to its long-term exploitation; they provided immediate profit in the form of plunder. If there was a longer-term perspective, it usually went no further than the annual extraction of tribute from defeated enemies.

The Frankish king Clovis (born 466; ruled 481–511) provides an excellent example of these developments. His very name meant "glory by combat" and his spectacular success in war was interpreted as a sign of divine favor (he converted to Christianity) that also brought him recognition from the Romans. The Byzantine emperor Anastasius made him consul after his victory over the Visigoths at the Battle of Vouillé in 507. Nonetheless, his campaigns did not usually consist of battles, which he fought rarely, but rather of yearly plunder raids deep into enemy territory.

632 to 972

The speed of the 7th-century Arab conquest still astonishes. The Prophet Muhammad established himself in the Arabian Peninsula in a period of little more than a decade. After his death in 632, Abu Bakr completed the conquest of the peninsula in two years. His successors moved into Egypt, Syria, Mesopotamia, and beyond. By 669, Arab forces had briefly laid siege to Constantinople. Before the century was out, they had penetrated deep into Persia, knocked at the gates of the Byzantine Empire in Asia Minor, and stood poised at the Straits of Gibraltar to move into Visigothic Spain.

Their main opponents, the Byzantines and Persians, had been greatly weakened by their interminable wars, and the Visigoths, Persians, and Byzantines were not closely integrated with the populations they ruled. For many it made no difference who their rulers were. Once defeated, one regime was easily replaced by another. Moreover, the Arabs were usually quite lenient in their treatment of conquered peoples. They required no conversion to Islam, only tribute, often at a rate lower than the tax burden imposed by the old regime.

Arab armies had a number of strengths. The traditional motive of lust for loot was reinforced by religious enthusiasm. With armies largely on horseback, they also possessed the twin advantages of initiative and mobility. Their knowledge of the desert enabled them to attack the old empires from a new direction. Rather than returning home every year, the Arabs, like the Vikings a little later, established armed camps along the way of their major expeditions from which they systematically launched further attacks. Famous examples with a long and distinguished future were Fustat in Egypt (which later grew into Cairo) and Basra in Iraq. Shorter-lived establishments were Qairawan, founded south of Carthage in 670; Cyzikos, just south of Constantinople (674–677); and Fraxinet, near Marseilles (circa 894–972).

The Arabs achieved another major feat in taking to the seas. In the 9th century, naval raids multiplied and led to long-term presences on Sardinia, Sicily, and Crete, as well as the Italian mainland and southern France.

Arab expansion appears to have faltered through a combination of geographic and socio-political factors. In Spain, Asia Minor, and Armenia, the Pyrenees, and the Taurus and Caucasus Mountains marked the limit respectively; in the east, the vast expanses of inner central Asia put a temporary halt to expansion. In addition, north of the Pyrenees and beyond the Taurus Mountains, the core areas of the Frankish and Byzantine realms were more loyal to their overlords than the frontier regions had been. Resistance stiffened and establishing a permanent presence became more difficult.

The Arabs also fell prey to their own internal bickering. There was no strong central power. By the 9th and 10th centuries, the Abbasid Caliphate had begun to fracture, and local dynasties seized power. In time, their divisions handed opportunities to enterprising individuals from Western Christendom and the Byzantine Empire to try and turn the tide back.

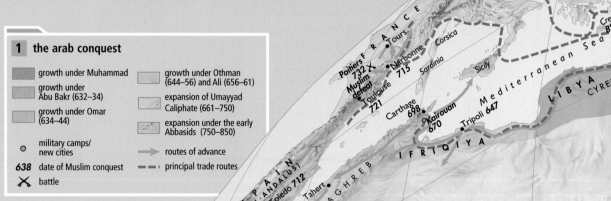

1 the arab conquest

- growth under Muhammad
- growth under Abu Bakr (632–34)
- growth under Omar (634–44)
- growth under Othman (644–56) and Ali (656–61)
- expansion of Umayyad Caliphate (661–750)
- expansion under the early Abbasids (750–850)
- ● military camps/ new cities
- **638** date of Muslim conquest
- ✕ battle
- → routes of advance
- – – – principal trade routes

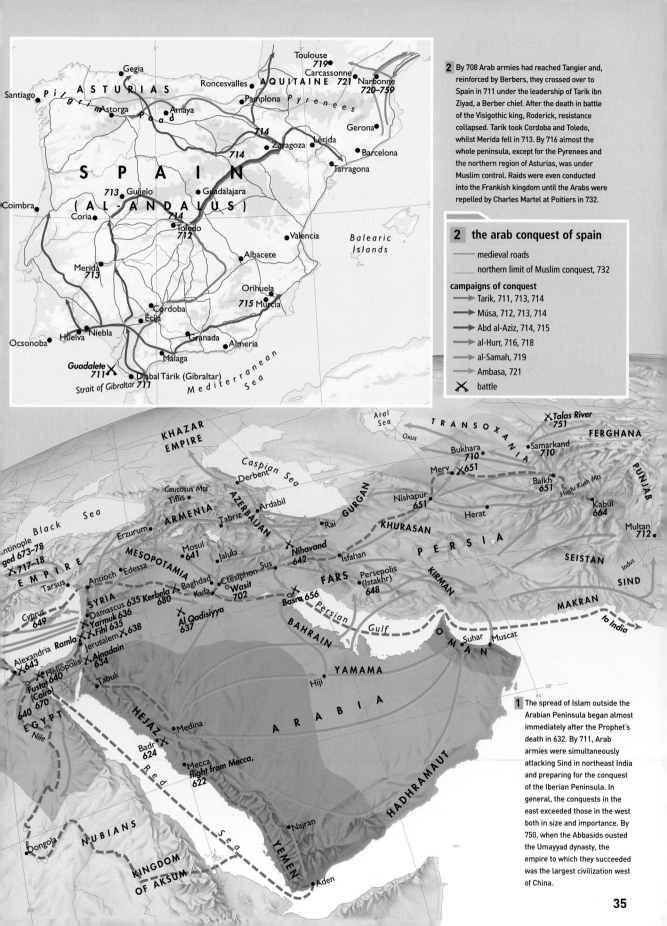

2 By 708 Arab armies had reached Tangier and, reinforced by Berbers, they crossed over to Spain in 711 under the leadership of Tarik ibn Ziyad, a Berber chief. After the death in battle of the Visigothic king, Roderick, resistance collapsed. Tarik took Cordoba and Toledo, whilst Merida fell in 713. By 716 almost the whole peninsula, except for the Pyrenees and the northern region of Asturias, was under Muslim control. Raids were even conducted into the Frankish kingdom until the Arabs were repelled by Charles Martel at Poitiers in 732.

2 the arab conquest of spain

— medieval roads
— northern limit of Muslim conquest, 732

campaigns of conquest
→ Tarik, 711, 713, 714
→ Músa, 712, 713, 714
→ Abd al-Aziz, 714, 715
→ al-Hurr, 716, 718
→ al-Samah, 719
→ Ambasa, 721
✕ battle

1 The spread of Islam outside the Arabian Peninsula began almost immediately after the Prophet's death in 632. By 711, Arab armies were simultaneously attacking Sind in northeast India and preparing for the conquest of the Iberian Peninsula. In general, the conquests in the east exceeded those in the west both in size and importance. By 750, when the Abbasids ousted the Umayyad dynasty, the empire to which they succeeded was the largest civilization west of China.

293
Emperor Diocletian divides the Roman Empire

6th century
expansion of empire under Justinian (527–65)

627
Heraclius defeats Persians at Nineveh

1071
Seljuk Turks defeat Byzantines at Manzikert

1096
the First Crusade

1204
Constantinople sacked by Fourth Crusade

1453
Turks capture Constantinople after siege; fall of the Byzantine Empire

The Byzantine Empire grew out of the partition of the Roman Empire by the Emperor Diocletian in 292. This division was made mainly for military reasons. Separate sectors, with their own armies and command structure, were intended to make the defence of the frontiers more effective. During the 5th century, the Eastern Empire was not as hard hit by invasions as the Western, and it managed to survive until its capital, Constantinople, finally fell to the Ottoman Turks in 1453.

The Byzantines inherited a well-educated military, with a core of long-serving, well-paid conscripts. The élite regularly reformed the military, partly in response to having to deal with different and changing enemies, and partly to adapt to the changing resources of the empire. Paying the army proved as much of a headache as fending off invaders. The chronic problem of raising sufficient tax money for wages led to a subdivision of the empire into "themes" in the mid-7th century. Each theme could raise a field army from soldiers who were given local land grants in return for military service. The land grant provided the soldier not only with a steady source of income, but also gave him a stake in the defense of the empire, or at least of that region. Although it helped reduce financial pressures, the themes gave rise to the problem of local armies that were effectively independent from the state. This encouraged

1 The Byzantines needed a significant tax and manpower base to support their armies. The Empire possessed this in Asia Minor, protected by mountains in the east and sea on the other sides. Nonetheless, enemies penetrated into Asia Minor and other parts of the Empire. Constantinople itself was besieged many times. Byzantine emperors tried to push the borders outward to keep the threats further away, gain access to more manpower and boost their revenue through loot and tribute. Much fighting thus took place beyond the Taurus Mountains and deep into the Balkans, as well as across the Mediterranean in Italy and North Africa.

2 The themes were administrative districts in which peasants were granted farms in exchange for service in the local army. Their establishment from the mid-7th century onwards stabilized recruitment problems. In effect the themes militarized the state by creating a capacity for a mobilization of manpower from all over the empire as well as a defense in depth.

2 **the development of the themes**

organization of *themes* in late 9th century

first five *themes* with date of foundation	the army in 840
Armeniac, 667	1,000 soldiers (a drungus)
Anatolic, 669	1,000 soldiers added in 809
Opsician, 680	1,000 soldiers added in 840
Carabisiani, 680	1,000 oarsmen
Thracian, 680	80 soldiers (an archontate)

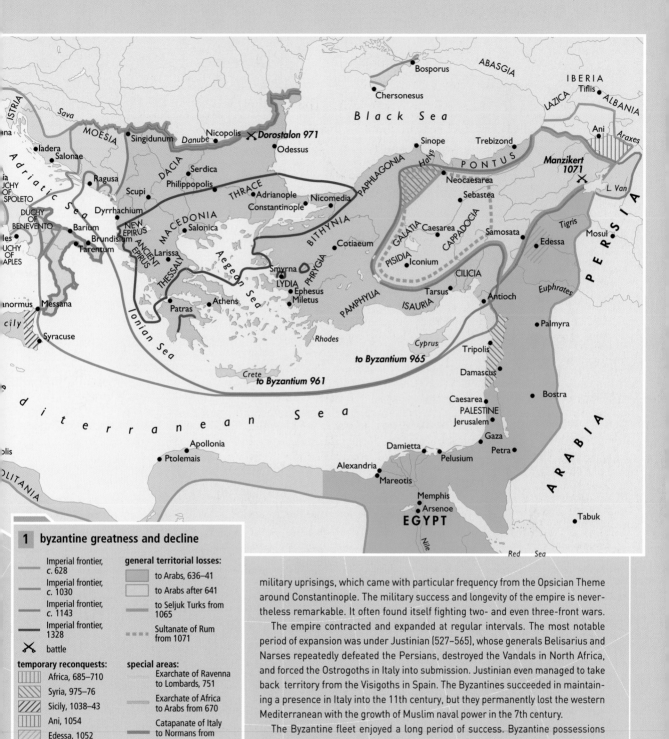

1 byzantine greatness and decline

Imperial frontier, c. 628

Imperial frontier, c. 1030

Imperial frontier, c. 1143

Imperial frontier, 1328

✕ battle

temporary reconquests:

Africa, 685–710

Syria, 975–76

Sicily, 1038–43

Ani, 1054

Edessa, 1052

Rum, c. 1118

general territorial losses:

to Arabs, 636–41

to Arabs after 641

to Seljuk Turks from 1065

Sultanate of Rum from 1071

special areas:

Exarchate of Ravenna to Lombards, 751

Exarchate of Africa to Arabs from 670

Catapanate of Italy to Normans from 1071

---

military uprisings, which came with particular frequency from the Opsician Theme around Constantinople. The military success and longevity of the empire is nevertheless remarkable. It often found itself fighting two- and even three-front wars.

The empire contracted and expanded at regular intervals. The most notable period of expansion was under Justinian (527–565), whose generals Belisarius and Narses repeatedly defeated the Persians, destroyed the Vandals in North Africa, and forced the Ostrogoths in Italy into submission. Justinian even managed to take back territory from the Visigoths in Spain. The Byzantines succeeded in maintaining a presence in Italy into the 11th century, but they permanently lost the western Mediterranean with the growth of Muslim naval power in the 7th century.

The Byzantine fleet enjoyed a long period of success. Byzantine possessions continued to dot the Italian and Balkan coasts, even when much of the interior was lost. The same was true for Asia Minor after the Seljuk Turks arrived in the 11th century and permanently breached the eastern defense. In 1071 the Byzantine emperor, Romanus IV, suffered a catastrophic defeat at the hands of the Seljuk sultan, Alp Arslan. This defeat ultimately spelled the end of the empire. Its territory began to contract to such an extent that it could no longer support adequate defenses. In the late 13th century, with the rise of the Ottoman Turks, the writing was on the wall. In the 1340s, on the invitation of a pretender in one of the interminable struggles for the Byzantine throne, they crossed into the Balkans. Soon only Constantinople's walls delimited the borders of the once-powerful empire.

the **carolingians**

732
Charles Martel defeats Arabs at Tours

768–814
reign of Charlemagne

774
Charlemagne conquers Lombard kingdom

788
Charlemagne annexes Bavaria

834
Viking attacks begin

899–955
Magyars launch 33 attacks against Germany, Italy, France, and Spain

955
Otto (the Great) defeats Magyars on the Lechfeld

The Carolingian Empire was founded on and brought down by war. The early rulers—Charles "the War Hammer" Martel (714–741), Pepin the Short (741–768), and the greatest of all, Charlemagne (768–814)—were outstanding warlords. Virtually every year of their reigns, the Carolingians led their armies in major military campaigns, gradually turning the direction of the campaigns outward—Saxons, Avars, Lombards, Moors and Bretons all suffered the depredations of the Franks, year after year. As these peoples realized that it was better to be inside than outside the Frankish realm, they began to submit and thus, particularly under Charlemagne, the empire expanded greatly. In 800, Charlemagne had himself crowned "Emperor of the Romans" by Pope Leo III in Rome.

However, after these submissions, the Franks found campaigning further east unrewarding. In Italy, geography hindered expansion, while in Spain, a strong Moorish presence made it difficult. The distances armies needed to cover to reach their enemies increased. Since armies needed to be mobilized anew for each campaign from all over the empire, more and more time was taken up by profitless travel. Cavalry became more important in Frankish armies, not so much because of their value in combat (this came later), but because mobility within the large empire was useful.

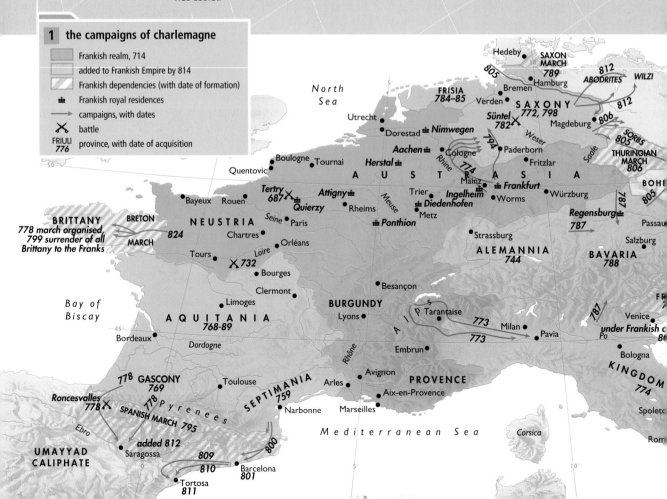

1 the campaigns of charlemagne

- Frankish realm, 714
- added to Frankish Empire by 814
- Frankish dependencies (with date of formation)
- ⚓ Frankish royal residences
- → campaigns, with dates
- ✗ battle
- FRIULI 776 province, with date of acquisition

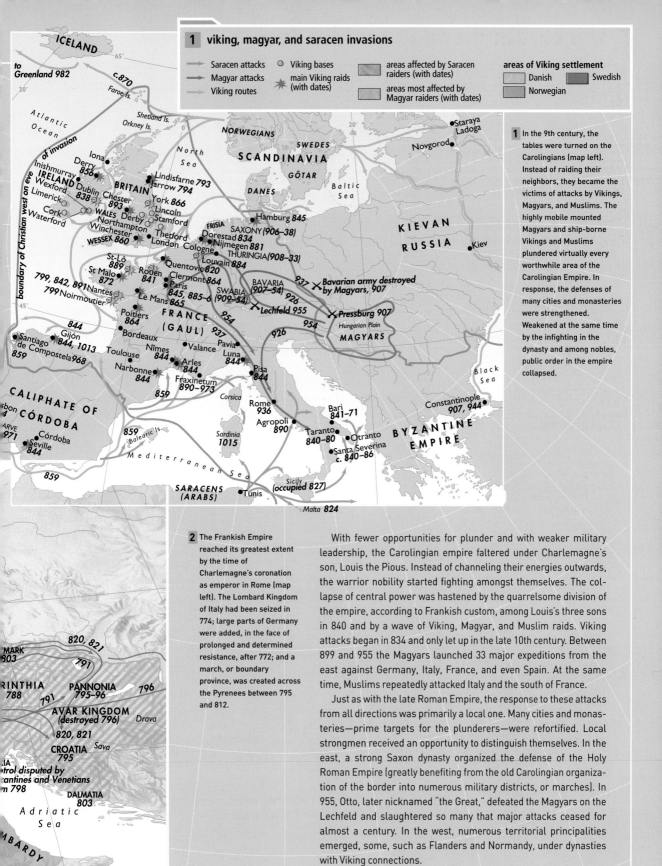

1 viking, magyar, and saracen invasions

→ Saracen attacks
→ Magyar attacks
→ Viking routes
○ Viking bases
✦ main Viking raids (with dates)
■ areas affected by Saracen raiders (with dates)
▨ areas most affected by Magyar raiders (with dates)

areas of Viking settlement
□ Danish
▨ Norwegian
▦ Swedish

1 In the 9th century, the tables were turned on the Carolingians (map left). Instead of raiding their neighbors, they became the victims of attacks by Vikings, Magyars, and Muslims. The highly mobile mounted Magyars and ship-borne Vikings and Muslims plundered virtually every worthwhile area of the Carolingian Empire. In response, the defenses of many cities and monasteries were strengthened. Weakened at the same time by the infighting in the dynasty and among nobles, public order in the empire collapsed.

2 The Frankish Empire reached its greatest extent by the time of Charlemagne's coronation as emperor in Rome (map left). The Lombard Kingdom of Italy had been seized in 774; large parts of Germany were added, in the face of prolonged and determined resistance, after 772; and a march, or boundary province, was created across the Pyrenees between 795 and 812.

With fewer opportunities for plunder and with weaker military leadership, the Carolingian empire faltered under Charlemagne's son, Louis the Pious. Instead of channeling their energies outwards, the warrior nobility started fighting amongst themselves. The collapse of central power was hastened by the quarrelsome division of the empire, according to Frankish custom, among Louis's three sons in 840 and by a wave of Viking, Magyar, and Muslim raids. Viking attacks began in 834 and only let up in the late 10th century. Between 899 and 955 the Magyars launched 33 major expeditions from the east against Germany, Italy, France, and even Spain. At the same time, Muslims repeatedly attacked Italy and the south of France.

Just as with the late Roman Empire, the response to these attacks from all directions was primarily a local one. Many cities and monasteries—prime targets for the plunderers—were refortified. Local strongmen received an opportunity to distinguish themselves. In the east, a strong Saxon dynasty organized the defense of the Holy Roman Empire (greatly benefiting from the old Carolingian organization of the border into numerous military districts, or marches). In 955, Otto, later nicknamed "the Great," defeated the Magyars on the Lechfeld and slaughtered so many that major attacks ceased for almost a century. In the west, numerous territorial principalities emerged, some, such as Flanders and Normandy, under dynasties with Viking connections.

warfare in the high middle ages

900 to 1500

10th–11th centuries
the Peace of God movement in France

1066
Battle of Hastings

1346
Battle of Crécy

1337–1453
Hundred Years' War between England and France

1415
Siege of Harfleur: Battle of Agincourt

1455–85
Wars of the Roses

Feudalism was a by-product of the extreme political fragmentation that Europe suffered with the collapse of Carolingian public order. Power became vested in a multitude of local strongmen who jealously guarded their recently acquired right to use force and administer justice. The symbols of these rights and the embodiment of their independence were the castle and the war-horse. A striking feature of medieval warfare was the extent to which it was subject to rules and rituals. This was nowhere more apparent than in siege warfare and pitched battles.

The church suffered considerably from the collapse of public order. The depredations of the 10th and early 11th centuries gave rise to a movement called the "Peace of God" in the south of France. Central to the movement was the call on knights to protect the unarmed: that is, clerics and common people. This gave rise to a code of conduct that became known as "chivalry." This was an ethos fostered partly in war and, in peacetime, through tournaments. These emerged in France in the middle of the 11th century and experienced their greatest popularity in the 12th century.

The set of laws governing siege warfare started from the premise, provided by the Bible in Deuteronomy 20:13–14, that in towns or castles that had resisted, "all males" should, on surrender, be "put to the sword" and "the loot divided among the army." This harsh principle, meant to induce immediate surrender, was tempered by the equally uncompromising principle that immediate surrender constituted treason to one's own party, which was also punishable by death. As a result, an intricate body of customs emerged by the late Middle Ages that allowed resistance and surrender

1 Castles proliferated in the 11th century (map right). The Charente is a good example of an early start. The number of castles multiplied by a factor of three to five, in some cases even many times that in a century. In Maine, there were none before 1000, 11 by 1050, and 62 by 1100. It used to be thought that this was in response to the Viking invasions. In fact, the surge began after these attacks stopped. The root cause was a failure by central, or even regional, authorities to control the process. This is suggested by such counter-examples as Normandy, which was ruled by powerful dukes. There, castle numbers increased at a much slower pace, from 12 in 1035 to just 20 in 1100. All were controlled by the duke, who prevented nobles from building castles without his permission.

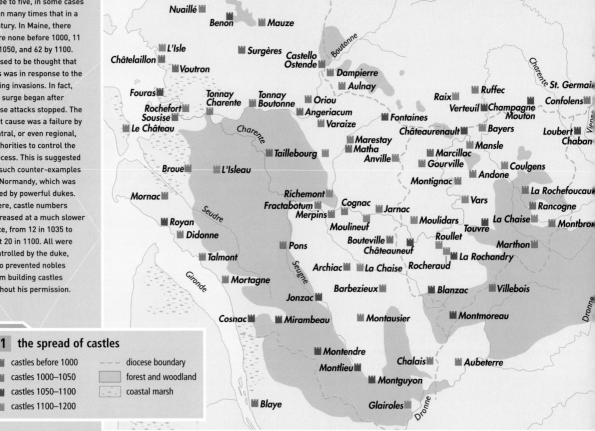

1 the spread of castles

- castles before 1000
- castles 1000–1050
- castles 1050–1100
- castles 1100–1200
- diocese boundary
- forest and woodland
- coastal marsh

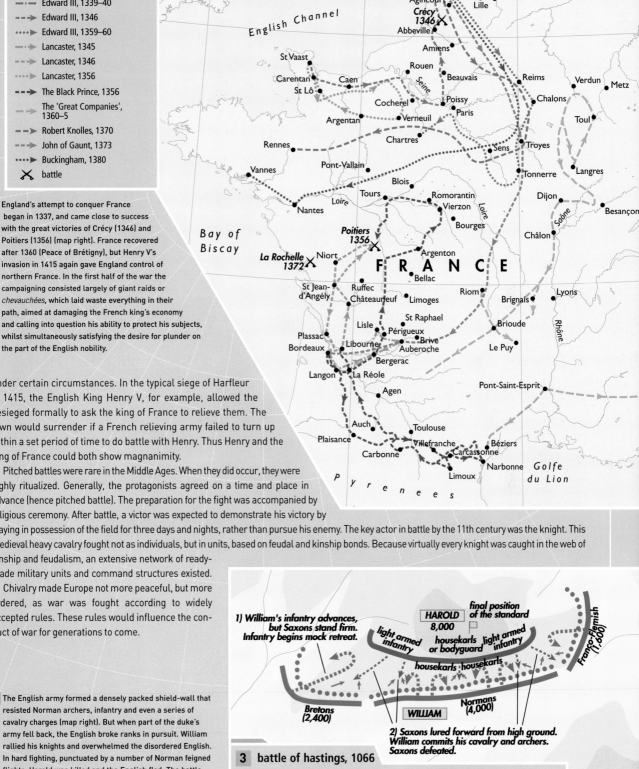

2 the hundred years war – early years, 1339–80

- —·—·→ Edward III, 1339–40
- —·—·→ Edward III, 1346
- ········→ Edward III, 1359–60
- ——→ Lancaster, 1345
- ———→ Lancaster, 1346
- ········→ Lancaster, 1356
- —·—·→ The Black Prince, 1356
- ———→ The 'Great Companies', 1360–5
- —·—·→ Robert Knolles, 1370
- —·—·→ John of Gaunt, 1373
- ········→ Buckingham, 1380
- ✕ battle

2 England's attempt to conquer France began in 1337, and came close to success with the great victories of Crécy (1346) and Poitiers (1356) [map right]. France recovered after 1360 (Peace of Brétigny), but Henry V's invasion in 1415 again gave England control of northern France. In the first half of the war the campaigning consisted largely of giant raids or *chevauchées*, which laid waste everything in their path, aimed at damaging the French king's economy and calling into question his ability to protect his subjects, whilst simultaneously satisfying the desire for plunder on the part of the English nobility.

under certain circumstances. In the typical siege of Harfleur in 1415, the English King Henry V, for example, allowed the besieged formally to ask the king of France to relieve them. The town would surrender if a French relieving army failed to turn up within a set period of time to do battle with Henry. Thus Henry and the king of France could both show magnanimity.

Pitched battles were rare in the Middle Ages. When they did occur, they were highly ritualized. Generally, the protagonists agreed on a time and place in advance (hence pitched battle). The preparation for the fight was accompanied by religious ceremony. After battle, a victor was expected to demonstrate his victory by staying in possession of the field for three days and nights, rather than pursue his enemy. The key actor in battle by the 11th century was the knight. This medieval heavy cavalry fought not as individuals, but in units, based on feudal and kinship bonds. Because virtually every knight was caught in the web of kinship and feudalism, an extensive network of ready-made military units and command structures existed.

Chivalry made Europe not more peaceful, but more ordered, as war was fought according to widely accepted rules. These rules would influence the conduct of war for generations to come.

3 The English army formed a densely packed shield-wall that resisted Norman archers, infantry and even a series of cavalry charges (map right). But when part of the duke's army fell back, the English broke ranks in pursuit. William rallied his knights and overwhelmed the disordered English. In hard fighting, punctuated by a number of Norman feigned flights, Harold was killed and the English fled. The battle between the two claimants for the English throne is depicted in the accounts of the time as a divine judgement.

1) William's infantry advances, but Saxons stand firm. Infantry begins mock retreat.

2) Saxons lured forward from high ground. William commits his cavalry and archers. Saxons defeated.

HAROLD 8,000 — final position of the standard

light armed infantry — housekarls or bodyguard — light armed infantry

housekarls · housekarls

Franco-Flemish (1,600)

Bretons (2,400)

WILLIAM

Normans (4,000)

3 battle of hastings, 1066

- ▬▬ Harold's position
- ·····➤ Saxon movement from high ground
- ▬▬ Norman cavalry and infantry, deployed at 9 a.m.
- ●●● Norman archers
- ▪▪▪➤ Norman infantry advance and retreat
- —→ Norman cavalry and archer attacks

41

the **crusades**

1095 to 1291

1096–99
First Crusade

1146–48
Second Crusade

1189–92
Third Crusade

1202–04
Fourth Crusade

1228–29
Fifth Crusade

1248–54
Sixth Crusade

1395
Crusade of Nicopolis

1444
Crusade of Varna

Towards the end of the 11th century the chivalric idea culminated in its supreme expression: the Christian enterprise of the Crusade. The church offered remission of sins for those who would fight to liberate and defend the Holy Land. The Crusades were the most ambitious military operations undertaken by the Christian West in the Middle Ages. Beginning in 1095, with the preaching of a crusade by Pope Urban II, and ending in 1291, with the loss of the last outpost in Palestine, Christian warriors attempted to restore Jerusalem and the surrounding Holy Land to Christianity.

First and foremost, the Crusades were the expression of an idea. All the material motives usually ascribed to crusaders—lust for power, land and, loot—were secondary to this religious purpose, the liberation of Jerusalem. Since the material motives could have been satisfied much closer to home, without an arduous journey across inhospitable lands and seas, it required considerable conviction for the tens of thousands of crusaders to undertake the dangerous and expensive expedition. Nonetheless, land and loot were important subsidiary considerations. Both provided an attractive and expected bonus to the spiritual salvation offered by the church.

The crusaders have often been criticized for their lack of unity. The army of the First Crusade (1096–99) started out with perhaps 4,500 knights and 30,000 foot soldiers. It not only suffered serious casualties in an astonishingly high number of 12 battles and four sieges before reaching Jerusalem, but also lost significant numbers to the ambitions of such leaders as Baldwin, Bohemond of Taranto, and Raymond of Toulouse who sought to create principalities around Edessa and Antioch. The army that took Jerusalem may have counted only 1,200 knights and 12,000 infantry. The new principalities, however, served an important purpose by providing strategic depth to the defense of the new Kingdom of Jerusalem.

Later crusaders sought to avoid the difficult land journey to and from Palestine and, instead, traveled by sea. When the center of Muslim power shifted to Egypt in the 13th century, the direction of the later Crusades (the Fifth, 1228–29, and Sixth, 1248– j54) changed accordingly. The best sources of plunder automatically led to strategically important areas and

2 battle of arsuf, 1191

☐ Crusaders ☐ Muslims

1 *Hospitallers*
2 *Burgundians*
3 *Champagnois*
4 *Poitevins*
5 *Angevins*

0   1 km
0   I mile

N

skirmishers

KING RICHARD

Arsuf

2 Marching from Acre to Jaffa in September 1191, a crusading army under Richard "Coeur de Lion" met the army of Saladin (map left). Richard advanced with infantry and crossbowmen protecting the cavalry from Muslim archers. The right flank was protected by the sea, the left by cavalry, so that they and the cavalry in the center could sally forth to beat off attacks or smash the main body of the enemy. On 7 September, Saladin's forces closed in but were shattered by three successive charges.

1 Beginning with the First Crusade, preached by Pope Urban II at the Council of Clermont (1095), the crusading movement inspired Christian Europe's struggle against the enemies of the faith—both internal and external—for four centuries (map above). Even after the fall of the last stronghold in Palestine in 1291, Crusades were fought to defend the Balkans against the Ottoman Turks, to complete the Reconquista in Spain, and against pagans around the Baltic.

Reconquista: grad conquest of southern of Iberian Peninsul completed by 1492

PORTUGAL

Lisbon

Las Na Tolosa
GRANADA
(1238–1492)
Granada

A L M O R A V
A L M O H A D
(1140–1269)

42   the **crusades**

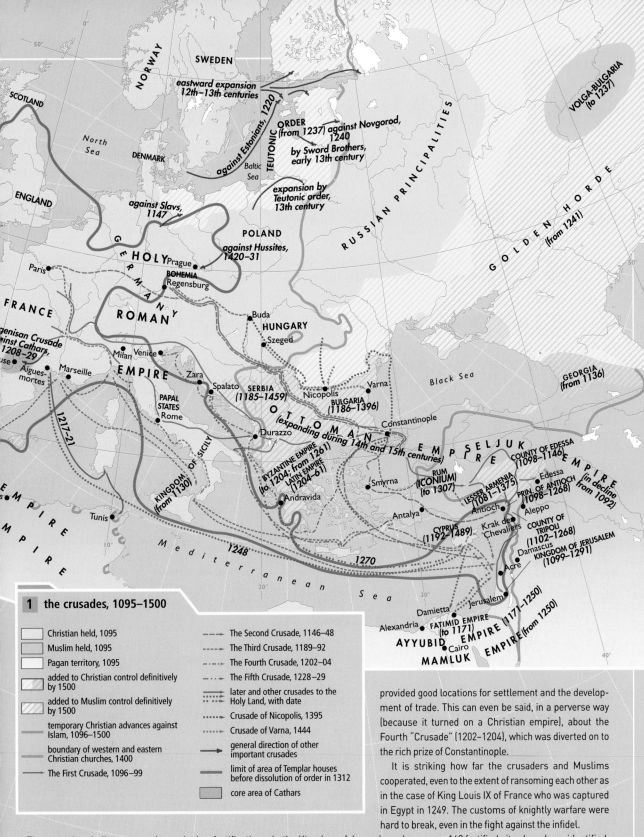

SCOTLAND

North
Sea

ENGLAND

NORWAY

SWEDEN

DENMARK

Baltic
Sea

eastward expansion 12th–13th centuries

against Estonians, 1220

TEUTONIC ORDER
(from 1237) *against Novgorod,
1240*

*by Sword Brothers,
early 13th century*

*against Slavs,
1147*

*expansion by
Teutonic order,
13th century*

RUSSIAN PRINCIPALITIES

VOLGA-BULGARIA
(to 1237)

GOLDEN HORDE
(from 1241)

FRANCE

Paris

G E R M A N Y
HOLY
Prague
BOHEMIA
Regensburg

POLAND
*against Hussites,
1420–31*

R O M A N

EMPIRE

Milan Venice

Marseille

Aigues-
mortes

1217–21

*Igensian Crusade
inst Cathars,
1208–29*
use

Zara

PAPAL
STATES
Rome

KINGDOM
(from 1130)

OF SICILY

Tunis

Buda

HUNGARY

Szeged

Spalato

SERBIA
(1185–1459)

Durazzo

Nicopolis

BULGARIA
(1186–1396)

Varna

Black Sea

GEORGIA
(from 1136)

O T T O M A N

(expanding during 14th and 15th centuries)

Constantinople

BYZANTINE EMPIRE
(to 1204; from 1261)
LATIN EMPIRE
(1204–61)

Andravida

Smyrna

RUM
(ICONIUM)
(to 1307)

E M P I R E SELJUK

LESSER ARMENIA
(1081–1375)

Antalya

CYPRUS
(1192–1489)

Antioch

Krak des
Chevaliers

COUNTY OF EDESSA
(1098–1146)

Edessa

PRIN. OF ANTIOCH
(1098–1268)

Aleppo

COUNTY OF
TRIPOLI
(1102–1268)

Damascus

E M P I R E
(in decline
from 1092)

Mediterranean Sea

1248

1270

Acre

KINGDOM OF JERUSALEM
(1099–1291)

EMPIRE

EMPIRE

Damietta

Jerusalem

Alexandria

FATIMID EMPIRE
(to 1171)

Cairo

AYYUBID

MAMLUK

EMPIRE (1171–1250)

EMPIRE (from 1250)

---

1 the crusades, 1095–1500

☐ Christian held, 1095	- - -▷ The Second Crusade, 1146–48
☐ Muslim held, 1095	- - - - The Third Crusade, 1189–92
☐ Pagan territory, 1095	-·-·- The Fourth Crusade, 1202–04
☐ added to Christian control definitively by 1500	- - - The Fifth Crusade, 1228–29
☐ added to Muslim control definitively by 1500	⟶ later and other crusades to the Holy Land, with date
── temporary Christian advances against Islam, 1096–1500	····· Crusade of Nicopolis, 1395
── boundary of western and eastern Christian churches, 1400	······ Crusade of Varna, 1444
── The First Crusade, 1096–99	⟶ general direction of other important crusades
	── limit of area of Templar houses before dissolution of order in 1312
	▨ core area of Cathars

provided good locations for settlement and the development of trade. This can even be said, in a perverse way (because it turned on a Christian empire), about the Fourth "Crusade" (1202–1204), which was diverted on to the rich prize of Constantinople.

It is striking how far the crusaders and Muslims cooperated, even to the extent of ransoming each other as in the case of King Louis IX of France who was captured in Egypt in 1249. The customs of knightly warfare were hard to break, even in the fight against the infidel.

The crusaders built many castles and other fortifications. In the Kingdom of Jerusalem alone some 162 fortified sites have been identified. However, one lost battle could easily lead castles to fall like dominoes—as indeed happened after the Battle of Hattin in 1187.

PART III | **THE MILITARY RENAISSANCE 1500-1650**

the **italian** wars

The rediscovery of classical Greek and Roman thought, known as the Renaissance, affected warfare as well as painting, literature, and architecture. Fifteenth-century Italy had the most sophisticated culture in Europe. Its well-developed economy also supported the most mature military institutions. Wealthy city-states blended military professionalism and civil administration to secure political stability, and for a while the military capability of great powers. Italy's disunity and wealth, however, were an irresistible temptation to her neighbours.

Italy lay at the crossroads of regionally distinctive military traditions. The French invaders had the best heavy cavalry and field artillery in the world. The offensive capability of Swiss pikemen, rare in medieval infantry, inspired imitation by German *landsknechts*. Spanish armies that traditionally relied on infantry quickly adopted the pike, and replaced their crossbows with the arquebus or *hackenbusche*. The arquebus was the key weapon of the military renaissance. Requiring little training, it was readily transferable across national borders, unlike the pike, which the French never mastered. It revolutionized the soldier's equipment and killed regardless of social class or armor. The rapid spread of

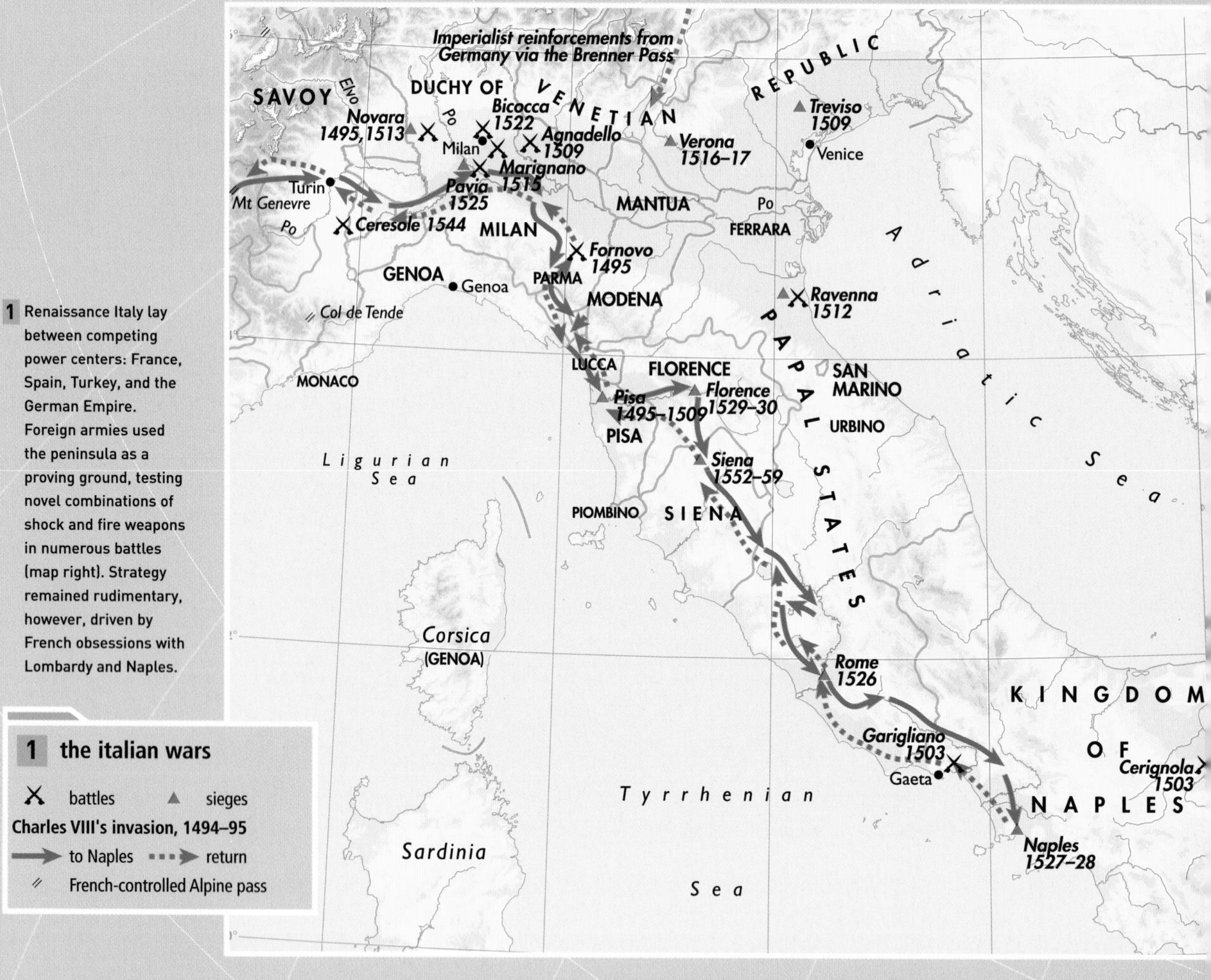

1 Renaissance Italy lay between competing power centers: France, Spain, Turkey, and the German Empire. Foreign armies used the peninsula as a proving ground, testing novel combinations of shock and fire weapons in numerous battles (map right). Strategy remained rudimentary, however, driven by French obsessions with Lombardy and Naples.

1 the italian wars

✕ battles   ▲ sieges

Charles VIII's invasion, 1494–95

➡ to Naples   ┅➤ return

⁄⁄ French-controlled Alpine pass

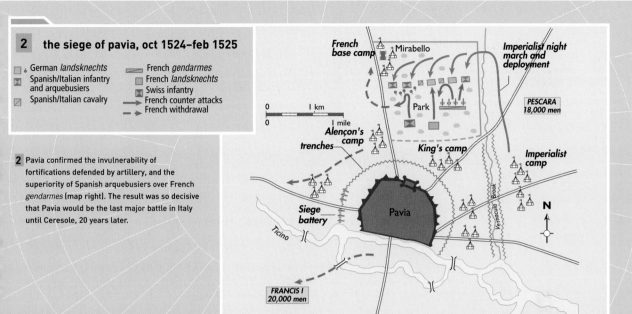

2 **the siege of pavia, oct 1524–feb 1525**

- ▫ German *landsknechts*
- ▨ Spanish/Italian infantry and arquebusiers
- ▨ Spanish/Italian cavalry
- ▱ French *gendarmes*
- ▨ French *landsknechts*
- ▨ Swiss infantry
- → French counter attacks
- ⇠ French withdrawal

0   1 km

0   1 mile

2 Pavia confirmed the invulnerability of fortifications defended by artillery, and the superiority of Spanish arquebusiers over French *gendarmes* (map right). The result was so decisive that Pavia would be the last major battle in Italy until Ceresole, 20 years later.

mass-produced handguns fuelled the growth of armies, paid for by loans and higher taxes. The proportion of infantry carrying firearms rose steadily, from 30% at Venice in 1548 to 60 % in the Spanish army of 1600. Commentators in the 1590s thought hand-to-hand combat a rarity.

The battles of the Italian Wars show the development of the new European tactical consensus, as the arquebus transformed the dominant mode of combat from shock to attrition. The opening battle at Fornovo (6 July 1495) recalled the chivalric past. French *gensdarmes* rode down similar Italian heavy cavalry, disordered by an unexpectedly flooded stream. Cerignola (April 1503) saw the first combination of arquebus and fieldworks to checkmate heavy cavalry, but at Ravenna (11 April 1512) cannon appeared to be the antidote to Spanish trenches. Field artillery played a decisive battlefield role for the first time, although it was the French heavy cavalry who clinched victory by penetrating the Spanish defenses to take their infantry in the rear. Novara (6 June 1513) and Marignano (13/14 September 1515) revolved around Swiss attempts to forestall the deadly combination of field artillery and heavy cavalry, but Bicocca (27 April 1522) vindicated the Spanish defensive school. Prosper Colonna, a typically cautious *condottiere* (mercenary commander), placed pikemen close behind his entrenched arquebusiers, to win the handgun's first major victory. Pavia (24 February 1525) confirmed the tactical dominance of firearms, this time in the open. Furious cavalry charges failed to break Spanish pikemen supported by arquebusiers, who shot down the French nobility around their king. So decisive was the Spanish victory that the French exchanged their crossbows for the arquebus.

europe and the ottoman empire

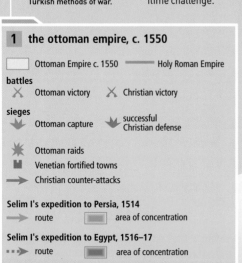

The main threat to the military renaissance lay outside Europe. The Ottoman Empire more than doubled in size during the early 16th century and under Suleiman the Magnificent (1520–66) overran Hungary. Turkish corsairs raided as far west as Spain. Distance limited Ottoman expansion, however, while their military institutions stagnated.

The Ottoman Empire followed a different military model to Western Europe. The sultan ruled a monolithic state. His refusal to recognize other rulers as equals provoked conflict with Christian and Muslim powers alike. Turkish armies reflected this centralization of authority. Turkish tactics combined the defensive power of infantry and guns with the fluidity and resilience of nomad light cavalry. They changed little between Kosovo in 1389 and Kerestes in 1596. The Turks adopted firearms, but these were neither essential nor a Turkish monopoly. The system worked as well against the Hungarians at Mohács who had guns, as against the Persians at Çaldiran (23 August 1514), who did not.

The sultan's absolute power of life and death and the inspiration of Islam forged a discipline unknown in other armies, whose disunity was a major factor in Ottoman success. Treachery contributed to the Mameluke defeat at Mercidabik (24 August 1516). Less than half the Hungarian army turned up for Mohacs, while Hungarian renegades accompanied Suleiman to Vienna in 1529. The most crucial defection was that of France. Habsburg–Valois rivalry diverted Charles V from defending Vienna, and destabilized the Mediterranean. Turkish galleys were short-range vessels with large crews and fragile hulls. A French alliance allowed them to winter in Marseilles, and raid the Spanish and Italian coasts, turning the Habsburg flank when the Danubian front stabilized in the 1530s. The capture of Malta would have perpetuated the Turkish naval presence in the western Mediterranean. However, the island's new fortifications and hard fighting by the Knights of St. John, the last of the Crusading Orders, halted the Ottoman advance in 1564. At the Battle of Lepanto (7 October 1571), the largest naval action since Actium, a coalition of Christian naval powers ended the Turkish maritime challenge.

1 The Ottoman Empire (map right) expanded rapidly in the early 16th century, exploiting weak and divided opposition. After the 1520s increased distances from the center of power at Constantinople to the frontiers prevented further expansion, while tactics and fortifications developed in Italy proved superior to stereotyped and inflexible Turkish methods of war.

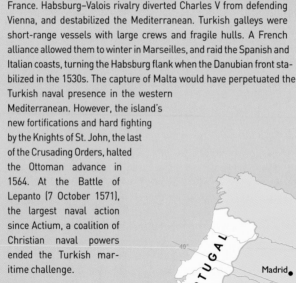

1 the ottoman empire, c. 1550

☐ Ottoman Empire c. 1550   ── Holy Roman Empire

battles
✕ Ottoman victory   ✕ Christian victory

sieges
⬇ Ottoman capture   ⬇ successful Christian defense

✺ Ottoman raids
◼ Venetian fortified towns
➡ Christian counter-attacks

Selim I's expedition to Persia, 1514
➡ route   ▭ area of concentration

Selim I's expedition to Egypt, 1516–17
┅➡ route   ▭ area of concentration

FRANCE

Bru•

50°

SW
SAVO

NAVARRE

PORTUGAL

Madrid•

40°

SPAIN   ARAGON

Marseilles
Turkish fleet over-winters 1543–4

Rosas 1543
Palamos 1543
Barcelona•

Minorca
1536
Majorca

Ibiza

M

Tangier•   •Gibraltar
•Ceuta

Melilla•

SULTANATE OF
MOROCCO

Oran
1563

Algiers
1541

Bugia•
1555

Bona•

B

ALGERIA
Ottoman vassal from 1537

0°

Or

Me

Geography and political centralization limited Ottoman expansion. The sultan's personal household troops were the basis of Turkish invincibility, and he could fight only on one front. As the empire grew, the campaigning season, when grass was available, grew shorter. Vienna was saved by its distance from the center of Ottoman power in Constantinople. Turkish armies could not fight in winter; horses died, and janissaries mutinied. A predominantly cavalry force easily overran the open spaces of Hungary and Syria, but suffered heavy losses in the mountains of Styria and Armenia. Bastioned fortifications defied the Turks' energetic but unscientific siege techniques. Rhodes surrendered for want of gunpowder, and Famagusta through treachery. Abortive sieges at Vienna and Malta mark the maximum reach of the Ottoman Empire. Suleiman died of dysentery during the siege of Szigeth (August–September 1566), ending the most serious external threat to Europe for 400 years.

2 Ottoman armies used similar tactics against Hungarians, Mamelukes, and Persians, supplementing the standard wagon laager of steppe warfare with cannon and professional infantry (map right). This firebase broke up enemy attacks, and provided a rallying point for the swarms of Turkish light cavalry.

SULTAN SELIM c. 60,000 men

SHAH ISMAIL c. 50,000 men

Turkish camp

Zaveyeh

Persian camp

Dize

2 battle of çaldiran, 1514

Turkish forces
- ⚑ Sultan Selim
- Timariot cavalry
- Janissaries
- Spahis
- irregular infantry

Persian forces
- Persian cavalry

SMALL STATES

LUSATIA SILESIA

POLAND

BOHEMIA

BAVARIA

MORAVIA

HUNGARY

Innsbruck Vienna 1529

AUSTRIA

TYROL STYRIA

Buda 1529

TRANSYLVANIA

MOLDAVIA

JEDISAN

KHANATE OF CRIMEA

ÇERKES

death of Suleiman the Magnificent, Szigeth 1566

VENICE

Senj CROATIA

Zara

DALMATIA

Trau Spalato

Mohács 1526

Belgrade 1521

WALLACHIA

Kosovo 1389

Nicopolis 1396

Black Sea

GEORGIA

Erzerum 1552

AZERB

PAPAL STATES

Rome

Cattaro 1538

Scutari

REP. OF RAGUSA

OTTOMAN

Constantinople

Çaldiran 1514

Naples 1544

NAPLES

Brindisi

Otranto 1480

Valona 1537

ALBANIA

Corfu 1537

Preveza 1538 Lepanto 1571

Chios gained from Genoa, 1566

ANATOLIA

EMPIRE

Lipari Is. 1544

Palermo

Sicily

Reggio 1534, 1541

Levkas

Cephalonia

Zante

Navarino

Action

MOREA

Nauplia

Samos

Tenos

Merjdabik 1516

Modon gained from Venice, 1500

Corone

Monemvasia

Naxos gained from Venice, 1566

Malta 1565

Cerigo gained from Venice, 1540

Crete

Rhodes gained from Knights Hospitallers, 1522

Cyprus

Nicosia 1551

Famagusta 1570–1

SYRIA conquered 1517

Tripoli 1551

Younis Khan

warfare in india and china

1500 to 1650

1526
Battle of Panipat: Babur conquers Delhi sultanate and founds Mughal Empire; seizes control of Hindustan

1550
Mongol threat re-emerges. Japanese pirate attacks on China increase

1644
Ming Dynasty toppled

The largest states of the early modern world lay in the Far East. Both Ming China and Mughal India were regional superpowers. They possessed gunpowder weapons, but these only reinforced existing military patterns, preventing the type of change seen in the West.

Chinese and Indian military establishments ran into millions, but structural weaknesses limited effectiveness. The Hindu caste system prevented *sowars* doing menial jobs usually undertaken by troopers. The Mughal army with which Babur seized control of Hindustan in 1526 was a lean outfit, hardened by campaigns in central Asia.

Ming China, with its bureaucratic tradition, had permanent training camps to prepare provincial units for expeditions or service on the northern border, but standards of training and equipment declined in the 16th century. Attempts to recruit competent leaders by examination failed, since educated Chinese despised military service. Unpaid garrisons took up banditry or farming. Raids from Mongolia imposed a stifling burden. The aggressive forward policy of the early 15th century cost three times the emperor's annual revenue, but subsequent withdrawal behind the Great Wall deprived the Ming of influence and vital intelligence. Famine and banditry destabilized late Ming society to the point where only an external force could restore order. The Manchu, like the Mughals, were seen as an army of occupation. Socially conservative, they had no taste for destabilizing military innovation.

The Chinese had invented gunpowder weapons in the late 13th century, but the speed and strategic flexibility of their nomadic opponents outweighed theoretically superior weaponry. In the disastrous T'umu campaign (July–August 1449) 20,000 Mongols wiped out a Ming army of half a million and captured the emperor.

1 the confucian triumph

- —— Grand Canal
- ⊡ national capital
- ⊙ provincial capitals
- ✕ battle
- ⟶ Cheng Ho's expeditions, 1405–33

Ming frontier defenses
- ∿∿∿ Great Wall
- ▫ border garrisons
- ◼ guard units

Yung-lo's expeditions
- – – ▸ 1410
- ·····▸ 1414
- – ·– ▸ 1424

Ming offensives
- ····▸ in Korea, 1593
- ⟶ disasters against Nurhaci, 1619
- ✕ Korean naval successes
- ✕ Japanese naval successes

Japanese offensives
- ⟶ pirate raids, 1540–65
- ▢ invasions after 1550
- ⟶ in Korea, 1592
- ····▸ in Korea, 1597

Litzu Cheng's revolt
- ▢ focus of revolt, 1539–40
- – – ▸ raids
- ⟶ advance on Peking

consolidation of Manchu rule
- – – ▸ 1645
- – –▸ 1646
- ·····▸ 1647–50

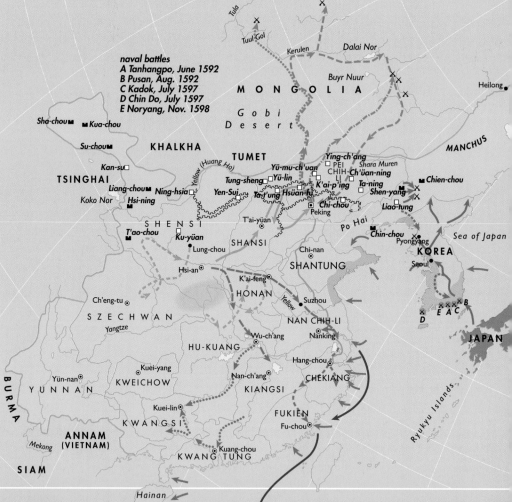

naval battles
A Tanhangpo, June 1592
B Pusan, Aug. 1592
C Kadok, July 1597
D Chin Do, July 1597
E Noryang, Nov. 1598

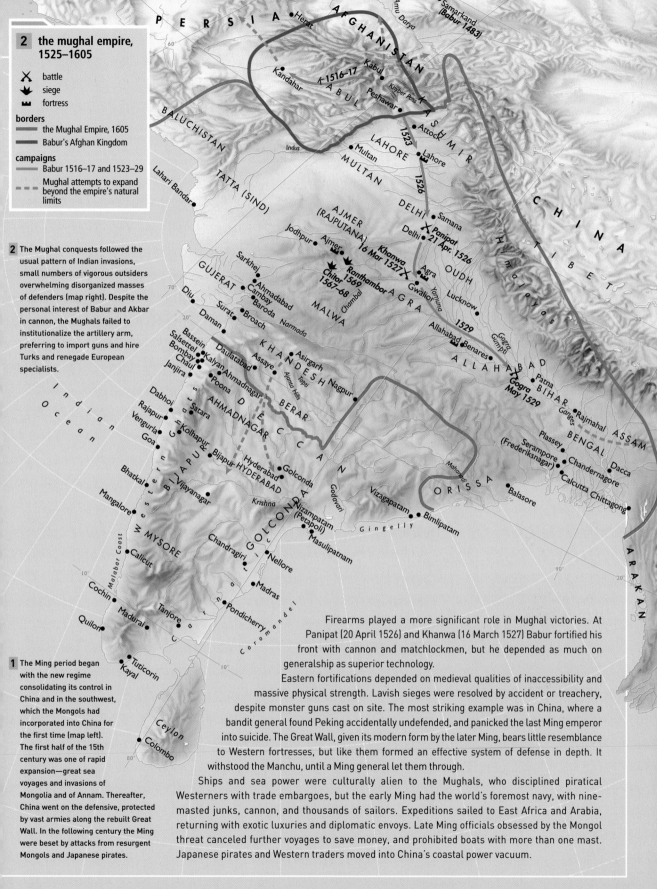

2 the mughal empire, 1525–1605

✕ battle
🔱 siege
♛ fortress

borders
⎯⎯ the Mughal Empire, 1605
⎯⎯ Babur's Afghan Kingdom

campaigns
⎯⎯ Babur 1516–17 and 1523–29
- - - Mughal attempts to expand beyond the empire's natural limits

2 The Mughal conquests followed the usual pattern of Indian invasions, small numbers of vigorous outsiders overwhelming disorganized masses of defenders (map right). Despite the personal interest of Babur and Akbar in cannon, the Mughals failed to institutionalize the artillery arm, preferring to import guns and hire Turks and renegade European specialists.

1 The Ming period began with the new regime consolidating its control in China and in the southwest, which the Mongols had incorporated into China for the first time (map left). The first half of the 15th century was one of rapid expansion—great sea voyages and invasions of Mongolia and of Annam. Thereafter, China went on the defensive, protected by vast armies along the rebuilt Great Wall. In the following century the Ming were beset by attacks from resurgent Mongols and Japanese pirates.

Firearms played a more significant role in Mughal victories. At Panipat (20 April 1526) and Khanwa (16 March 1527) Babur fortified his front with cannon and matchlockmen, but he depended as much on generalship as superior technology.

Eastern fortifications depended on medieval qualities of inaccessibility and massive physical strength. Lavish sieges were resolved by accident or treachery, despite monster guns cast on site. The most striking example was in China, where a bandit general found Peking accidentally undefended, and panicked the last Ming emperor into suicide. The Great Wall, given its modern form by the later Ming, bears little resemblance to Western fortresses, but like them formed an effective system of defense in depth. It withstood the Manchu, until a Ming general let them through.

Ships and sea power were culturally alien to the Mughals, who disciplined piratical Westerners with trade embargoes, but the early Ming had the world's foremost navy, with nine-masted junks, cannon, and thousands of sailors. Expeditions sailed to East Africa and Arabia, returning with exotic luxuries and diplomatic envoys. Late Ming officials obsessed by the Mongol threat canceled further voyages to save money, and prohibited boats with more than one mast. Japanese pirates and Western traders moved into China's coastal power vacuum.

the **wars** of religion

1562 to 1598

1562–63
French Protestants' struggle for freedom of worship and the right of establishment begins first civil war

1572
Massacre of Saint Bartholomew's Day

1577
Catholics persuade Henry III to repeal the edict of toleration

1585–89
War of the Three Henrys

1598
Wars conclude with Edict of Nantes in France and with the Treaty of Vervins with Spain

The French Religious Wars arose from a triangular struggle between the Crown and two factions, the Catholic League and Protestant Huguenots. Both sought to control a royal government weakened by the struggle with the Habsburgs, and a by succession of minors.

The Huguenots lacked the siege guns to complete victories won by their superior cavalry, but held too many towns themselves for the league to take them all. Protected by salt marshes or mountains, Huguenot redoubts at La Rochelle and in the Cevennes only fell to a revived royal government in the late 1620s. The crushing Huguenot defeat at Moncontour (3 October 1569) should have ended the war then, but the local nature of the struggle reduced the significance of pitched battles. Warlordism was endemic. Local gentry perpetuated instability for amusement and profit. The primacy of religious over national feeling encouraged and legitimized foreign intervention, which sustained the combatants whenever domestic support faltered.

The infrequency of battles in the later Italian Wars devalued traditional heavy cavalry. They were useless for sieges, and worn out by campaign duties like reconnaissance or raiding. The old French companies of *gensdarmes*

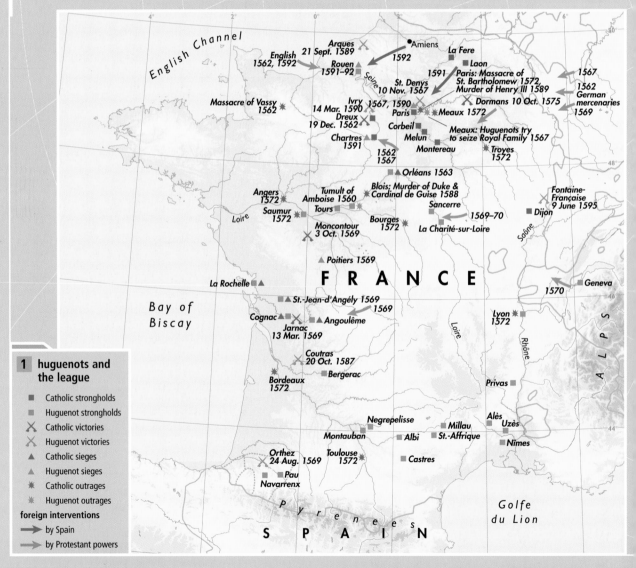

1 **huguenots and the league**

- ■ Catholic strongholds
- ■ Huguenot strongholds
- ✕ Catholic victories
- ✕ Huguenot victories
- ▲ Catholic sieges
- ▲ Huguenot sieges
- ✳ Catholic outrages
- ✳ Huguenot outrages

foreign interventions
- → by Spain
- → by Protestant powers

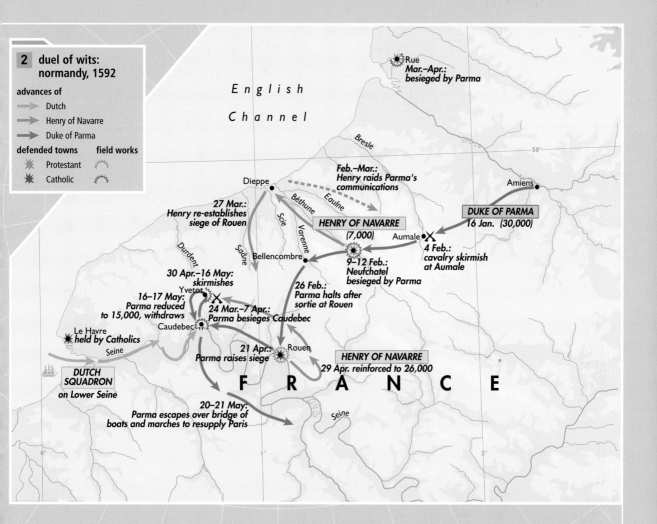

2 duel of wits: normandy, 1592

advances of
→ Dutch
→ Henry of Navarre
→ Duke of Parma

defended towns   field works
✳ Protestant   〜 (light field works)
✴ Catholic   〜 (dark field works)

English Channel

Rue
Mar.–Apr.:
besieged by Parma

Bresle

Amiens

Dieppe

Feb.–Mar.:
Henry raids Parma's
communications

Béthune   Eaulne

27 Mar.:
Henry re-establishes
siege of Rouen

DUKE OF PARMA
16 Jan. (30,000)

Scie   Varenne

HENRY OF NAVARRE
(7,000)

Aumale ✕

Durdent   Saâne

Bellencombre

4 Feb.:
cavalry skirmish
at Aumale

9–12 Feb.:
Neufchatel
besieged by Parma

30 Apr.–16 May:
skirmishes

Yvetot ✕

26 Feb.:
Parma halts after
sortie at Rouen

16–17 May:
Parma reduced
to 15,000, withdraws

Caudebec

24 Mar.–7 Apr.:
Parma besieges Caudebec

Le Havre
held by Catholics

Seine

21 Apr.:
Parma raises siege

Rouen

HENRY OF NAVARRE
29 Apr. reinforced to 26,000

DUTCH
SQUADRON
on Lower Seine

F R A N C E

20–21 May:
Parma escapes over bridge of
boats and marches to resupply Paris

Seine

2 Individual campaigns displayed high standards of generalship and maneuver (map above). Henry IV was unable to force Parma to fight at a disadvantage, but refused to do so himself, despite his personal preference for reckless cavalry charges.

1 The Wars of Religion lacked stable fronts or clear lines of operation (map left). Like 20th-century ideological conflicts they took their shape from atrocities, local rivalries, and foreign interventions. Widespread gangsterism and mutual distrust prolonged hostilities that served little rational purpose.

from the Hundred Years' War were in decline before the Religious Wars, as great nobles opted for the comforts of civilian life. In their place appeared less heavily armored cavalry carrying firearms, known as *Reiters* from the area of their origin. German heavy cavalry had often been worsted by French *gensdarmes*, and readily adopted the *pistala*, a single-handed arquebus that appeared in the 1540s. Such cavalry had a dual capability: they could ride arquebusiers down in the open, or shatter unsupported pike formations with their pistols. *Reiters* were vulnerable while reloading, and their skirmishing tactics encouraged unenthusiastic soldiers to fire uselessly at long range.

Infantry had become the dominant arm in Italy, but cavalry could still exploit the tactical discontinuity between marching and fighting order. Infantry could resist cavalry when suitably arrayed, but faced disaster if caught on the march by more mobile horsemen. Imperialist cavalry destroyed two-thirds of a French army retiring from St. Quentin (10 August 1557). France had more open country than Italy, and the haphazard circumstances of civil war suited cavalry equipped with firearms. Most of the battles of the Religious Wars were cavalry actions, with the infantry hardly engaged. The Wars of Religion served to reverse the numerical decline of French cavalry. From 46% in 1495 to 16% in the Metz campaign of 1552, one-quarter of the forces engaged at Ivry in 1590, when Henry of Navarre smashed the Leaguers' army, were cavalry. Except for a few Spanish lancers, most of these were armored pistoleers, now the standard European heavy cavalryman. After a thousand years the man-at-arms had lost his predominance. One of Henry of Navarre's first acts as Henry IV was to disband the surviving *compagnies d'ordonnance*.

the **dutch** revolt

1559 to 1648

21 July 1568
Battle of Jemmingen: rebels shot by Duke of Alva's veterans

October 1573
relief of Leyden

October 1576
'Spanish Fury' at Antwerp: rebellion against the Duke of Alva, Spanish viceroy in the 1560s, and his soldiers due to their policy of terror

31 January 1578
Battle of Gemblours: Spanish rebels killed or captured 5,000 retreating rebels

July 1584– August 1585
Spanish army besieges Antwerp

1593
Dutch capture Gertruidenberg

1629
Dutch army siege of s'-Hertogenbosch

The prosperous towns and dank swamps of Netherlands provide a surprising setting for the next step in the military renaissance. The burghers of the Low Countries not only fought the most powerful military machine of the day, the Spanish Army of Flanders, to a standstill, they also developed a new style of army, the prototype of professional military forces today.

The Dutch Revolt is a fine example of the advantages of the defensive. The obstinate resistance of every Dutch town gained time for the strategic balance to shift against Spain through the action of allies and the development of Dutch sea power, which enriched the Dutch while the Army of Flanders mutinied for want of pay. Delay brought all the country's resources into play: its numerous defensible towns, dykes, ponds, and difficult passages, and the inaccessible national redoubt of Holland, so waterlogged that ships sailed across flooded fields to relieve Leyden (October 1573). The Duke of Alva, Spanish viceroy in the 1560s, alienated popular support by his policy of terror. Wherever his victorious soldiers went, they swelled the ranks of his enemies. The "Spanish Fury" at Antwerp (October 1576) even drove the loyal Roman Catholics of the southern provinces to rebel.

The war in Netherlands had its own rules. Lack of space reinforced the contemporary preference for sieges. Battles were uniquely scarce, after early demonstrations of the crushing superiority of Spanish arms. At Jemmingen (21 July 1568) Alva's veterans lured the rebels out of their trenches, and shot them down like wild fowl. At Gemblours (31 January 1578) Spanish cavalry killed or captured 5,000 retreating rebels, unable to defend themselves on the march. A conciliatory viceroy exploited Gemblours to pacify the southern provinces, but the action was atypically decisive. Like other civil wars the Dutch Revolt was fought out at a local level. Small garrisons squabbled over individual villages, with no fixed front line. "La Guerre aux Vaches" generated widespread insecurity, and was perhaps more typical of the 16th-century experience of war than battles and marches.

s'-Hertogenbosch

ditches

N

2 The 17th-century experience of war in Western Europe was of sieges rather than battles. Superior siege techniques swung the balance in favour of attackers by the mid-1620s. Both sides could predict the progress of a siege, often resulting in surrender before a practicable breach had been made.

2 siege of s'-hertogenbosch, 1629

- Spanish defenses
- Dutch entrenched camps
- Dutch line of circumvallation (face outwards)
- Dutch line of contravallation (face outwards)
- Dutch approaches

1 the dutch revolt, 1566–1609

battles
- ✕ Spanish success
- ✕ Dutch success

sieges
- ▲ Spanish success
- ✳ Spanish massacre
- ▲ Dutch success

Dutch defensive lines
- ••••• Oude Hollandsche Waterlinie
- –•–•– river Ijssel 1605–06

regions
- **I** Catholic redoubt in North East until 1590s
- **II** Dutch inner redoubt
- **III** Dutch outer redoubt
- **IV** open cavalry country in Catholic south

support
- → Spanish
- → Protestant

1 The Dutch matched the Netherlands' strategic resources against superior Spanish tactics (map right). Numerous towns and inundations prolonged resistance, while the long frontier with Germany and the North Sea coast were always open to foreign assistance but closed to the Spanish. Maurice of Nassau's offensives followed the fortified river lines that determined the final borders of the rebel republic.

Map labels:
North Sea
Jemmingen 21 July 1568
Groningen May–July 1594
Heiligerlee 23 May 1568
Steenwijk May 1592
Coevorden July–Sept. 1592
Alkmaar Aug.–Oct. 1573
Deventer July 1591
Haarlem Dec. 1572–July 1573
Amsterdam
relief by sea
Naarden
Zutphen June 1591
Leyden Oct. 1573–Oct. 1574
Sea Beggars 1572
NETHERLANDS
Nijmegen Oct. 1591
Mookerheyde 14 Apr. 1574
Gertruidenberg June 1593
English support 1585
Spanish reinforcements by sea
s'-Hertogenbosch 1629
Spanish attempts to turn the river lines
Breda 1624–25
DUCHY of CLEVES
SMALL
Ostend 1601–04
Hulst Sept. 1591–96
Antwerp July 1584–Aug. 1585
Turnhout 24 Jan. 1597
Protestant German support
Rhine
Nieupoort 2 July 1600
Mechelen
Maastricht
LIMBURG
Brussels
Liège
STATES
SPANISH
Gemblours 31 Jan. 1578
BISHOPRIC OF LIÈGE
Mons 1572
NETHERLANDS
Spanish reinforcements overland by the Spanish Road
Huguenots
FRANCE
LUXEMBURG

The years of attrition paid off in the 1590s. Dutch forces became strong enough to launch a counter-offensive, while half the Army of Flanders was absent fighting Huguenots. The great rivers were more than military obstacles. The Dutch used barges to shift siege guns rapidly on internal lines, reducing enemy fortresses in short sharp sieges: Zutphen in seven days, Deventer in 11, Hulst in five, and Nijmegen in six. Maurice of Nassau consolidated the Netherlands' southern border, eliminated the Roman Catholic enclave in the northeast, and pushed the Dutch border 50 miles east of the river Ijssel. In 1598 the Dutch counter-offensive reached its culminating point along the modern frontier. The Army of Flanders returned, English help dwindled, and the Dutch army made little headway in the hostile open countryside of what is now Belgium.

the **thirty years war**

1618 to 1632

1618
revolt of Protestant nobles in Prague

1623
Imperialist victory at Stadtlohn

17 September 1631
Swede Gustavus victorious against Catholics at Breitenfeld

3 September 1632
Gustavus defeated at Alte Veste

16 November 1632
Battle of Lützen; Gustavus dies in action

6 September 1634
Spanish army defeats the Swedes at Nordlingen

17 May 1648
Turenne destroys last Imperialist army at Zusmarshausen

The Thirty Years War began in Central Europe, but religious divisions and hostility between the Habsburgs and the French and Dutch broadened the conflict.

The unlimited aims of the Holy Roman Emperor Ferdinand II, intent on enforcing religious uniformity in Germany, made the war "a fight between God and the Devil" with no third way. Gustavus Adolphus threatened Habsburg Silesia to draw the Imperial General Tilly away from Magdeburg, Sweden's only ally, but Tilly's army stormed Magdeburg anyway, killing five-sixths of the population. Despite Sweden's marginal location, Gustavus created the modern military hierarchy, grouping companies in battalions permanently affiliated to regiments, some of whose successors exist in the modern Swedish Army.

Gustavus' victory at Breitenfeld (17 September 1631) destroyed Tilly's army, but a single battle was insufficient to knock out the empire and its Spanish allies. Gustavus did not march directly on Vienna after Breitenfeld. Despite his personal taste for action, Gustavus was cautious, fighting only at an advantage or from behind entrenchments. He expanded his base into the Rhineland, simultaneously reducing Imperial resources. His ensuing campaign in South Germany, however, degenerated into an indecisive raid on Bavaria, when he failed to storm Ingolstadt's bastions. Gustavus had an army of Napoleonic proportions, but as the leader of a coalition Gustavus lacked Napoleon's freedom to maneuver regardless of the interests of his allies. Wallenstein's advance against Nuremberg in July 1632 forced Gustavus to respond with a fraction of his strength (20,000 out of 150,000) or risk another atrocity like Magdeburg. Wallenstein avoided action, starving the Swedes out of their trenches. Gustavus attacked over ground unfavorable to combined arms tactics, and suffered his first defeat at the Alte Veste. Wallenstein persisted with a strategy of diversion. Raiding into Saxony, he compelled Gustavus to postpone an invasion of Austria.

1 Strategists of the Thirty Years' War maneuvered to dominate areas of logistical importance, rather than to gain tactical advantage (map right). Despite the Swedish army's superiority on the battlefield, Gustavus Adolphus pursued similar logistical objectives to his enemies, seeking to build up an economic base in North Germany.

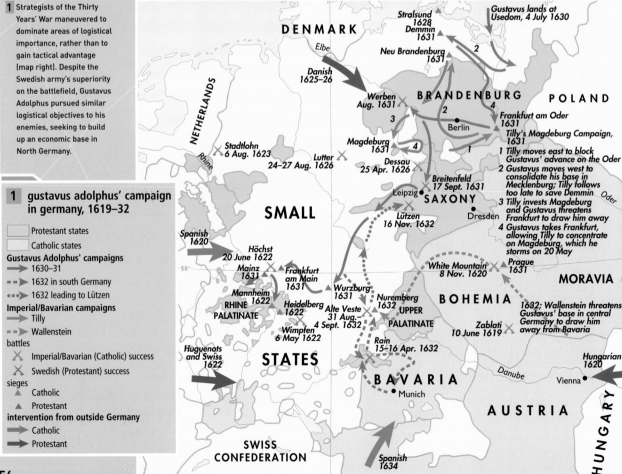

1 gustavus adolphus' campaign in germany, 1619–32

- Protestant states
- Catholic states

Gustavus Adolphus' campaigns
- 1630–31
- 1632 in south Germany
- 1632 leading to Lützen

Imperial/Bavarian campaigns
- Tilly
- Wallenstein

battles
- ✕ Imperial/Bavarian (Catholic) success
- ✕ Swedish (Protestant) success

sieges
- ▲ Catholic
- ▲ Protestant

intervention from outside Germany
- Catholic
- Protestant

Gustavus lands at Usedom, 4 July 1630

Stralsund 1628
Demmin 1631

DENMARK

Elbe

Neu Brandenburg 1631

BRANDENBURG

POLAND

Danish 1625–26

Werben Aug. 1631

2

4

Frankfurt am Oder 1631

Berlin

Tilly's Magdeburg Campaign, 1631

1 Tilly moves east to block Gustavus' advance on the Oder
2 Gustavus moves west to consolidate his base in Mecklenburg; Tilly follows too late to save Demmin
3 Tilly invests Magdeburg and Gustavus threatens Frankfurt to draw him away
4 Gustavus takes Frankfurt, allowing Tilly to concentrate on Magdeburg, which he storms on 20 May

3

NETHERLANDS

Rhine

Stadtlohn 6 Aug. 1623

Lutter 24–27 Aug. 1626

Magdeburg 1631

4

1

Dessau 25 Apr. 1626

Breitenfeld 17 Sept. 1631

Oder

SMALL

Leipzig

SAXONY

Dresden

Lützen 16 Nov. 1632

Spanish 1620

Höchst 20 June 1622

Mainz 1631

Frankfurt am Main 1631

Wurzburg 1631

Nuremberg 1632

UPPER PALATINATE

White Mountain 8 Nov. 1620

Prague 1631

BOHEMIA

MORAVIA

Mannheim 1622

RHINE PALATINATE

Heidelberg 1622

Alte Veste 31 Aug.– 4 Sept. 1632

1632; Wallenstein threatens Gustavus' base in central Germany to draw him away from Bavaria

Wimpfen 6 May 1622

Rain 15–16 Apr. 1632

Zablati 10 June 1619

Huguenots and Swiss 1622

STATES

BAVARIA

Munich

Danube

Hungarian 1620

Vienna

AUSTRIA

HUNGARY

SWISS CONFEDERATION

Spanish 1634

-50°-

1 The later course of the Thirty Years' War showed the primacy of politics over religion, and logistics over tactics (map below). A French cardinal struggled to stop Catholic Spain intervening in Protestant Germany and Holland. Turenne's militarily brilliant campaigns were finally decisive, because Germany was too exhausted for the war to continue.

The ensuing Battle of Lützen (16 November 1632) destroyed the last Imperial army, but Gustavus' chance death in action prevented an immediate advance on Vienna. Deprived of the Swedish Hercules, Cardinal Richelieu, the French chief minister, adopted a logistical strategy, attacking the communications between scattered Habsburg possessions in Italy, Germany, and the Netherlands. The "Spanish Road," by which reinforcements reached the Army of Flanders from the Habsburg Duchy of Milan, was a remarkable example of Renaissance military logistics. The troops followed routes surveyed by military engineers, skirting trouble spots like Calvinist Geneva. Henry IV cut the original Spanish Road through Franche Comté, and Dutch sea power threatened the maritime route through the English Channel, but the Spanish found another route through the Grisons valleys. A Spanish army reached south Germany to defeat the Swedes at Nordlingen (6 September 1634), but French occupation of Alsace permanently cut the Spanish Road, dashing Habsburg ambitions for a unified Catholic Europe. Political plurality continued to ensure Europe's economic and military development, unconstrained by the command style of economy that crippled Europe's monolithic competitors in the east.

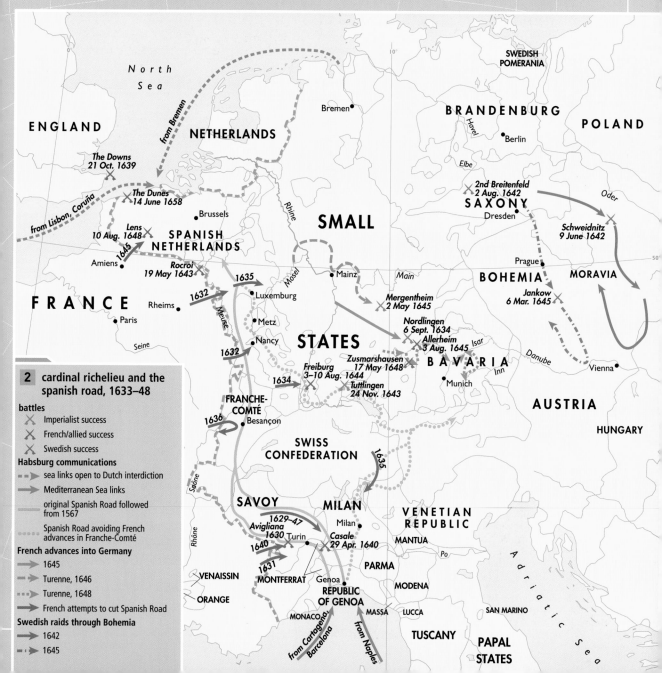

2 cardinal richelieu and the spanish road, 1633–48

battles
✕ Imperialist success
✕ French/allied success
✕ Swedish success

Habsburg communications
▰▰▰ sea links open to Dutch interdiction
→ Mediterranean Sea links
━━━ original Spanish Road followed from 1567
⋯⋯ Spanish Road avoiding French advances in Franche-Comté

French advances into Germany
➤ 1645
➤ Turenne, 1646
➤ Turenne, 1648
➤ French attempts to cut Spanish Road

Swedish raids through Bohemia
➤ 1642
➤ 1645

13 August 1704
Battle of Blenheim

1704
British capture Gibraltar

1706
Eugene's victory at Turin; French evacuation of northern Italy. Marlborough's triumph at Ramillies

11 July 1708
Battle of Oudenarde

11 September 1709
Battle of Malplaquet: allies suffer heavy defeat

1713
France, Britain, and Holland sign Peace of Itrecht; Charles VI of Austria continues war with France

1714
Charles VI agrees to treaties of Rastatt and Baden

Only the most skilful generals could achieve far-reaching success within the constraints of early 18th-century warfare. The Duke of Marlborough did so during the War of the Spanish Succession, by deception and variations of standard tactical procedures.

Marlborough's Blenheim campaign was kept secret even from his allies. The march to the Danube wrong-footed hostile Franco-Bavarian forces and kept Britain's key ally, Austria, in the war. Logistical preparations even extended to replacement shoes. Marlborough extracted supplies from towns along his route by a smooth mixture of threats and promises. Payment was assured by Britain's sound war finances, symbolized by the foundation of the Bank of England in 1694. His tactical victory at Blenheim broke the aura of French invincibility, and secured major allied war aims: the Spanish Netherlands and Naples fell into allied hands.

At Blenheim, Marlborough diverted the attention of the Franco-Bavarian armies to their flanks, then broke through the unstable center. Almost two-thirds of the defeated armies became casualties, the highest attrition of any 18th-century battle. Marlborough used the same grand tactics at Ramillies (23 May 1706). Diversions on the flanks preceded a central break-through, while improvised cavalry reserves moved under cover to

1 **marlborough's march to the danube (may–june 1704), and subsequent campaigns**

→ Marlborough's march to the Danube
⇢ diversions
⋯▸ Marlborough's new communications
⊸ Marlborough's 1708 campaign
→ allied troops moving to join Marlborough
➤ French reaction
● towns falling to allies after Ramillies
⬇ sieges
⊸ French evacuation of Flanders after Oudenarde
┅┅ *Ne Plus Ultra* lines forced by Marlborough, 26 July–4 August 1711

troop concentrations	major battles
Marlborough	✕ allied success
allies	✕ French success
French	

Map

VILLEROI 46,000 men

OVERKIRK 50,000 men

MARLBOROUGH 21,000 men

19 May

HANOVERIANS 5,000 men

H O L Y   R O M A N   E M P I R E

SPANISH NETHERLANDS

Oudenarde 11 July 1708
Brussels
Maastricht
Bonn
26 May
Koblenz

Lille 1708
Valenciennes 1712
Mons 1709
Ramillies 23 May 1706
Malplaquet 11 Sept. 1709
Denain 24 July 1712

Mainz 3 June

DANES & PRUSSIANS 14,000 men
Nuremberg

DE COIGNE 10,000 men
7 June

12 June

Oise
Aisne
Marne

F R A N C E

L O R R A I N E

A L S A C E

Paris

Moselle
Meuse

TALLARD 36,000 men
Strasburg
1 July

BADEN & EUGENE 64,000 men

22 June

Blenheim 13 Aug 1
Augsbu

Aube
Seine
Rhône

Meurthe

V o s g e s

Rhine

S c h w a r z w a l d
Schwäbische Alb
Ulm
29 July

18 July
Danube

BAVARIAN 26,000 men
Lech

Ruhr
Rhine
Ohm
Fulda
Werr
Main

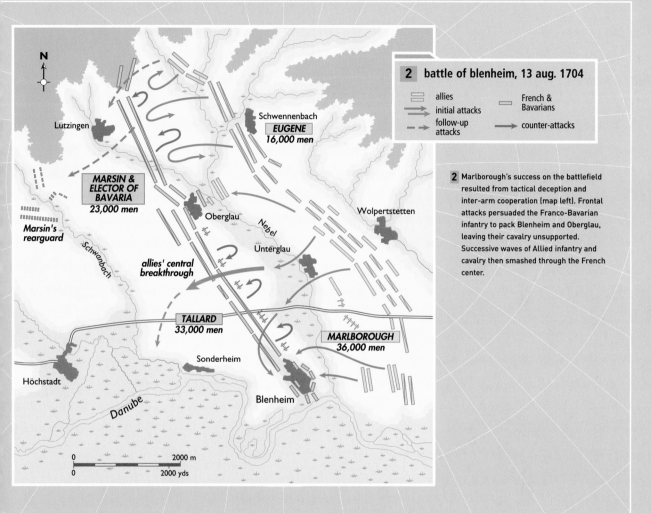

N

2 **battle of blenheim, 13 aug. 1704**

| | allies | | French & Bavarians |
| initial attacks | follow-up attacks | counter-attacks |

Lutzingen

Schwennenbach

EUGENE
16,000 men

MARSIN & ELECTOR OF BAVARIA
23,000 men

Marsin's rearguard

Oberglau

Nebel

Wolpertstetten

allies' central breakthrough

Unterglau

Schwanbach

TALLARD
33,000 men

MARLBOROUGH
36,000 men

Höchstadt

Sonderheim

Blenheim

Danube

| 0 | | 2000 m |
| 0 | | 2000 yds |

2 Marlborough's success on the battlefield resulted from tactical deception and inter-arm cooperation (map left). Frontal attacks persuaded the Franco-Bavarian infantry to pack Blenheim and Oberglau, leaving their cavalry unsupported. Successive waves of Allied infantry and cavalry then smashed through the French center.

1 A protégé of Turenne, Marlborough was one of the few commanders able to overcome the strategic limitations of his day (map left). The ambiguous nature of Marlborough's maneuvers deceived both allies and the enemy, but demanded sound logistical practice, which earned him the affection of his troops.

the decisive point. However, Marlborough's methods became predictable. Marshal Villars inflicted heavy losses on the allies at Malplaquet (11 September 1709). During a summer of mainly inconclusive maneuvering, the Allies captured Tournai and threatened Mons, which Villars was ordered to hold. Marlborough and Eugene forces Villars's army to retreat after a specially hard-fought battle.

Marlborough could risk offensive battles because tactical developments were in his favor. French successes in the 1690s had made them complacent. The remorseless advance and controlled fire of Allied battalions demoralized their opponents.

Even Marlborough could not avoid the frustrations of siege warfare. In ten campaigns he fought four battles, two actions, and 30 sieges. Fortresses in Western Europe were too close together to be ignored, and armies lacked the numbers to mask them as Napoleonic generals would do a century later. The siege of Lille in 1708 required 80 heavy guns, 20 mortars, and 3,000 wagonloads of stores. The siege lasted 120 days, and cost the allies five times the casualties of the Battle of Oudenarde (11 July 1708), which had made the operation possible.

1683 to 1721

1700
Denmark, Saxony–Poland, and Russia form an alliance and attack Sweden

20 November 1700
Swedes defeat Russians at Narva. Denmark knocked out of the war by Sweden

1701
Swedes invade Polish Courland

1702
Swedes enter Warsaw and depose Augustus II

1706
Swedes force Saxony to make peace at Altrastadt

January 1708
Charles XII, king of Sweden, invades Russia

8 July 1709
Peter (the Great) destroys Charles's army at Poltava. Brandenburg-Prussia, Hanover, and Denmark join Russia in a struggle for Sweden's Baltic empire

While Western Europe experimented with the balance of power, the East saw a strategic revolution. The export of the military renaissance to Russia created a new power from nothing. A well-armed Russia ended forever the nomadic incursions that had terrorized Europe throughout the Middle Ages. Turkey, the most recent intruder from the steppe, rejected modern military techniques, to the advantage of a resurgent Austria.

Russia was the first Asian country to import the military renaissance wholesale, forming European-style regiments in the 1630s. They made up two-thirds of the Russian army by 1682, replacing the *streltsi*, an obsolescent corps of rebellious musketeers. German loan words, such as *soldat* or *junker*, reveal the foreign inspiration of Russia's military expertise. Peter the Great crushed the *streltsi* with exemplary cruelty, before accelerating military and social change to meet a strategic challenge from Sweden. Charles XII, the youthful king of Sweden, compensated for his small army with the most aggressive tactics in Europe. His cavalry gave up armor and charged at a gallop, when even Marlborough's horse trotted into contact. Swedish infantry advanced to 40 paces from the enemy without firing, fired two volleys, and closed with the bayonet.

A Russian defeat at Narva (20 November 1700) showed their inability to withstand such shock tactics. Russian infantry ran about like stampeded cattle, while the Swedes, outnumbered five to one, took so many prisoners they had to let them go. Peter's response was to raise 50 new infantry regiments. When Charles XII invaded Russia in January 1708, advancing over the frozen rivers, the Russians avoided battle. They wore out the Swedes, destroying the countryside ahead of them. Charles's hopes of exploiting internal opposition to Peter were disappointed; the new Russian regiments could at least suppress dissidents. At Poltava (8 July 1709) Peter destroyed Charles's attenuated army, much to the Swedes' surprise. Other powers quickly recognized the emergence of a new military power. In the 1730s a Russian army marched into Germany and defeated a French force at Danzig. Russian and Chinese forces met in central Asia, ending the freedom of the steppe nomads. The forcible imposition of Western military institutions upon Russia exacted a terrible price. Brutally suppressed risings became a feature of the regime. The only reliable arm of government was the army, recruited more effectively and repressively than anywhere else. The military renaissance in the West tamed the man on horseback, but in Russia's militarized society it imposed new chains.

1 the eastern front, 1683–1721

→ Austrian allied relief of Vienna, and counter-attacks

→ Russian campaign in Moldavia, 1711

- - ▶ Russian raids

•••••• Russian defences, 1708–09

▨ Russian winter quarters, 1708–09

→ Swedish campaigns

•••••▶ Swedish campaign in Russia, 1708–09

▨ Swedish winter quarters, 1708–09

- -▷ Swedish retreat after Poltava

→ Turkish campaigns

- - ▶ Turkish raids

battle victories
✕ Austrian
✕ Russian
✕ Swedish
✕ Turkish

sieges
⬤ Austrians besieging Turkish city
⬤ Turks besieging Austrian city
⬤ Danes besieging Swedish city
⬤ Swedes besieging Danish city

1 Sweden's aggressive empire-building made it many enemies. When Sweden was attacked by Russia, Denmark, and Saxony–Poland in 1700, Charles XII launched a series of brilliant campaigns, which saw him defeat Denmark, devastate Poland, and invade Saxony before catastrophic defeat at Poltava ended his invasion of Russia (map right). The Swedish army's tactical pre-eminence was no substitute for the strategic strength that Peter the Great of Russia was able to mobilize.

Trondhjem

NORWAY
(Danish)

S W E D E N

KARELIA

Christiania

Frederiksten
Nov. 1718
Death of Charles XII
Stockholm

Nystad
Åbo
Helsingfors
St. Petersburg

Gangut
6 Aug. 1714 ✕
Revel

INGRIA
Narva
20 Nov. 1700

R U S S I A N

Russian raids on
Swedish coast
1719–20

ESTONIA
Hummelsdorf
18 July 1702
1701

Errestfer
7 Jan. 1702 ✕
Pskov

Gothenburg

LIVONIA
Riga

Moscow

Tula

Helsingborg
Feb. 1710
DENMARK
Aarhus
Frederiksborg
Copenhagen
Malmö
✕ 1700

Baltic
Sea

1700

COURLAND

Dyneburg

Vitebsk
1708
Holovsin
4 July 1708
1708

Smolensk

E M P I R E

Gadebusch
1712 ✕
Stralsund
1713
Hamburg
SWEDISH
POMERANIA
Stettin

Königsberg

PRUSSIA

L I T H U A N I A

Minsk
Lesnaya
9–10 Oct. 1708

Kursk

Wilno

Gdansk

PRUSSIA
Berlin
Poznan
Lodz
Toruń
Pultusk
13 Apr. 1703
1703 ✕
Warsaw

1709

Elbe

P R U S S I A
Breslau
Dresden
Fraustadt
3 Feb. 1706
SAXONY
1706
Leipzig
Frankfurt

Vistula

Brest-Litovsk

1709
Kharkov
1709
Cossacks

Kliszow
2 July 1708 ✕

P O L A N D
(in personal union with Saxony)

HETMANATE
Kiev
8 July 1709
Poltava

Oder

SILESIA
BOHEMIA
Prague

MORAVIA
Brünn

Cracow

Lvov

Winnica

Dnieper

Zaporogian Cossacks

Stuttgart

BAVARIA
Munich
Salzburg
urich

Danube

1683
AUSTRIA
Vienna
Pozsony
Buda
1686
Pest
Debrecen

Dniester
1711

MOLDAVIA
Jassy

Tartars

KHANATE
OF
CRIMEA
Bakhchisaray

HABSBURG POSSESSIONS
Graz

HUNGARY
1687
Szeged
Zenta
11 Sept. 1697 ✕
Temesvár
1716

Kolozsvár

Pruth
July 1711

Milan

Trieste

Venice

Zágráb

TRANSYLVANIA
Brassó

VENETIAN

1689

Bologna

Zara

Bosna Saray

Belgrade
30 Aug. 1689,
16 Aug. 1717
1738–39
Nish

WALLACHIA

Bucharest

Ruschuk
1711

Black Sea

Florence

Spalato

PAPAL
Rome

STATES

KINGDOM
OF
NAPLES
Naples
Bari
Taranto

Mostar

REPUBLIC
OF RAGUSA

MONTENEGRO

1689
Üsküb

O T T O M A N

Sofia

Varna

Burgas

Danube

Philippopolis
Adrianople

Salonica

Janina

E M P I R E

Constantinople

Angora

AND

SICILY

(Military administration)

naval warfare under the ancien régime

1652 to 1762

1652–54
First Anglo-Dutch War

1691
Act of parliament required the Royal Navy to exceed the combined strength of its nearest rivals, the French and the Dutch

28 May–2 June 1692
spectacular naval victory for British at Barfleur and La Hogue

24 August 1704
Battle of Malaga: French withdraw to avoid combat

1739
War of Jenkins's Ear: struggle between England and Spain, growing out of commercial rivalry

22 February 1744
Battle of Toulon

20 May 1756
Battle at Minorca: Admiral Byng defeated, then executed by his own side

18–19 August 1759
Battle of Lagos: British under Admiral Boscawen defeat the French

Improved sailing warships and professionalization of Europe's navies introduced the classic age of fighting sail. The First Anglo-Dutch War of 1652–54 saw more naval actions than the preceding 150 years, a trend continued in a series of maritime wars that defined the modern concepts of naval strategy. Fleets of sailing warships bound together European and colonial rivalries, causing the first 'world wars'.

A 1691 Act of Parliament required the Royal Navy to exceed the combined strength of its nearest rivals, the French and Dutch. By 1762 the Royal Navy had emerged as the most powerful in the world with 84,000 men and 300 ships. Government dockyards supported the growing fleets, becoming the largest industrial enterprises in the world.

Naval architecture reflected different national strategies. The British built slower, stronger ships to enhance seakeeping; the clean scientific lines of French ships made them faster but less durable. Shallow coastal waters handicapped the Dutch when heavier rates appeared with 100 or more guns. They fell behind in the naval arms race.

Spanish and Portuguese monopolies of trade with the Indies and America had provoked English, French, and Dutch incursions since the 16th century. Viewed by the occupying powers as pirates and smugglers, the interlopers gained respectability as officially sponsored companies and expeditions replaced the early buccaneers.

Security of merchant shipping was a dividend of sea power. Land transport was prohibitively expensive, so goods traveled by sea. Navies defeated in battle reverted to the medieval strategy of attacking trade. After Barfleur, heavy units of the French Navy participated in a systematic *guerre de course*, taking over 4,000 vessels. The Brest fleet captured 90 ships from one convoy off Cadiz in 1693. The English organized convoys from the 1660s to deter state-sponsored Dutch and French privateers, and freelance corsairs operating off North Africa and the West Indies. Parliamentary legislation, such as the Cruisers and Convoys Act of 1708,

2 European sailing navies created global oceanic empires, inspiring and spreading conflict (map below). Admirals were innocent of Mahanian doctrines of sea power but had a clear understanding of its practical value. They sought to protect their own trade, while damaging that of the enemy, launched amphibious operations around the world, and blockaded enemy ports to prevent them doing the same.

1 Naval warfare was a way of breaking the strategic stalemate ashore, but fleets were often too large for decisive defeat, and imposed a new deadlock (map above). The frequent Anglo-Dutch battles of the three wars of the 1650s–70s made way for long periods without fleet actions.

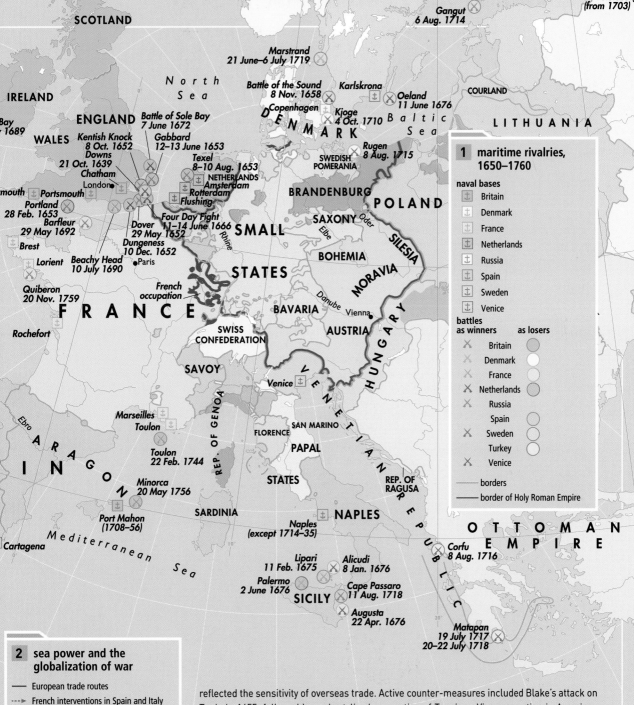

reflected the sensitivity of overseas trade. Active counter-measures included Blake's attack on Tunis in 1655, followed by a short-lived occupation of Tangiers. Vigorous action in American waters against the Brethren of the Coast persuaded some buccaneers to move as far away as Madagascar. Jean Bart, the great practitioner of *guerre de course* in the 1690s, hoped to divert sufficient Anglo-Dutch resources to allow a new French challenge for control of the sea. Dispersal of French warships as commerce raiders, however, allowed the British to strengthen convoy escorts and patrol the Western Approaches. The Royal Navy swept French ships off the sea, taking 2,200 in two years (1710–12). The collapse of French trade in the 1740s helped end the War of the Austrian Succession. Great Britain, her own trade intact, was the only power not to face financial ruin during the Seven Years War.

mid-18th-century europe

Eighteenth-century warfare was formal, but not static. Professional officers endlessly refined the skills of their men. International competition for power encouraged European armies to improve continually. However, logistical constraints on the conduct of war remained unresolved.

Peacetime armies optimized infantry firepower by constant drill. The British perfected a walking fire technique that nearly brought them victory at Fontenoy (11 May 1745). The Prussians streamlined their soldiers' coats, gave them paper cartridges and iron ramrods, and taught them to fire five rounds a minute. Trained musketry dominated the battlefield. The proportion of cavalry in European armies continued to decline: from one-third in 1650, to one-quarter in 1750, and one-sixth in 1810.

French officers, disgusted with the slaughter at Malplaquet, turned away from conventional linear tactics. Maurice de Saxe was the only reformer to put his ideas into practice. At Fontenoy he defeated British offensive fire tactics with Malplaquet-style fieldworks and a sophisticated artillery fire plan, including a dedicated reserve of 12 guns, a unique idea in the 1740s. At Roucoux and Lauffeld, Saxe took the offensive.

The inspiration for Saxe's skirmishers came from irregular troops, known as Croats, on their military frontier with Turkey. The appearance of Croats in Alsace inspired the Legion de Grassin, a French irregular corps that fought at Fontenoy. The British also learned about light troops outside Europe. Native North Americans, used to wood fighting, were tactically superior to local militia and regular troops imported from Europe. In 1755, Native North Americans destroyed a numerically superior British force at the Monongahela. Subsequently, the British formed irregular corps like Roger's Rangers, who beat the Native North Americans at their own game. British regulars in North America lightened their equipment, cut down their hats, and learned to fight from cover.

Enhanced tactical mobility did not benefit strategy. Physical limits on maneuver remained the same. Large armies could not disperse to subsist, as detachments lacked the command structure and mixture of arms to fight

2 battle of lauffeld, 2 july 1747

allied troops
- British
- Austrian/Dutch
- French

2 Some generals tried to play strength against weakness. The French marshal Maurice de Saxe doubled his line at Lauffeld to attack the exposed part of a defending line with heavy columns. In a precursor of Frederick the Great's celebrated oblique order, the French cavalry moved around the open Allied flank.

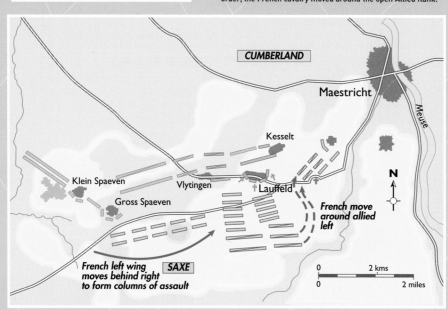

1 The Austrian branch of the Habsburg dynasty was founded by Charles V's brother Ferdinand, elected king of Bohemia and Hungary in 1526. For 200 years, the Habsburgs disputed possession of Hungarian territory with the Ottomans. After the Turkish defeat at the siege of Vienna (1683), the Habsburgs extended control rapidly down the Danube, consolidating their gains by the Treaties of Carlowitz (1699) and Passarowitz (1718). Austria lost Silesia to Russia in the War of the Austrian Succession (1740–48) and failed to recover it in the Seven Years' War (1756–63). Croat irregular troops, long used to guard the frontier with the Turks, proved highly effective against the Prussians—their guerrilla tactics helped ensure the Prussians did not make inroads into Bohemia.

separately. Nor could they advance rapidly by a single line of operation. Inadequate roads delayed convoys, and low agricultural productivity inhibited requisitions. The numerous horses that moved an army ate immense quantities of fodder, so campaigns began when the grass grew in April. By the time one side had won a battle, it would be too late to do more than pick up a fortress or two before winter allowed the beaten army to recover. The allied reconquest of the Spanish Netherlands after Ramillies (23 May 1706) was a rare opportunity to exploit a victory at the start of the campaigning season. Nevertheless, wars did cause major political shifts. Turkey was excluded from Europe and French ambitions were curbed, despite the limited capabilities of 18th-century armies.

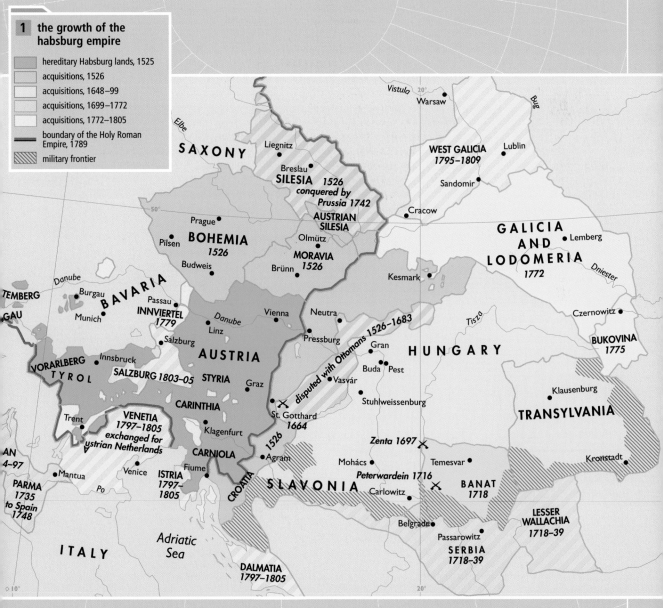

1 the growth of the habsburg empire

- hereditary Habsburg lands, 1525
- acquisitions, 1526
- acquisitions, 1648–99
- acquisitions, 1699–1772
- acquisitions, 1772–1805
- boundary of the Holy Roman Empire, 1789
- military frontier

the **first colonial wars**

The Mughal Empire collapsed when internal decay invited external attack. Increasing intolerance of non-Muslims alienated the Rajputs and inspired Sikh militancy. Mughal generals seized power for themselves, such as the Nizam at Hyderabad. After the last great emperor, Aurangzeb, died in 1707, the Marathas of the Deccan took control of northern India, even taking Portuguese bases at Bassein and Chaul. An army of Afghan heavy cavalry inflicted a disastrous defeat on the Marathas at Panipat (14 January 1761). However, the Afghans lacked the numbers or political support to control India and withdrew, leaving chaos from which the British would profit.

French and British coastal enclaves in India needed control of the sea for supplies and military reinforcements. Their proximity provoked numerous naval actions. Linear tactics prevented loss of ships, yet as in European waters inconclusive battles had disproportionate effects. A French naval victory at Negapatam (25 July 1746) allowed them to seize Madras, but British reinforcements under Boscawen saved their nearby base at Fort St. George. The British then besieged the French base Pondicherry, until the monsoon drove Boscawen off station. In the 1750s an outnumbered British squadron inflicted enough damage in three "indecisive" actions to compel the French admiral to withdraw to distant Mauritius to refit. Pondicherry surrendered in 1761, having no hope of relief by sea. Naval power allowed the British to move forces between the Carnatic and Bengal. When the Nawab of Bengal occupied Calcutta in 1756, the British mounted a joint operation from Madras to retake it. A squadron of battleships then pushed 21 miles up the river Hooghly, to bombard the French factory at Chandernagore (23 March 1757). Victory in India opened new strategic possibilities for the British. The 1762 expedition to Manila sailed from Madras. Calcutta developed a naval dockyard, building European-style warships in local teak.

Europeans revolutionized Indian land warfare. In the 1730s the French introduced light field guns, and trained their factory watchmen to fight with musket and bayonet, their *cipahis* defeating a Mughal successor army at St. Thomé (3 November 1746). The British imitated the French, depending heavily on Indian troops to extend and consolidate British rule beyond the range of their fleets. At Plassey (23 June 1757) Colonel Robert Clive defeated 50,000 Mughal-style troops with 3,200 men, two-thirds of them sepoys. Traditional Indian armies had no tactical answer to well-drilled bayonets and mobile field guns firing case shot. Only the Marathas' strategy of retreating into ground unsuitable for artillery and harassing British communications had any success. By 1805 the East India Company employed 150,000 sepoys. Britain had become a major Asian land power, combining European military techniques with Indian numbers. The new style of Indian soldier would be a mainstay of British imperial power.

2 The destruction of the Army of Hindustan followed the political defeat of its Maratha owners. Unlike traditional Indian armies, de Boigne's regiments could change front during a battle, and their well-served field guns inflicted heavy losses on their British opponents before the 2,000 surviving sepoys surrendered.

N
0   1 km
0   1 mile

Mohalpur

MAHRATTAS
9,000 men

Mahratta cavalry

LAKE

Laswari

British infantry approach

Hussowly

2 **battle of laswari, 1 november 1803**

British cavalry at start of action

British cavalry during infantry battle

British attacks

Mahratta 1st position

Mahratta final position, refusing right flank

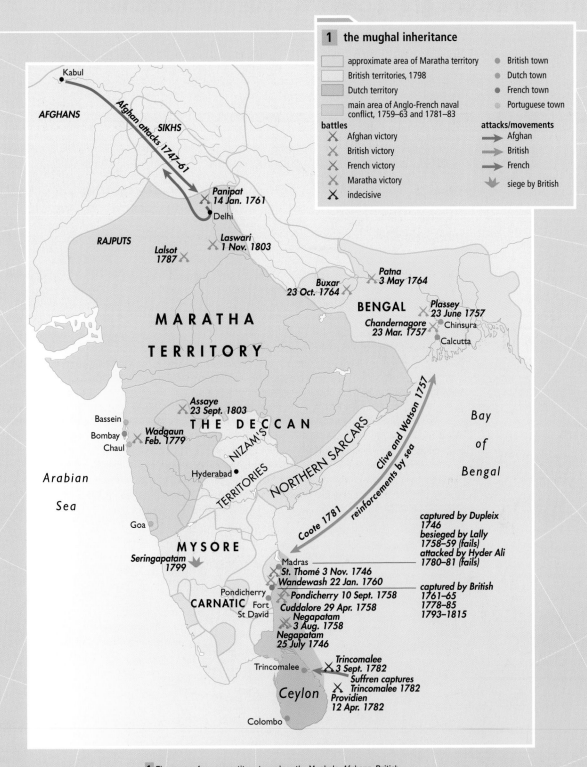

1 the mughal inheritance

approximate area of Maratha territory	● British town
British territories, 1798	● Dutch town
Dutch territory	● French town
main area of Anglo-French naval conflict, 1759–63 and 1781–83	● Portuguese town

battles
- ✕ Afghan victory
- ✕ British victory
- ✕ French victory
- ✕ Maratha victory
- ✕ indecisive

attacks/movements
- → Afghan
- → British
- → French
- ↓ siege by British

Kabul

AFGHANS

SIKHS

Afghan attacks 1747–61

Panipat
14 Jan. 1761

Delhi

RAJPUTS

Lalsot
1787

Laswari
1 Nov. 1803

Patna
3 May 1764

Buxar
23 Oct. 1764

BENGAL

Plassey
23 June 1757

Chandernagore
23 Mar. 1757

Chinsura

Calcutta

MARATHA
TERRITORY

Assaye
23 Sept. 1803

THE DECCAN

Bassein

Bombay

Chaul

Wadgaun
Feb. 1779

NIZAM'S

TERRITORIES

Hyderabad

NORTHERN SARCARS

Clive and Watson 1757

reinforcements by sea

Coote 1781

Bay
of
Bengal

Arabian
Sea

Goa

MYSORE

Seringapatam
1799

Madras

St. Thomé 3 Nov. 1746

Wandewash 22 Jan. 1760

Pondicherry 10 Sept. 1758

Cuddalore 29 Apr. 1758

Negapatam
3 Aug. 1758

Negapatam
25 July 1746

CARNATIC

Pondicherry

Fort
St David

captured by Dupleix
1746
besieged by Lally
1758–59 (fails)
attacked by Hyder Ali
1780–81 (fails)

captured by British
1761–65
1778–85
1793–1815

Trincomalee

Trincomalee
3 Sept. 1782

Suffren captures
Trincomalee 1782

Providien
12 Apr. 1782

Ceylon

Colombo

1 There were four competitors to replace the Mughals: Afghans, British, French, and Marathas. Anglo-French commercial rivalry concealed the strength of the outsiders, short-sightedly seen as allies or puppets. Sea power was crucial to British success, allowing them to shuttle reinforcements between Bombay and Bengal, while French lack of naval bases settled indecisive sea battles against them.

frederick the great and the prussian expansion

1756
Prussians invade Saxony and begin Seven Years War

1757
Prussians inflict 50% losses on a stronger Austrian army at Leuthen (6 December)

1759
British victorious at Battle of Minden (1 August)

1759
Battle of Kunersdorf (13 August)

1763
Frederick II makes terms with Saxony and Austria, begins reforms in Prussia

1764
Treaty of Alliance between Prussia and Russia

The genius of Frederick the Great and the training of his soldiers preserved Prussia from the combined efforts of Austria, France, and Russia. Prussian battalions were so reliably drilled that Frederick the Great's armies could march across the enemy front, wheel into line, and go straight into an attack. This processional deployment formed the basis of Frederick's famous "oblique order." Trained to charge long distances at a gallop, Prussian cavalry set the standard for mounted tactics, until rifled small arms rendered them obsolete in the 19th century. The Prussians were the first totally professional army.

Frederick's opponents soon countered his tactics. At Kolin (18 June 1757) Austrian light troops hung about the Prussian flank, provoking a premature advance. At Zorndorf (25 October 1758) encircled Russians faced about to convert the battle into another frontal attack, with ghastly results: 35% Prussian losses against 53% Russian. All armies had improved rates of fire, making frontal attacks terribly costly. Artillery had also improved. New casting techniques made guns lighter but more effective. The Russians and Austrians reformed their artillery in the early 1750s. Their new guns outclassed the Prussians in number, range, and weight of fire, and massacred Prussian infantry at Prague and Kolin. Frederick strengthened his own artillery, deploying 12-pounder fortress guns at Leuthen. He broadened the capability of his gunners with field howitzers and horse artillery. Frederick's horse artillery formed a mobile reserve of firepower, foreshadowing Napoleon's use of reserve artillery.

The Seven Years War does not fit the stereotype of 18th-century limited warfare. Prussia faced dismemberment if defeated. Frederick's pre-emptive occupation of Saxony drew in France, expanding a Central European conflict into a world war. Frederick's internal position and the tactical superiority of his army enabled him to attack his geographically dispersed enemies one at a time. He defeated a French army at Rossbach (5 November 1757), then marched 170 miles in 12 days to beat the Austrians at Leuthen. Frederick's early victories paralyzed opposing generals. They were slow to exploit his absence, or their own successes. An Austro-Russian army failed to occupy Berlin, and end the war, after their victory at Kunersdorf (12 August 1759). Frederick, on the other hand, could not follow up his victories as he always needed the troops elsewhere. Strategic weakness forced him into offensive battles, accepting heavy casualties to keep the enemy at

1 Frederick's well-drilled Prussians (map right) "walked round the Austrians like a washerwoman at a tub," and smashed through the resulting angle in the Austrian line. Oblique order was not an infallible recipe for success. A similar attack at Kolin, seven weeks later, failed with heavy losses.

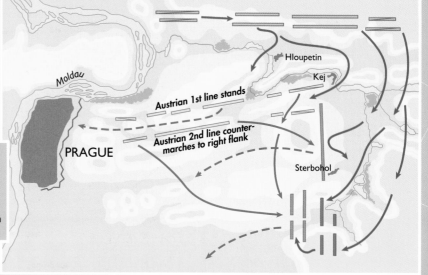

2   battle of prague, 6 may 1757

Prussian cavalry 1st and 2nd position

Austrian cavalry 1st and 2nd position

Prussian turning movement

Austrian infantry 1st and 2nd position

Austrian reaction

Austrian retreat

Moldau

PRAGUE

Hloupetin

Kej

Austrian 1st line stands

Austrian 2nd line counter-marches to right flank

Sterbohol

bay. However, he had little choice. Prussia lacked the fortifications that limited offensives in traditional seats of war, and Frederick could not risk losing territory by defending obstacles until outmaneuvered. As long as he controlled Prussia's revenues and received British subsidies, Frederick could hire fresh mercenaries, while even a Prussian defeat wrecked the opposing army. Despite his tactical genius, however, Frederick came to regard battles as an expedient of the unimaginative. He was saved, accidentally, by the political breakdown of the opposing coalition.

1 Threatened by a numerically superior coalition, Frederick sought to defeat his enemies separately (map below). He maneuvered on internal lines and exploited the tactical superiority of his army in offensive battles. Later opponents of geographically dispersed alliances, such as the German Wehrmacht or Israeli Defence Force, would also combine a strategic defensive with offensive tactics.

1 the miracle of the hohenzollerns, 1756–63

fortresses
- Austrian
- Prussian
- Swedish
- captured by Austrians
- captured by Russians

battles
- Austrian victory
- Austro-Russian victory
- French victory
- Prussian victory
- Russian victory

advances
- Frederick's movements during the 1757 Rossbach/Leuthen campaign
- Austrian advance
- French advance
- Russian advance
- Swedish advance

The American War of Independence is commonly seen as defying the military conventions of the day. The strategy and tactics of the war, however, were not unusual. British defeat revealed the shortcomings of maritime power confronted with popular resistance on a continental scale while distracted by a strategic threat closer to home.

The British war machine of the 1770s was soundly financed, with a competent army experienced in colonial warfare and the largest navy in the world. It was defeated by a popular revolt that printed worthless paper money, created an army from nothing, and never possessed a navy beyond privateers. The initial weakness of the rebels was to their advantage, as the British government underestimated the response required. North America was simply too large to occupy with the troops available. British strategic mobility was low. They could make amphibious descents upon New York or Charleston, but once ashore lacked transport, and moved at the speed of a foot soldier. British defeats became disasters, while defeated American forces had space to withdraw, protected by difficult terrain.

Political factors constrained British conduct of the war in ways familiar today: opposition to the war within Britain was vocal; counter-insurgency forces faced the choice between ineffective half measures and extremes that alienated moderates; and revolutionary militia dominated the countryside, their political role in suppressing Loyalist dissent exceeding their value on the battlefield. The militia symbolized the dispersal of political authority in the United States. This made for poor strategic direction of the American war effort, but increased British difficulties in suppressing a many-headed revolt. Their capture of Philadelphia, the seat of Congress, lacked the political resonance of occupying a European capital.

Washington's success in keeping his army together deprived the British of victory, but French intervention won the war. The Royal Navy had too few resources to intimidate the rebels, or isolate North America, as it had in the Seven Years' War. Ships were rotten and the best admirals politically disaffected. Many ships remained in home waters to deter a combined Franco-Spanish battle line that outnumbered the British 140:120. The French had no European diversions, and usurped the Royal Navy's amphibious monopoly, sending an expedition to assist the Americans. In August 1781 Washington

1 maritime vs. continental power, 1776–82

→ allied (French/American) 1776–80
⇢ allied 1781
→ British 1776–80
⇢ British 1781

battles
✕ allied success
✕ British success

blockades
⛴ allied
⛴ British

sieges
↓ Successful American attack
↓ Successful British defense

Guildford C
Ho
15 Mar. 1

Great Smoky Mts.

Cowpens
17 Jan. 1781

Cornwa
1780–8

Camden
16 Aug. 1780

Augusta
29 Jan. 1779

SOUTH
CAROLINA

Charleston

GEORGIA

Savannah
Sept.–Oct. 1779

Can
D'Esfaing
Sept.–Oct.

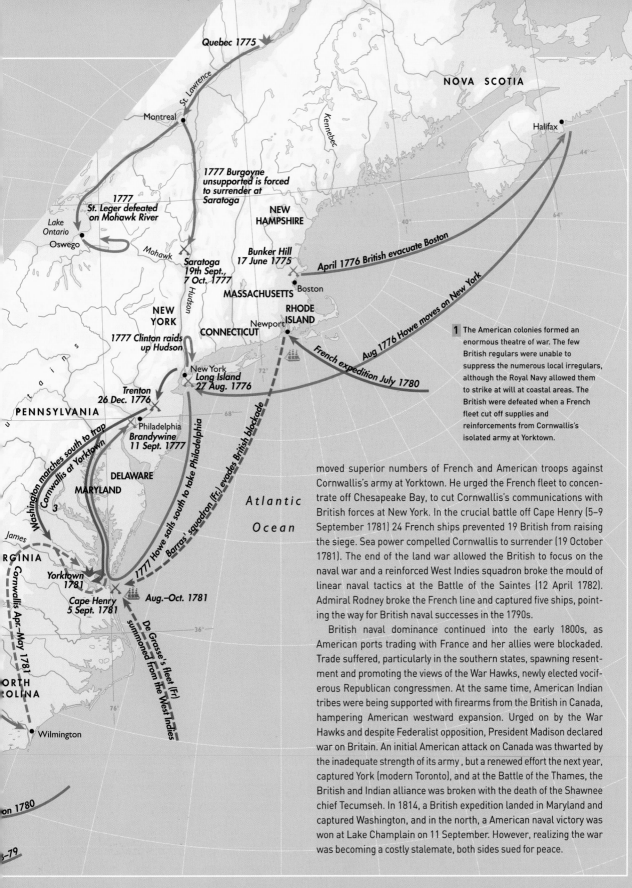

Quebec 1775

NOVA SCOTIA

St. Lawrence

Montreal

Halifax

Kennebec

Lake Ontario

Oswego

1777 St. Leger defeated on Mohawk River

1777 Burgoyne unsupported is forced to surrender at Saratoga

NEW HAMPSHIRE

Mohawk

Saratoga 19th Sept., 7 Oct. 1777

Hudson

Bunker Hill 17 June 1775

April 1776 British evacuate Boston

MASSACHUSETTS   Boston

NEW YORK

1777 Clinton raids up Hudson

CONNECTICUT

Newport   RHODE ISLAND

Aug 1776 Howe moves on New York

French expedition July 1780

1 The American colonies formed an enormous theatre of war. The few British regulars were unable to suppress the numerous local irregulars, although the Royal Navy allowed them to strike at will at coastal areas. The British were defeated when a French fleet cut off supplies and reinforcements from Cornwallis's isolated army at Yorktown.

New York   Long Island 27 Aug. 1776

Trenton 26 Dec. 1776

PENNSYLVANIA

Philadelphia

Brandywine 11 Sept. 1777

Washington marches south to trap Cornwallis at Yorktown

3

DELAWARE

MARYLAND

Barras' squadron (Fr.) evades British blockade

1777 Howe sails south to take Philadelphia

Atlantic

Ocean

James

VIRGINIA

Cornwallis Apr.–May 1781

Yorktown 1781

Cape Henry 5 Sept. 1781

Aug.–Oct. 1781

De Grasse's fleet (Fr) summoned from the West Indies

NORTH CAROLINA

Wilmington

on 1780

8–79

moved superior numbers of French and American troops against Cornwallis's army at Yorktown. He urged the French fleet to concentrate off Chesapeake Bay, to cut Cornwallis's communications with British forces at New York. In the crucial battle off Cape Henry (5–9 September 1781) 24 French ships prevented 19 British from raising the siege. Sea power compelled Cornwallis to surrender (19 October 1781). The end of the land war allowed the British to focus on the naval war and a reinforced West Indies squadron broke the mould of linear naval tactics at the Battle of the Saintes (12 April 1782). Admiral Rodney broke the French line and captured five ships, pointing the way for British naval successes in the 1790s.

British naval dominance continued into the early 1800s, as American ports trading with France and her allies were blockaded. Trade suffered, particularly in the southern states, spawning resentment and promoting the views of the War Hawks, newly elected vociferous Republican congressmen. At the same time, American Indian tribes were being supported with firearms from the British in Canada, hampering American westward expansion. Urged on by the War Hawks and despite Federalist opposition, President Madison declared war on Britain. An initial American attack on Canada was thwarted by the inadequate strength of its army , but a renewed effort the next year, captured York (modern Toronto), and at the Battle of the Thames, the British and Indian alliance was broken with the death of the Shawnee chief Tecumseh. In 1814, a British expedition landed in Maryland and captured Washington, and in the north, a American naval victory was won at Lake Champlain on 11 September. However, realizing the war was becoming a costly stalemate, both sides sued for peace.

the **french** revolutionary wars

1792 to 1796

1792
French National Assembly declares war on Austria

1792–94
French conquest of the Low Countries and the left bank of the Rhine

1793
threatened with invasion, the French government orders a *levée en masse*

18 May 1794
Battle of Tourcoing: French mount a 60,000-strong force against the allies

1796
Jourdan and Moreau invade Germany

The French Revolution profoundly changed the art of war. It released social forces that combined explosively with late-18th-century military trends. Unlike other "military revolutions" these trends were not technological in origin, but tactical.

French Army officers despaired of rivaling the precision of the Prussian drillmasters who had defeated them at Rossbach (1757). Instead they exploited the native flexibility of the French soldier by integrating skirmishers with the line of battle. Skirmishers screened the movement of columns unable to use their own weapons, and prepared the advance with accurate individual fire. Aimed fire was more dangerous than that of men jammed together in close order, while skirmishers presented a less vulnerable target. Dispersed skirmishers could thus achieve fire superiority over formed troops armed with similar weapons. This system became official French Army doctrine in 1791 and by 1815 it had spread to all European armies, forming the basis for a new tactical consensus. The French Army's system of all-arms divisions further enhanced tactical articulation.

Battles were less deadly, but there were more of them: 713 battles took place in Europe between 1790 and 1820, compared with 2,659 for the period 1480 to 1790. Enthusiastic French armies suffered more casualties than the regular troops they defeated. Their losses were replaced by compulsion. Threatened with invasion in August 1793, the government in Paris proclaimed a *levée en masse*. Half a million Frenchmen were under arms by the end of the year, in 11 separate armies. Such numbers were hard to maintain, falling to 227,000 in 1799. Battlefield strengths rarely exceeded those of the Seven Years War; Tourcoing (18 May 1794) was exceptional. Nevertheless, the increased total size of armies made it essential to feed them at the enemy's expense. A ring of annexed territories and puppet republics surrounded France by 1796, a system fundamental to Napoleon's empire.

French expansion was slow, until Napoleon focused revolutionary energies. Republican armies often failed to cooperate. When Jourdan and Moreau invaded Germany in 1796, the Austrian Archduke Karl beat them in detail, and chased them back to the Rhine. However, the conquest of the Low Countries and the left bank of the Rhine in three years (1792–94) compares strikingly with Louis XIV's decades of fighting fruitlessly for the same objectives. The contrast suggests the decisive potential of revolutionary warfare, when it was directed in a coordinated manner.

The new tactical methods exploited a profound shift in political attitudes. War was no longer the exclusive concern of kings or governments. It demanded popular participation, and soldiers who could be trusted not to desert when dispersed to forage or skirmish. Other European armies distrusted light infantry as socially subversive, and wished to avoid the economic dislocation caused by living off the country. They were slow to make the same demands of their soldiers and populations as the French.

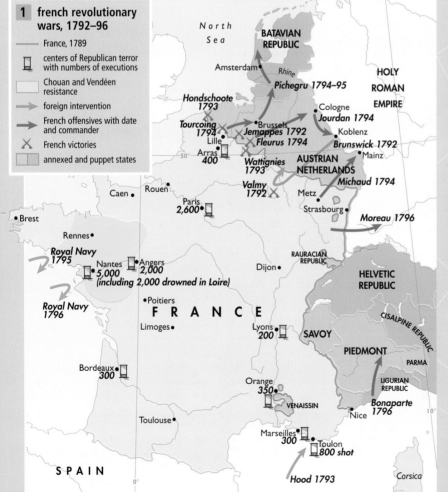

1 french revolutionary wars, 1792–96

- France, 1789
- centers of Republican terror with numbers of executions
- Chouan and Vendéen resistance
- foreign intervention
- French offensives with date and commander
- French victories
- annexed and puppet states

North Sea

BATAVIAN REPUBLIC

Amsterdam
Rhine

HOLY ROMAN EMPIRE

Pichegru 1794–95

Hondschoote 1793
Cologne
Jourdan 1794

Tourcoing 1794
Brussels
Jemappes 1792
Lille
Fleurus 1794
Koblenz
Arras **400**
Brunswick 1792
Mainz

Wattignies 1793
AUSTRIAN NETHERLANDS

Valmy 1792
Metz
Michaud 1794
Strasbourg
Moreau 1796

Caen
Rouen
Paris **2,600**

Brest
Rennes

Royal Navy 1795
Nantes **5,000 (including 2,000 drowned in Loire)**
Angers **2,000**
Dijon

RAURACIAN REPUBLIC

HELVETIC REPUBLIC

Royal Navy 1796
Poitiers
F R A N C E
Limoges

Lyons **200**
SAVOY

CISALPINE REPUBLIC

PIEDMONT
PARMA

Bordeaux **300**

Orange **350**
VENAISSIN
LIGURIAN REPUBLIC
Nice
Bonaparte 1796

Toulouse

Marseilles **300**
Toulon **800 shot**

S P A I N

Corsica

Hood 1793

1 Austria and Prussia invaded France in 1792, but the Duke of Brunswick's half-hearted campaign ended after an indecisive action at Valmy. After executing King Louis XVI in January 1793, the republic declared war on Britain, Holland, and Spain too (map opposite left). To the surprise of the allies, the French republican armies repelled each invasion and exported their revolution to the Low Countries, the west bank of the Rhine, and northern Italy.

2 The campaigns of the 1790s saw both sides disperse their forces over wide frontages, ready to concentrate for battle (map top right). At Tourcoing the French defeated the Allies in detail, acting on interior lines to concentrate against York's forces. However, both sides' losses were about 8%: decisive victories proved elusive.

3 In 1796 Archduke Karl of Austria exploited his central position to defeat two French invasions of southern Germany (map below). Jourdan was driven back and compelled to seek an armistice after the Battle of Würzburg.

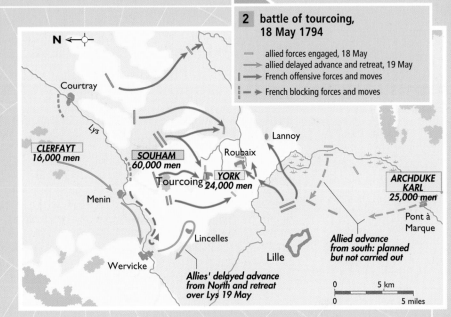

2 battle of tourcoing, 18 May 1794

- ▬ allied forces engaged, 18 May
- → allied delayed advance and retreat, 19 May
- → French offensive forces and moves
- ⇢ French blocking forces and moves

Courtray

Lys

CLERFAYT 16,000 men

SOUHAM 60,000 men

Tourcoing

YORK 24,000 men

Roubaix

Lannoy

ARCHDUKE KARL 25,000 men

Menin

Pont à Marque

Lincelles

Lille

Allied advance from south: planned but not carried out

Wervicke

Allies' delayed advance from North and retreat over Lys 19 May

0   5 km
0   5 miles

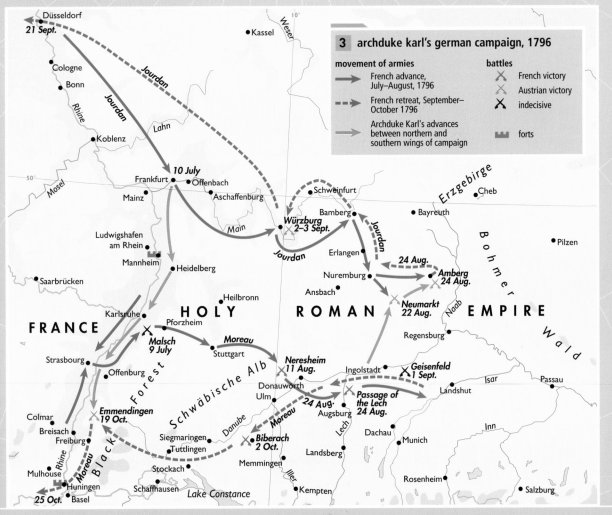

3 archduke karl's german campaign, 1796

movement of armies

- → French advance, July–August, 1796
- ⇢ French retreat, September–October 1796
- → Archduke Karl's advances between northern and southern wings of campaign

battles

- ✕ French victory
- ✕ Austrian victory
- ✕ indecisive
- ▣ forts

Düsseldorf 21 Sept.

Kassel

Weser

Cologne

Bonn

Jourdan

Rhine

Lahn

Koblenz

Jourdan

10 July

Frankfurt

Offenbach

Aschaffenburg

Schweinfurt

Cheb

Erzgebirge

Bayreuth

Mosel

Mainz

Main

Würzburg 2–3 Sept.

Bamberg

Jourdan

Pilzen

Ludwigshafen am Rhein

Mannheim

Heidelberg

Jourdan

Erlangen

Nuremburg

Ansbach

24 Aug.

Amberg 24 Aug.

Bohmer

Saarbrücken

Heilbronn

Neumarkt 22 Aug.

Naab

Wald

EMPIRE

Karlsruhe

HOLY

Pforzheim

Malsch 9 July

Moreau

Stuttgart

ROMAN

Regensburg

FRANCE

Strasbourg

Offenburg

Black Forest

Neresheim 11 Aug.

Ingolstadt

Geisenfeld 1 Sept.

Isar

Passau

Schwäbische Alb

Donauwörth

Ulm

24 Aug.

Augsburg

Passage of the Lech 24 Aug.

Landshut

Emmendingen 19 Oct.

Moreau

Danube

Lech

Dachau

Inn

Colmar

Breisach

Freiburg

Siegmaringen

Tuttlingen

Biberach 2 Oct.

Memmingen

Landsberg

Munich

Rosenheim

Salzburg

Rhine

Moreau

Mulhouse

Huningen

25 Oct.

Basel

Stockach

Schaffhausen

Lake Constance

Iller

Kempten

1796 to 1800

1796
Bonaparte's first campaign in Italy

1797
Treaty of Tolentino; Napoleon defeats Austrians at Neumarkt and Unzmarkt

1797
French occupation of Venice

1798
Bonaparte's Egyptian campaign: Mamluks defeated at Battle of Pyramids

1799
Austria (supported by Britain, Russia, Naples, and Portugal) declares war on France

1800
French army crosses Alps in the Marengo campaign, and gains a narrow victory over the Austrians

The armies of the Revolution contained the seeds of Napoleon's success. General Bonaparte's first campaign in Italy in 1796 showed his grasp of the potential of divisional organization and skirmishing tactics. In his first campaign, Bonaparte showed the originality of his genius, defeating larger, better-equipped armies with two strategies that became Napoleonic trademarks: the Strategy of the Central Position, and the Envelopment or *la manoeuvre sur les derrières*.

The first allowed inferior numbers to divide a superior enemy army, and defeat its wings in detail. It worked best against allied armies, more concerned with their own safety than for their ally. When the Austrians fell back behind the Po and Ticino, Bonaparte used his now superior numbers to implement the more ambitious *manoeuvre sur les derrières*. Screened by the river Po, Bonaparte gained the Austrian rear between Piacenza and Lodi, precipitating an immediate Austrian withdrawal from Lombardy. The French advanced 100 miles in two weeks, and seized Milan with enormous quantities of loot, resolving their own logistical difficulties. The crossing of the Alps in the Marengo campaign of 1800 was an even more impressive demonstration of the envelopment strategy. The Austrians had regained northern Italy, and were pressing against the French frontier on the Riviera. Bonaparte, now the French head of state, crossed the Alps behind the Austrians. The French re-occupied Milan, cutting Austrian communications, while maintaining their own through Switzerland.

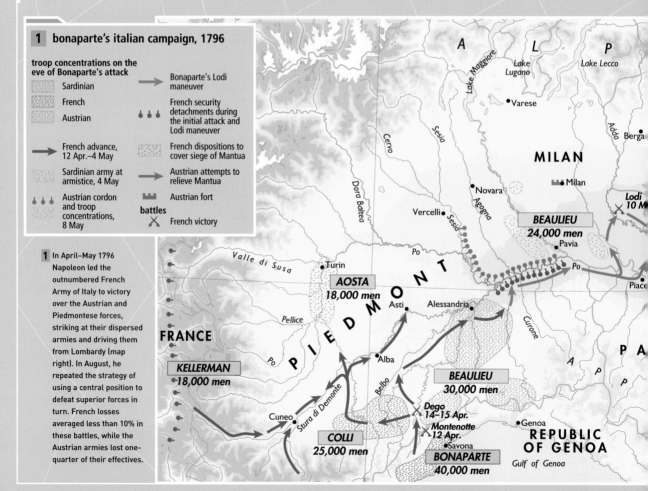

1 **bonaparte's italian campaign, 1796**

troop concentrations on the eve of Bonaparte's attack

- Sardinian
- French
- Austrian

→ French advance, 12 Apr.–4 May

Sardinian army at armistice, 4 May

Austrian cordon and troop concentrations, 8 May

→ Bonaparte's Lodi maneuver

French security detachments during the initial attack and Lodi maneuver

French dispositions to cover siege of Mantua

→ Austrian attempts to relieve Mantua

Austrian fort

battles
✕ French victory

1 In April–May 1796 Napoleon led the outnumbered French Army of Italy to victory over the Austrian and Piedmontese forces, striking at their dispersed armies and driving them from Lombardy (map right). In August, he repeated the strategy of using a central position to defeat superior forces in turn. French losses averaged less than 10% in these battles, while the Austrian armies lost one-quarter of their effectives.

Map labels:
A L P
Lake Maggiore
Lake Lugano
Lake Lecco
•Varese
Adda
Berga
Cervo
Sesia
MILAN
ılı Milan
Lodi 10 M
Dora Baltea
Agogna
•Novara
BEAULIEU 24,000 men
•Pavia
Vercelli•
Sesia
Po
Po
Piace
Valle di Susa
•Turin
P I E D M O N T
AOSTA 18,000 men
Asti•
Alessandria•
Curone
Pellice
Po
FRANCE
•Alba
A P P
KELLERMAN •18,000 men
Stura di Demonte
Belbo
BEAULIEU 30,000 men
P A
Cuneo
Dego 14–15 Apr.
Montenotte 12 Apr.
•Genoa
COLLI 25,000 men
•Savona
REPUBLIC OF GENOA
BONAPARTE 40,000 men
Gulf of Genoa

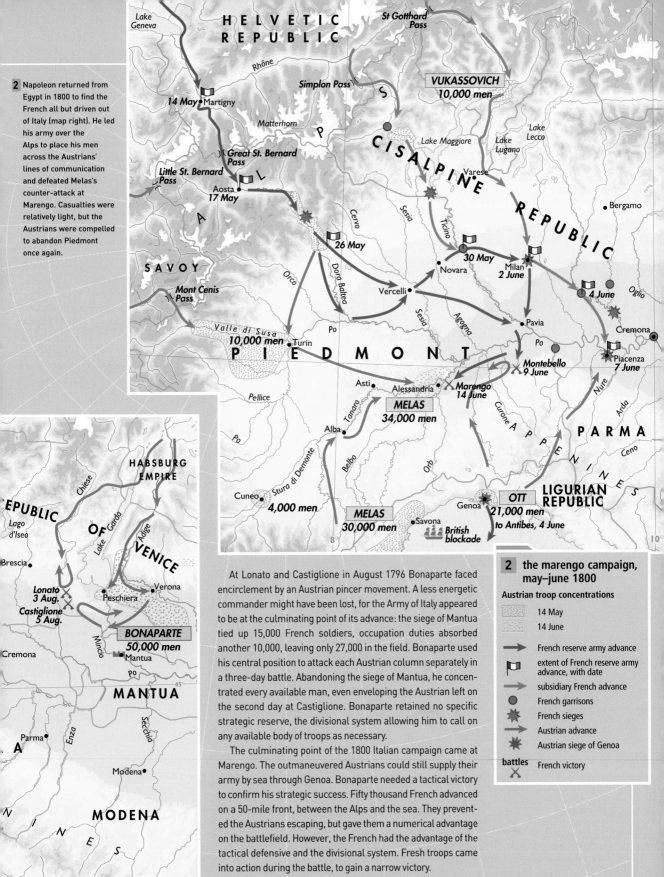

2 Napoleon returned from Egypt in 1800 to find the French all but driven out of Italy (map right). He led his army over the Alps to place his men across the Austrians' lines of communication and defeated Melas's counter-attack at Marengo. Casualties were relatively light, but the Austrians were compelled to abandon Piedmont once again.

HELVETIC REPUBLIC

St Gotthard Pass

VUKASSOVICH
10,000 men

Lake Geneva

Rhône

Simplon Pass

S

14 May • Martigny

Matterhorn

P

Great St. Bernard Pass

Little St. Bernard Pass

Lake Maggiore

CISALPINE

Lake Lugano

Lake Lecco

L

Aosta
17 May

A

SAVOY

Varese

• Bergamo

REPUBLIC

26 May

Cervo

Sesia

Ticino

30 May

Milan
2 June

4 June

Oglio

Novara

Mont Cenis Pass

Orco

Dora Baltea

Vercelli

Sesia

Agogna

Pavia

Po

Cremona

Valle di Susa
10,000 men

Po

Turin

PIEDMONT

Montebello
9 June

Piacenza
7 June

Nure

Pellice

Asti

Alessandria

Marengo
14 June

Curone

A

PARMA

Ceno

Alba

Belbo

Tanaro

Orb

MELAS
34,000 men

P

P

E

N

Arda

Cuneo

Stura di Demonte

4,000 men

MELAS
30,000 men

Savona

Genoa

OTT
21,000 men
to Antibes, 4 June

LIGURIAN REPUBLIC

N

E

S

British blockade

Inset map (bottom left):

HABSBURG EMPIRE

Chiese

REPUBLIC

Lago d'Iseo

Brescia

OF

Lake Garda

Adige

VENICE

Lonato
3 Aug.

Castiglione
5 Aug.

Peschiera

Verona

Cremona

Mincio

BONAPARTE
50,000 men

Mantua

Po

MANTUA

Parma

Enza

Secchia

Modena

A

MODENA

N

E

S

At Lonato and Castiglione in August 1796 Bonaparte faced encirclement by an Austrian pincer movement. A less energetic commander might have been lost, for the Army of Italy appeared to be at the culminating point of its advance: the siege of Mantua tied up 15,000 French soldiers, occupation duties absorbed another 10,000, leaving only 27,000 in the field. Bonaparte used his central position to attack each Austrian column separately in a three-day battle. Abandoning the siege of Mantua, he concentrated every available man, even enveloping the Austrian left on the second day at Castiglione. Bonaparte retained no specific strategic reserve, the divisional system allowing him to call on any available body of troops as necessary.

The culminating point of the 1800 Italian campaign came at Marengo. The outmaneuvered Austrians could still supply their army by sea through Genoa. Bonaparte needed a tactical victory to confirm his strategic success. Fifty thousand French advanced on a 50-mile front, between the Alps and the sea. They prevented the Austrians escaping, but gave them a numerical advantage on the battlefield. However, the French had the advantage of the tactical defensive and the divisional system. Fresh troops came into action during the battle, to gain a narrow victory.

Legend:

2 the marengo campaign, may–june 1800

Austrian troop concentrations

14 May

14 June

→ French reserve army advance

⚑ extent of French reserve army advance, with date

→ subsidiary French advance

● French garrisons

✳ French sieges

→ Austrian advance

✳ Austrian siege of Genoa

battles
✕ French victory

1804
General Bonaparte becomes emperor

20 October 1805
27,000 Austrians surrender at Ulm

2 December 1805
bBattle of Austerlitz: Austria sues for peace and Napoleon's army occupies south Germany

1806
Prussia declares war on France

14 October 1806
Battle of Jena-Auerstadt: Napoleon victorious against Prussians

14 June 1807
Battle of Friedland: Russians seek peace after heavy losses

Napoleon Bonaparte became emperor of France in 1804. Lacking legitimacy, except the bayonets of his followers, he had to ensure their continued support. He plundered Europe for the benefit of the French Army, perpetuating international instability. The Grande Armée began as the Army of England, but in 1805 it turned upon Napoleon's continental rivals, Austria and Russia.

The Grande Armée advanced with seven corps to the Danube. The Austrian high command fatally underestimated the threat. General Mack occupied an exposed position at Ulm in Bavaria, a French ally. He expected a direct advance through the Black Forest. Meanwhile, the mass of the Grande Armée swung north of Ulm, reaching the Danube between Ulm and the Austrian base at Vienna. Twenty-seven thousand Austrians surrendered on 20 October 1805. Napoleon's 2:1 numerical superiority made his success a rare example of a bloodless triumph.

The Allies were unable to defend Vienna, its arsenals falling into French hands. Napoleon caught up with a combined Austro-Russian army at Austerlitz, 70 miles

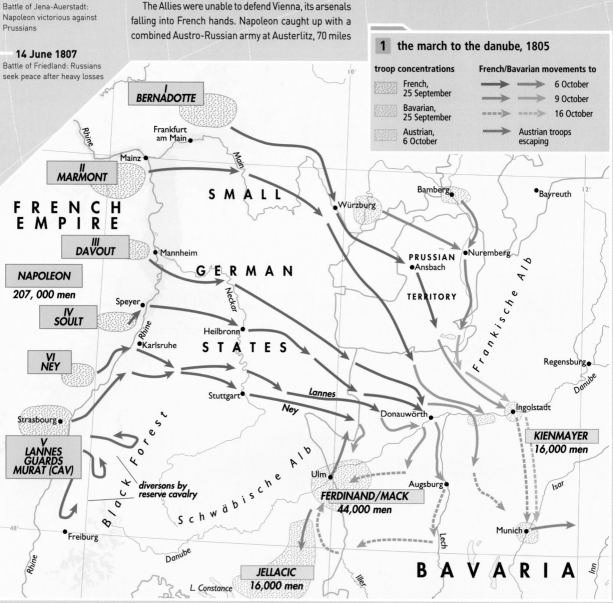

1 **the march to the danube, 1805**

troop concentrations

- French, 25 September
- Bavarian, 25 September
- Austrian, 6 October

French/Bavarian movements to
- 6 October
- 9 October
- 16 October
- Austrian troops escaping

north of Vienna. Napoleon outwitted the Allies, but their defeat required hard fighting. The French owed their final success to the tactical superiority of their veterans. This second defeat, in the heart of his country, persuaded the Austrian emperor to make peace. Napoleon had knocked Austria out of the war in just three months' fighting.

The Grande Armée occupied south Germany after Austerlitz, to oversee creation of the French-dominated Confederation of the Rhine. In response Prussia occupied Saxony and Hesse-Kassel, north of the Main. The Prussians made a dangerous flank march across Napoleon's front to regain the Elbe, their divisions strung out along a single road, unlike the French who moved by several roads on a broad front.

Napoleon's tactics brought on the double battle of Jena-Auerstadt. The Prussians outnumbered Davout's corps on the right at Auerstadt 2:1 but he beat them off. Bernadotte's corps then intercepted the Prussian withdrawal near Apolda, converting it into a rout. The devastating consequences of the French victory made clear the implicit message of Marengo: an army losing its lines of communications and suffering a decisive defeat would be ruined.

The large French army quickly overran the small kingdom of Prussia, but resistance continued in Poland and East Prussia, with Russian help. Strategic success eluded Napoleon in the roadless wastes of Eastern Europe. The Grande Armée had to fight bloody frontal actions against the traditionally obstinate Russians, whose unpredictable movements sometimes enabled them to seize the initiative. For the first time Napoleon had failed to gain the type of rapid decisive victory that he needed. The Treaty of Tilsit (July 1807), signed on a raft on the River Niemen, was the high-water mark of his empire.

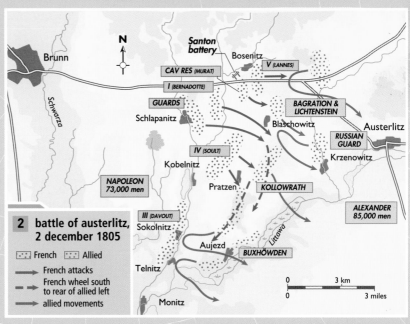

2 battle of austerlitz, 2 december 1805

.::. French   .::. Allied
→ French attacks
⇢ French wheel south to rear of allied left
⇨ allied movements

1 Napoleon opened the 1805 campaign with a far larger army than he had previously commanded, outnumbering the enemy by 2:1 (map left). His Grande Armée carried little baggage, invading enemy territory at harvest time and marching far faster than the Austrians anticipated. Before they realized what was happening, the French had slipped past Ulm and Mack's army was obliged to surrender.

2 At Austerlitz Napoleon tempted the cumbersome Austro–Russian army to attack his right flank, weakening its own center (map above right). Napoleon broke through the middle of the Allied army, which broke up with 30% losses. It was militarily and politically decisive: Austria sued for peace.

3 The Austrians demonstrated just how much they had improved at Wagram: although defeated by 6 July, with 45,000 casualties, it had been a "near run thing" and Napoleon's loss of 34,000 cut deeply into the ranks of his veterans (map right). The Grande Armée would never be quite the same again.

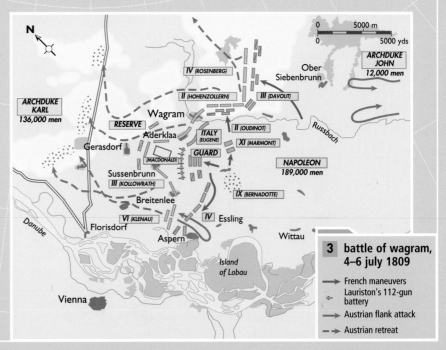

3 battle of wagram, 4–6 july 1809

→ French maneuvers
⇉ Lauriston's 112-gun battery
→ Austrian flank attack
⇢ Austrian retreat

naval warfare in the age of napoleon

28 May–1 June 1794
the Glorious First of June

14 February 1797
Battle of St. Vincent: Sir John Jervis outmaneuvers a Spanish fleet of superior numbers

21 October 1805
Battle of Trafalgar: Nelson's 27 ships against a 33-strong Franco–Spanish fleet; 18 Franco–Spanish ships were taken or sunk

Sea warfare in the 1790s underwent no revolution comparable to that ashore. Occasional battles and invasion scares punctuated years of blockade and privateering in a pattern familiar from the 1690s. A century of Anglo-French naval rivalry was about to reach a climax.

The French Revolution showed the irrelevance of the Nation in Arms concept to organizing a fleet in wartime. Eighty per cent of French naval officers emigrated, leaving ships and dockyards in chaos. France's main naval ally, Spain, could never recruit enough trained seamen to man her extensive inventory of well-constructed ships. Half-trained crews could not match the rapid broadsides of well-drilled British seamen-gunners. The allies' tactical inferiority encouraged a preference for pursuing strategic aims while avoiding a decisive battle. The Glorious First of June (1 June 1794) appeared to justify this approach. The British had the better of the fighting, but the French secured a vital grain convoy, saving the Revolution.

The Battle of St. Vincent (14 February 1797) underlined the tactical value of British seamanship. Sir John Jervis exploited a gap in a Spanish fleet to achieve local superiority of numbers. Outnumbered 2:1 overall, he captured four ships, breaking off the action before numbers began to tell. Nelson repeated Jervis's' tactical concentration at the Nile, against a French squadron at anchor, reversing the strategic balance of power in the Mediterranean.

Trafalgar was the culmination of this series of British successes. Nelson concentrated all his 27 ships against 23 of the combined Franco-Spanish strength of 33. He attacked in two divisions to break the enemy line, cutting off the center and rear. Eighteen Franco-Spanish ships were taken or sunk.

Napoleon's plan for the Trafalgar campaign was to concentrate his fleets in the West Indies. This threat to a vital economic region might draw off enough British ships to give the combined fleets numerical superiority in the Channel. However, Napoleon's naval forces lacked the Grande Armée's professionalism, and he did not allow for the greater friction of war at sea, with its variable weather and erratic communications. His subsequent attempt to return to the Mediterranean gave Nelson the chance to put an end to French strategic machinations, by destroying the French fleet in combat.

The Continental System was Napoleon's admission of defeat at sea. The extent of his empire allowed him to reverse the British blockade by excluding them from European ports. The British responded by developing markets outside Europe. Maritime supremacy brought prosperity. The British subsidized opposition to Napoleon, while mounting expeditions against the periphery of the empire, at Copenhagen, Sicily, and Spain. The Royal Navy's aggressive combat strategy had given the British strategic freedom. The limited-risk strategy of the French had lost them the ability to pursue even restricted strategic goals at sea.

Map labels:

Atlantic Ocean

Ballinamuck 1796

Tory 179...

UNIT...

Dublin · Liverpo...

KIN...

Bantry Bay 1796

Glorious First of June 28 May–1 June 1794

Plymouth

Portsm...

Villeneuve's return from West Indies (July 1805) and failure to join French fleet at Brest

17

Isle de Groix 23 June 1795

21 Brest

Lorient 3

Belle Isle 17 July

Ferrrol squadron joins Channel Fleet

Cape Finisterre 22 July 1805

Aix Roads 11–12 Apr. 1809

Rochefort

8

Ferrol 12

Corunna

Vigo

Santander 1813

Bordeaux

PORTUGAL

Douro

1807

Tagus

Lisbon

Madrid

Ebro

SPAIN

CATA...

Barce...

Madeira

Cape St. Vincent 14 Feb. 1797

Nelson's return from West Indies and junction with Channel Fleet

6

Cadiz 12 July 1801

Cadiz 7

Gibraltar British

Cartagena 6

Trafalgar 21 Oct. 1805

Algeciras 6 July 1801

Maj...

1797 Canary Islands Tenerife

MOROCCO

ALG...

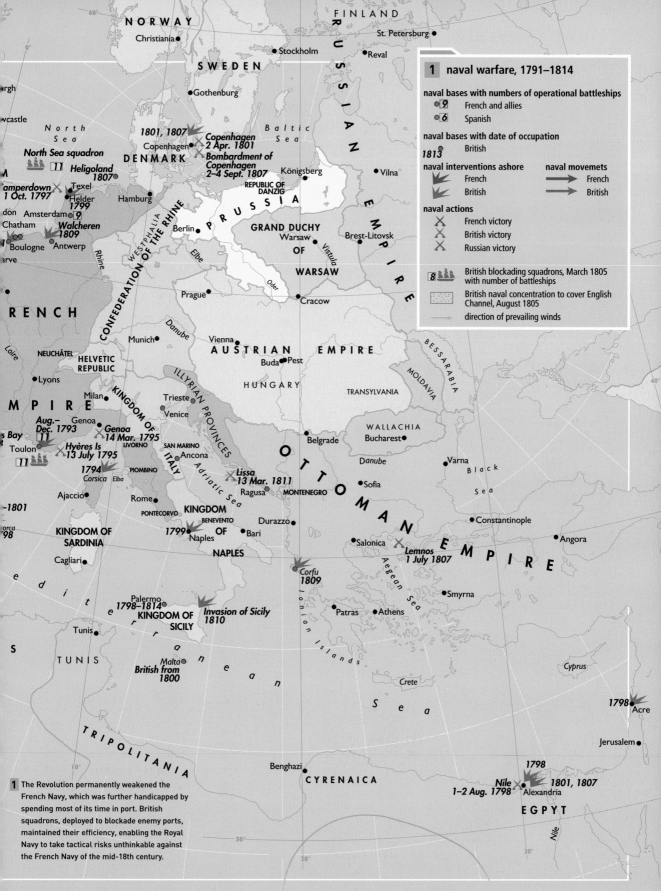

NORWAY

FINLAND

SWEDEN

St. Petersburg

Christiania

Stockholm

Reval

RUSSIAN EMPIRE

Gothenburg

North Sea

1801, 1807
Copenhagen

Baltic Sea

DENMARK

North Sea squadron

Heligoland 1807

Copenhagen 2 Apr. 1801

Bombardment of Copenhagen 2–4 Sept. 1807

Königsberg

Vilna

urgh

wcastle

Camperdown 1 Oct. 1797

Texel

Helder 1799

Hamburg

WESTPHALIA

CONFEDERATION OF THE RHINE

REPUBLIC OF DANZIG

PRUSSIA

don

Amsterdam 9

Chatham

Walcheren 1809

Boulogne Antwerp

Berlin

Elbe

GRAND DUCHY OF WARSAW

Warsaw

Brest-Litovsk

Oder

Vistula

arve

Rhine

Prague

Cracow

Loire

NEUCHÂTEL

HELVETIC REPUBLIC

Lyons

Munich

Danube

Vienna

AUSTRIAN EMPIRE

Buda Pest

BESSARABIA

MOLDAVIA

MPIRE

Milan

KINGDOM OF

ILLYRIAN PROVINCES

Trieste

Venice

HUNGARY

TRANSYLVANIA

Aug.–Dec. 1793

s Bay

Genoa

Genoa 14 Mar. 1795

LIVORNO

ITALY

San Marino

Ancona

Adriatic Sea

WALLACHIA

Bucharest

Toulon

Hyères Is 13 July 1795

1794

Corsica Elba

PIOMBINO

Rome

Belgrade

Danube

Varna

Black Sea

Ajaccio

PONTECORVO

KINGDOM

BENEVENTO

OF

Lissa 13 Mar. 1811

Ragusa

MONTENEGRO

Sofia

–1801

orca

98

KINGDOM OF SARDINIA

1799

Naples

Durazzo

Bari

NAPLES

OTTOMAN EMPIRE

Salonica

Constantinople

Angora

Cagliari

Corfu 1809

Lemnos 1 July 1807

Palermo 1798–1814

KINGDOM OF SICILY

Invasion of Sicily 1810

Ionian Islands

Aegean Sea

Smyrna

Patras

Athens

Tunis

TUNIS

Malta British from 1800

Mediterranean Sea

Crete

Cyprus

S

TRIPOLITANIA

1798 Acre

Jerusalem

Benghazi

CYRENAICA

1798

Nile 1–2 Aug. 1798

Alexandria

1801, 1807

EGPYT

Nile

1 The Revolution permanently weakened the French Navy, which was further handicapped by spending most of its time in port. British squadrons, deployed to blockade enemy ports, maintained their efficiency, enabling the Royal Navy to take tactical risks unthinkable against the French Navy of the mid-18th century.

the **peninsular war**

1808
British Expeditionary Force lands in Portugal

1809
John Moore dies at Corunna; British win at Oporto and Talavera

1810
Massena invades Portugal; Wellington holds the line at Torres Vedras

1811
Battle of Albuera (16 May)

1812
Battles of Ciudad Rodrigo, Salamanca (22 July) and, Badajoz; Wellington forced back to Portugal (October)

1813
Battle of Vitoria effectively ends war

The Napoleonic military system failed comprehensively in Spain. The country is large, divided by mountain ranges that run across the path of a French invader. There was no agricultural surplus like that in Central Europe, meaning that large armies starved. Good roads were few, hampering strategic combinations. Fortresses like Badajoz and Ciudad Rodrigo dominated such communications as there were, and could not be bypassed, giving sieges an unusual significance. A conservative people, suspicious of outsiders, found ideals of liberty and fraternity unattractive, depriving the French of the political support they had received in Italy and Germany.

Elsewhere in Europe, occupation of the capital soon brought a country to order. Spanish central government was weak and local particularism ensured that resistance continued regardless of the fall of Madrid. Even so, the centers of Spanish patriotic resistance would have fallen to French repression, or the more imaginative pacification measures pursued by Suchet in Catalonia, had it not been for British intervention.

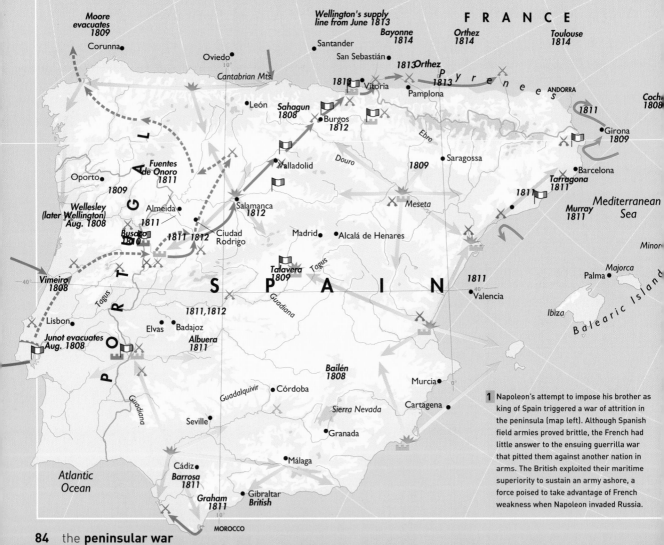

1 Napoleon's attempt to impose his brother as king of Spain triggered a war of attrition in the peninsula (map left). Although Spanish field armies proved brittle, the French had little answer to the ensuing guerrilla war that pitted them against another nation in arms. The British exploited their maritime superiority to sustain an army ashore, a force poised to take advantage of French weakness when Napoleon invaded Russia.

Britain's army was small, but it stopped the French finally crushing the guerrillas. They in turn prevented the French concentrating against the British. The British commander Sir Arthur Wellesley, later Duke of Wellington, exploited British financial and maritime strength to organize a supply train of Spanish muleteers and feed his army. He avoided alienating the local population by foraging, as the French did. When Napoleon withdrew his best troops for Russia, Wellington went on the offensive, using sea power to switch his base from Lisbon to ports in northern Spain.

Unlike Napoleon, Wellington did not depend on grand strategic combinations. His methods derived from an older tradition, based on direct control of formations by the commander. Like Frederick the Great, Wellington relied on his personal eye for country to exploit enemy mistakes. Marmont had outmaneuvered him in July 1812, forcing Wellington to retreat from Tordesillas on Salamanca. As the two armies raced side by side for a strategic river crossing, Wellington detected a gap in the French column, isolating their leading division. Within minutes he had organized an overwhelming attack on the head of the French column, not dissimilar to Frederick's demolition of the Austrian left flank at Leuthen. At Salamanca, however, both armies were moving, showing how dynamic battlefields had become with the general adoption of the divisional system.

Wellington had not cut off Marmont's retreat, so his victory was less decisive than Napoleon's strategic masterpieces at Austerlitz or Jena. Despite his humiliating defeat, Marmont was able to regroup his army and drive Wellington back to the Portuguese frontier in October 1812. Wellington lacked Napoleon's unlimited reserves of manpower, so he could never risk throwing his army across the enemy's rear. He depended on a Frederician strategy of attrition to wear down French strength, assisted by the country and the guerrillas.

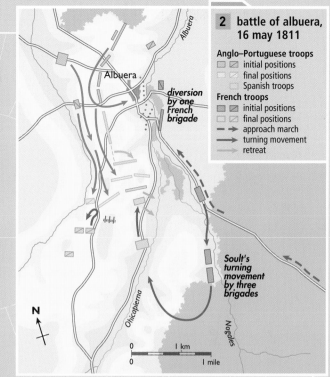

2 battle of albuera, 16 may 1811

Anglo–Portuguese troops
- ☐ initial positions
- ☐ final positions
- ☐ Spanish troops

French troops
- ☐ initial positions
- ☐ final positions
- ⇢ approach march
- → turning movement
- → retreat

2 Marshal Soult's attempt to raise the siege of Badajoz was bloodily repulsed at Albuera (map above), but not before French cavalry had wiped out one British infantry brigade and driven off much of the Spanish contingent.

3 At Salamanca, Marmont's army was caught out by the British assault; he and his successor were both wounded and the leaderless French army disintegrated.

---

1 the peninsular war, 1808–14

- Spanish insurrections, May 1808
- spread of Spanish revolt
- Spanish fortress
- Portuguese fortress
- French garrisons, 1808
- Moore's campaign, 1808–09
- line of Torres Vedras
- Wellington's campaign, 1813–14

battles and sieges
- ✕ British victory
- ✕ French victory (discounting numerous defeats of smaller Spanish units)
- ✕ Spanish victory

3 battle of salamanca, 22 july 1812

Anglo–Portuguese troops
- → lines of attack
- ⇢ concealed march of Pakenham's division and two cavalry brigades

French troops
- → approach march
- → counter-attacks
- ⊙⇢ final position and retreat

napoleon at bay

1812
Napoleon invades Russia (24 June); Battle of Borodino (7 September); retreat from Moscow (begins 19 October); disastrous French crossing of Berezina (26–28 November)

1813
Battle of Lützen (2 May); battle of Bautzen (20 May); Napoleon defeats allies at Dresden (26 August); Napoleon defeated at "Battle of the Nations" at Leipzig (16–19 October)

1814
the "Five Days" (10–14 February); allies enter Paris (30 March); Napoleon abdicates and is exiled to Elba

1815
Napoleon lands in France (1 March); "Hundred Days" begins; Waterloo campaign (16–18 June); battles of Ligny and Quatre Bras and Waterloo; Napoleon abdicates for second time (22 June)

All the factors that vitiated Napoleon's war in Spain applied in Russia. After two months his forces had lost 150,000 men from sickness and desertion. The Russians, aware of Napoleon's weaknesses, ordered a lengthy retreat, leading the Grande Armée into the infamous long marches, which sapped tits strength.

The Battle of Borodino (7 September 1812) marked the climactic point of 20 years of revolutionary and Napoleonic violence. The Russians lost more men at Borodino than any other modern army had yet suffered in one action. Nevertheless, the battle failed to shake the Russians' resolve. The French advanced to capture Moscow, but soon had no alternative but retreat.

The Battle of Maloyaroslavets persuaded Napoleon to withdraw by the Smolensk road, which had been swept bare of supplies during the advance. Fresh Russian forces, released from the south after peace with Turkey, threatened Napoleon's line of retreat, preventing him from wintering at Smolensk. The Cossacks prevented the French resting or dispersing to forage, while infuriated peasants murdered French stragglers. The Grande Armée's veteran cadres were lost.

Napoleon rejoined the remnants of the Grande Armée in April 1813. His last campaign in Germany began with a string of classic victories. The next 12 months, however, saw the initiative pass to his enemies. The allies, recognizing Napoleon's superior battlefield skills, concentrated against his subordinates. Gradually the allies closed the circle around Napoleon, who fell back on Leipzig.

Understanding how Napoleon's military success at Ulm, Jena, and Wagram had depended on their political disunity, the allies realized that, acting together, they could achieve numerical superiority without adopting radical ideas about the Nation in Arms. In the brief Waterloo campaign (16–18 June 1815) Napoleon took the initiative, invading Belgium to knock out his most inveterate

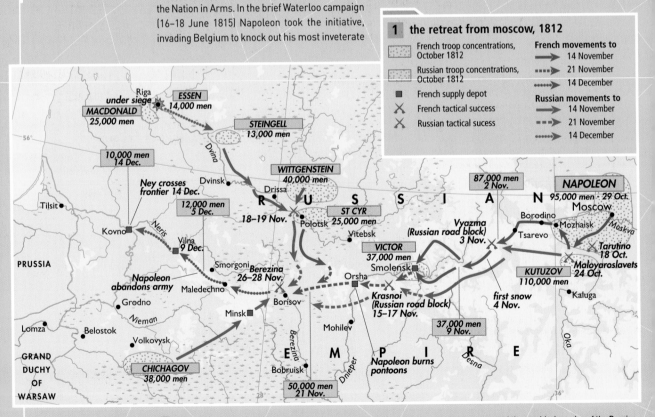

1 the retreat from moscow, 1812

French troop concentrations, October 1812	
Russian troop concentrations, October 1812	
French supply depot	
French tactical success	
Russian tactical sucess	

French movements to
→ 14 November
--→ 21 November
····→ 14 December

Russian movements to
→ 14 November
--→ 21 November
····→ 14 December

1 The Russians forced Napoleon to retreat over the route of his original advance after he evacuated the smoldering ruins of the Russian capital. The countryside had already been stripped bare and his soldiers found nothing left to plunder. Foraging parties fell prey to Cossack patrols that hovered like vultures around the French columns.

enemies, the Prussians and the British. Outnumbered almost 2:1, Napoleon naturally tried to seize a central position between them. Napoleon's attempts to drive the allies apart caused the double Battle of Ligny/Quatre Bras. One wing of the French held off Wellington, while Napoleon tried to crush Blücher. However, the Prussians were allowed to retreat and joined Wellington. The late Prussian arrival at Waterloo proved decisive. The appearance of the Prussians drew off Napoleon's reserve, leaving no infantry to support Ney's cavalry charges against the British center. Blücher's flank march gave him the central position. He used his interior position to extend Wellington's left flank and to envelop Napoleon's right. The direction of the Prussian advance combined with Wellington's pursuit of the columns of the Guard to precipitate a rout, decisively ending one of the few truly revolutionary periods in the history of war.

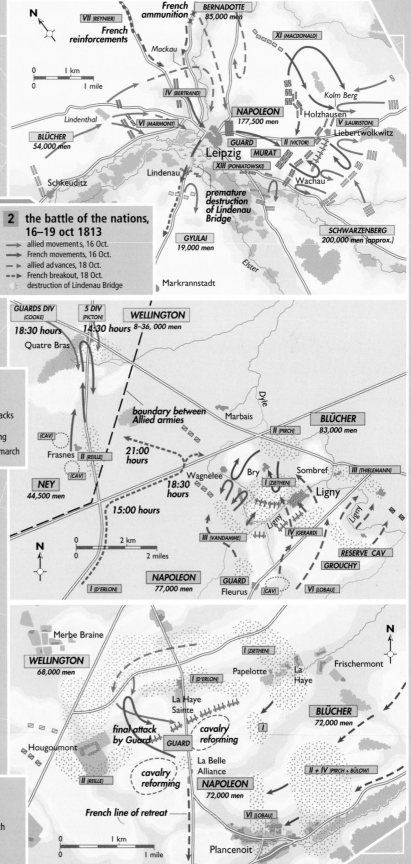

2 the battle of the nations, 16–19 oct 1813

→ allied movements, 16 Oct.
→ French movements, 16 Oct.
--→ allied advances, 18 Oct.
--→ French breakout, 18 Oct.
✶ destruction of Lindenau Bridge

3 battles of ligny and quatre bras, 17 june 1815

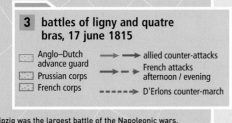

▫ Anglo–Dutch advance guard
▫ Prussian corps
▫ French corps
→ allied counter-attacks
→ French attacks afternoon / evening
--→ D'Erlons counter-march

2 Leipzig was the largest battle of the Napoleonic wars, on a scale that even the emperor could not control (top right). Some 185,000 French and allied troops held off nearly 300,000 Russian, Austrian, Prussian, and Swedish soldiers until the premature demolition of the Lindenau bridge turned a fighting retreat into disaster. French losses were around 30,000 with another 30,000 captured; their opponents lost over 50,000 men.

3 At the twin battles of Quatre Bras and Ligny, Napoleon sought to crush the Prussians while Marshal Ney dealt with the British advance guard (middle right). The Prussians were beaten and withdrew, but Ney's assault at Quatrebras was too late in the day to be decisive.

4 From his headquarters at La Belle Alliance, Napoleon could see little of the British position on the reverse slope of across the valley (bottom right). Clumsy infantry tactics and the frittering away of a whole corps in the battle for Hougoumont left Napoleon exposed to the Prussian flank attack that afternoon. Too late, he flung his Imperial Guard into a final assault on the British, only to see it broken.

4 battle of la belle alliance, 18 june 1815

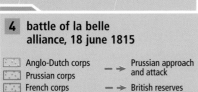

▫ Anglo-Dutch corps
▫ Prussian corps
▫ French corps
--→ Prussian approach and attack
--→ British reserves

NG TOM
T MAFEKING 1899

the **crimean war**

1853 to 1856

1853
Turkey declares war on Russia (5 October); British fleet enters Bosporus (30 October); Turkish fleet destroyed off Sinop (30 November)

1854
Britain and France declare war on Russia (28 March); allies land at Kalamata, north of Sevastopol (14 September); Battle of the Alma (20 September); siege of Sevastopol begins (17 October); Battle of Balaklava (25 October), sees charges of Light and Heavy Brigades; Russians defeated at Inkerman (5 November)

1855
second bombardment of Sevastopol (9 April); allies capture Kerch and Yenikale (25 May); Sevastopol falls after Russian evacuation (8–9 September); first use of ironclad warships, to bombard Kinburn (16 October)

1856
Treaty of Paris ends war (30 March)

The Tsar's ambitions in the Balkans culminated in a Russian naval attack on a much weaker Turkish squadron at Sinop (30 November 1853). Newly developed shell guns caused a "massacre," and inspired an Anglo-French alliance to keep the Russian fleet out of the eastern Mediterranean. Their natural war aim was to destroy the Russian Navy's dockyard at Sevastopol in the Crimea, although there were subsidiary operations in the Baltic and White Seas.

The allies could nourish their forces from the sea, while the Russians withered at the end of lengthy land communications. Fleets provided superior operational mobility, transporting allied armies directly across the Black Sea, before Russian troops on the Danube could reach the Crimea on foot. It was impossible to blockade Russia, but Allied gunboats interdicted coastal traffic through the Sea of Azov, which sustained Russian forces in the Crimea. Improving communications had other consequences. The telegraph paralyzed French commanders with contradictory orders from Paris. Newspapers inflamed public war fever, spurred governments to ill-considered action, and compromised operational security. The world's first war correspondent (William Howard Russell) made the British commander-in-chief a scapegoat for governmental neglect and muddle, but did heighten awareness of the human cost of war.

Crimean battles failed to match Napoleonic paradigms of brilliant maneuver or decisive success. All arms coordination was poor. Battles became slogging matches where increased firepower swelled casualty lists.

The Alma saw the first major use of muzzle-loading rifles in battle. The allied monopoly of the Minié rifle sufficed, with a 3:2 superiority of numbers, to drive the Russians out of a strong defensive position in a frontal attack. The allies lacked transport and cavalry to move inland to envelop the Russians, or mount an effective pursuit. The Russians took shelter behind improvised defenses at Sevastopol, armed them with guns from the Russian fleet, and baffled the allied armies for almost a year. Rifle pits and earthworks thrown up by Sevastopol's civilian population proved more effective than formal defenses. Trench warfare had made its unwelcome début. Mutual attrition was costly. The Royal Navy landed 140 32-pounder guns during the siege: 32 were destroyed and 73 condemned as worn out. Crowding large numbers of men together caused heavy losses from disease.

Battles at Balaklava (25 October 1854), Inkerman (5 November 1854), and the Traktir Bridge (16 August 1855) underlined the Russian inability to face allied firepower in the open. At

Transylvanian Alps

WALLACHI

Bucharest

Mar.
185
Oltenitza Silistria
4 Nov. 1854

Shumen
BULGARIA

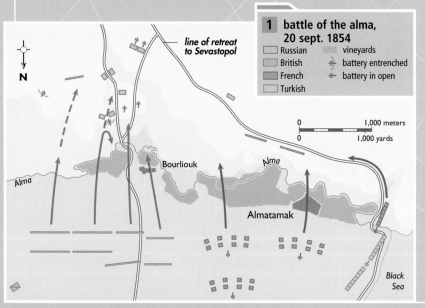

1 battle of the alma, 20 sept. 1854

☐ Russian	☐ vineyards
☐ British	⚔ battery entrenched
☐ French	⚔ battery in open
☐ Turkish	

line of retreat to Sevastopol

N

Bourliouk

Alma

Alma

Almatamak

0   1,000 meters
0   1,000 yards

Black Sea

1 Little changed from 1812, the Russian army occupied a strong position at the Alma, which it defended with traditional stubbornness (map left). Russian counter-attacks drove back part of the British army, but many allied regiments had muzzle-loading rifles that gave them a tremendous advantage. The Russians withdrew after serious casualties, but the numerically weak allied cavalry failed to convert retreat into rout.

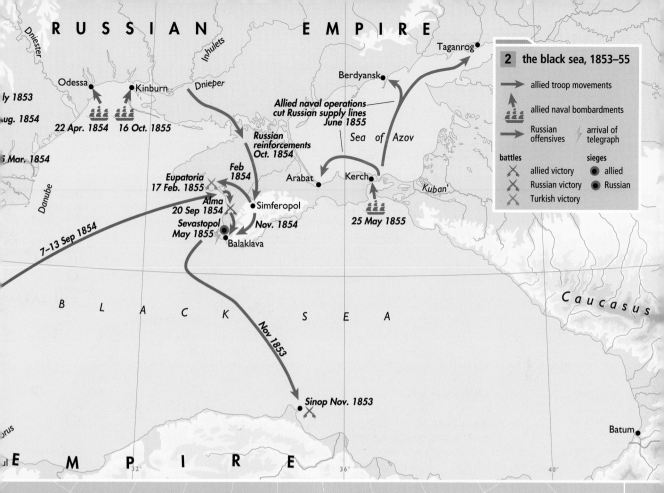

Odessa • Kinburn

ly 1853
aug. 1854

22 Apr. 1854   16 Oct. 1855

5 Mar. 1854

Dniester   Inhulets   Dnieper

Taganrog

Berdyansk

2 the black sea, 1853–55

→ allied troop movements

⚓ allied naval bombardments

→ Russian offensives   — arrival of telegraph

battles
✕ allied victory
✕ Russian victory
✕ Turkish victory

sieges
● allied
● Russian

Allied naval operations cut Russian supply lines June 1855

Sea of Azov

Russian reinforcements Oct. 1854

Eupatoria 17 Feb. 1855

Feb 1854

Arabat   Kerch

Kuban'

Alma 20 Sep 1854   • Simferopol

Sevastopol May 1855   *Nov. 1854*

25 May 1855

7–13 Sep 1854

Balaklava

B   L   A   C   K   S   E   A

C a u c a s u s

Nov 1853

Sinop Nov. 1853

orus

E M P I R E

Batum

32°   36°   40°

2 In 1853, Britain and France declared war on Russia following a dispute about who had custody over the Christian Holy Places in Ottoman-ruled Palestine (map above). Though the Anglo-French force was poorly equipped and undermined by disease and inter-allied squabbles, the Russian forces proved even more incompetent. Russian defeats at Balaklava and Inkerman in 1854 opened the way to the loss of the Black Sea base of Sevastopol in 1855. By highlighting Russian weaknesses, the war led to widespread reforms.

3 Unable completely to invest the port, the allies fell back on traditional siege warfare, with the heaviest guns yet seen (map right). However, Russian earthworks proved very resilient and their defenders resolute. The Russian army's attempt to relieve the siege was beaten off in a battle most famous for the Charge of the Light Brigade and the "Thin Red Line" of the 93rd Highlanders.

Balaklava their cavalry failed in a charge against a single battalion armed with the new rifle. Inkerman was fought in a fog, but edged weapons caused only 6% of the casualties. In the sixth and final bombardment, 183 allied guns and mortars fired 28,176 rounds in three days, an unprecedented display of firepower. Russian casualties exceeded 1,000 a day, before the Malakoff redoubt fell, persuading the Russians to evacuate Sevastopol's smoking ruins (8–9 September 1855). The Allies had won, but their armies left the Crimea only after another seven months of naval and diplomatic pressure, including the first use of ironclad warships to bombard Kinburn (16 October 1855).

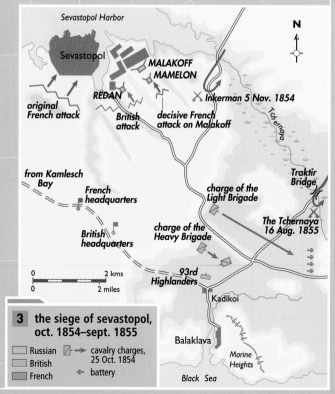

Sevastopol Harbor

N

Sevastopol

MALAKOFF MAMELON

REDAN

original French attack

British attack

decisive French attack on Malakoff

Inkerman 5 Nov. 1854

Tchernaya

from Kamlesch Bay

French headquarters

charge of the Light Brigade

Traktir Bridge

British headquarters

charge of the Heavy Brigade

The Tchernaya 16 Aug. 1855

93rd Highlanders

0   2 kms
0   2 miles

Kadikoi

3 the siege of sevastopol, oct. 1854–sept. 1855

☐ Russian   ▱→ cavalry charges, 25 Oct. 1854
☐ British   ⊨ battery
☐ French

Balaklava

Marine Heights

Black Sea

the **franco-austrian** war

Nationalism posed a particular threat to the multinational army of the Habsburg Empire, the antithesis of a Nation in Arms. In 1858 France allied with Sardinia, the largest independent Italian state, to drive the Austrians from the peninsula.

Bonapartist mythology had helped the emperor's nephew, Napoleon III, seize power. Like his uncle he needed to win a quick victory, but feared the Austrian army at Milan might overrun the outnumbered Sardinians before the French arrived. Steam power resolved both problems. Steamships carried French troops to Genoa. Other units went by rail to the foot of the Alps and marched to the Sardinian railhead, pre-empting a plodding Austrian advance on Turin.

The Austrians fell back, thinking Napoleon III would envelop their left flank. Instead he turned to their right, boldly transferring his army 60 miles across the Austrian front by rail. Napoleon III achieved a double first, using railways not only to move his army to the theater of war but to outmaneuver the enemy.

The Austrians retreated to the Ticino, where they surprised the allies by defending the river line, although French troops had already crossed further north. The result was an asymmetrical battle, fought astride the Ticino. Neither side's losses were decisive, but the Austrian corps withdrew eccentrically, unlike the Prussians after Ligny, becoming too scattered to resume action the next day.

The soldiers on both sides were conscripts, but many French soldiers re-engaged, becoming long-service professionals. Austrian recruits served only a short time. Their battlefield performance reflected this, with losses of only one-twelfth reducing Austrian units to hopeless disorder. Men from non-German regiments deserted in droves. Both sides used muzzle-loading rifles, but masses of fruit trees obscured the battlefield and limited their effect. Austrian reservists received their rifles only on the way to the front. They did not know how to load, let alone compensate for the weapon's high trajectory when aiming. French tactics speeded up to counteract the increased firepower of rifles. French light infantry, Chasseurs and Zouaves, became shock troops, closing rapidly with the enemy to avoid their fire effect.

2 The French infantry did not rely just on the Minié rifle, but on dash and élan, in sad contrast to the Austrian Army whose non-German regiments tended to melt away at indecent speed. The Austrian attempt to crush the French bridgehead over the Ticino collapsed in the face of furious counter-attacks. The eventual arrival of the French flanking force led the Austrians to break off the action (map right).

1 the campaign in lombardy, 19 may–2 july 1859

advances

- - → French concentration, 28 April–8 May

→ allied turning movement, 28 May–3 June and advance through Lombardy after Magenta

→ Garibaldi's operations and Sardinian advance to contact, 24 June

→ Austrian advance to contact, 2–4 June and 23–24 June

- - → advance of French V Corps from Tuscany, 27 June–2 July

▮ Austrian fort

Valle di Susa

Turin

45°

army positions, 19 May
- Sardinian
- French
- Austrian

army positions, 23 June
- Sardinian
- French
- Austrian

battles
- ✕ French victory
- ✕ Sardinian victory
- ✕ Austrian victory

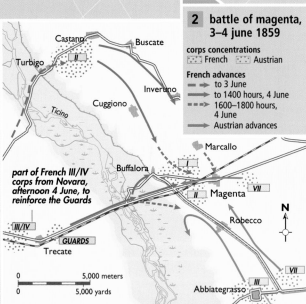

2 battle of magenta, 3–4 june 1859

corps concentrations
French Austrian

French advances
- - - to 3 June
— to 1400 hours, 4 June
- - - 1600–1800 hours, 4 June
— Austrian advances

Castano
Buscate
Turbigo
II
Inveruno
Ticino
Cuggiono
Marcallo
I
Buffalora
VII
II Magenta
Robecco
N
part of French III/IV corps from Novara, afternoon 4 June, to reinforce the Guards
III/IV
GUARDS
Trecate
VII
III
Abbiategrasso

| 0 | 5,000 meters |
| 0 | 5,000 yards |

When the Austrians launched a counter-offensive to catch the allies off balance at Solferino, the monolithic allied deployment made a frontal "soldier's battle" inevitable. Napoleon III went forward promptly. Austrian corps commanders failed to support their own brigades, let alone each other. The ground was open, allowing the French to use their new rifled field guns effectively for the first time. Massed in the Napoleonic style, they overpowered Austrian smooth-bore batteries before these came into action.

With moderate advantages in generalship and weaponry, aggressive French regulars smashed the Austrian center at Solferino in a typical Napoleonic central breakthrough. The defeated army escaped over the Mincio. Casualties in the largest battle since Leipzig shocked the two emperors into agreeing to peace terms.

1 The French Army was the first to effect a strategic concentration by steam power, shipping part of the army to Genoa while the rest traveled by rail. Once in Lombardy, the French outflanked the Austrians with another rail move, forcing them back to the river Ticino (map below). Defeated at Magenta, the Austrians fell back, reaching the Mincio before counter-attacking on 24 June. Throughout the campaign, the Austrians were handicapped by the poor training of their conscripts, who received their new rifles only on their way to the front.

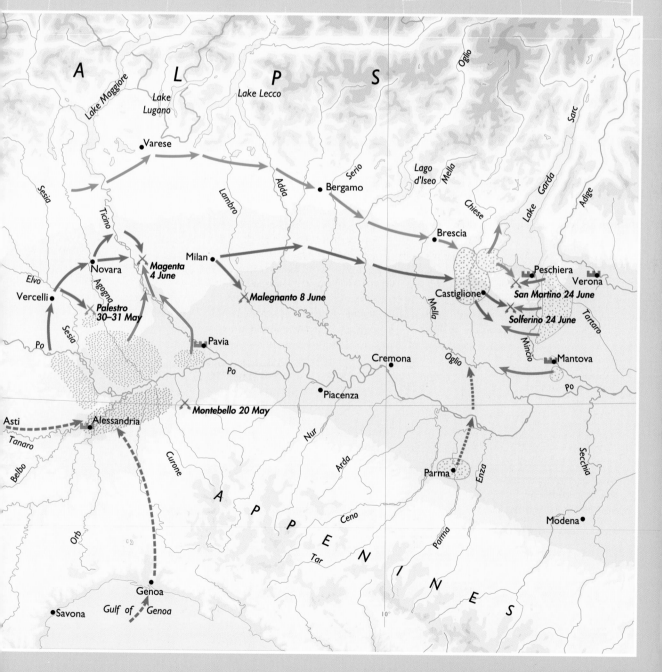

Prussia's destruction of the army of the French Second Empire in the summer of 1870 began a new military era. Helmut von Moltke was chief of Prussian general staff. His victory was strategic, for French tactics, morale, and weapons were in many respects superior to those of the Germans.

Moltke used railways to occupy broad defensive positions, which served as jumping-off points for a converging invasion of France's eastern provinces. Allied forces from south Germany increased his numerical superiority: 450,000 against 180,000. Moltke laid down the general order of advance, leaving its execution to army and corps commanders, guided by their staff. Their movements led to a series of battles that the high command may not have intended, but which they could exploit to their advantage. French commanders, starved of initiative by an over-centralized Napoleonic command style, failed to support each other.

The battle of Froeschwiller (6 August 1870) set the tactical pattern of the war. The French held a magnificent position, with splendid fields of fire for their Chassepot rifles, but the Germans trumped them with superior artillery. German frontal attacks and artillery fire pinned down the French, until neighboring corps enclosed the French cen-

2 The first major action set the pattern: Prussian infantry attacks were pressed home with great gallantry, supported by their powerful artillery (map left). Fierce French counter-attacks collapsed in the face of unprecedented firepower and the army retreated. Recriminations followed, with accusations of betrayal in the air. Within weeks, the cries of "to Berlin" seemed very hollow.

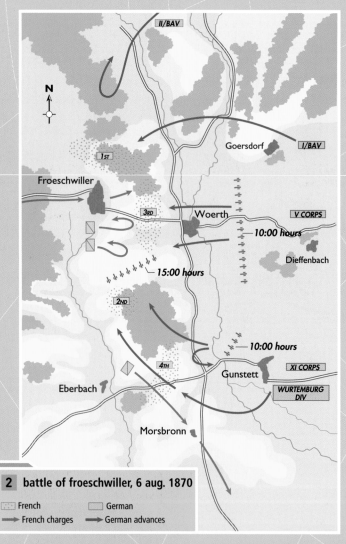

2 battle of froeschwiller, 6 aug. 1870

- ⬚ French
- ⬚ German
- ➡ French charges
- ➡ German advances

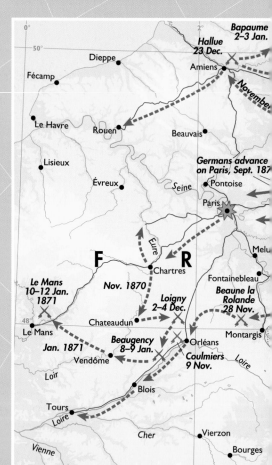

ter in a circle of fire. Some French infantry units lost three-quarters of their numbers in ferocious counter-attacks. The French rifle outranged the Dreyse, but German skirmish lines presented a dispersed target allowing them to close the range without disproportionately heavy losses.

French commanders were intellectually ill-prepared to command armies far larger than the corps they had led previously, and lacked effective staffs to help them. The weight of responsibility paralyzed the experienced Marshal Bazaine, who allowed his army to be surrounded at Metz. The Paris government ordered Marshal MacMahon, hero of Magenta, to relieve Bazaine with a turning movement that exposed his own communications. Moltke exploited his central position between the two marshals to concentrate against MacMahon, forcing him to surrender at Sedan. MacMahon's predictable destruction shows the dangers of political demands that ignore military realities.

A Republican government seized power after Sedan, with a conscious appeal to the Nation in Arms. By the end of the war the French had called up as many men as the Germans. However, French numbers proved no substitute for skill in raising the German siege of Paris. Past besieging forces had been vulnerable to attack by relieving forces. Now the tactical superiority of the defense, coordinated by telegraph, allowed the Germans to defeat separate attacks launched from unoccupied French territory. At Coulmiers, the only French victory of the war, the defeated Bavarians escaped with limited casualties, despite French superiority of numbers of more than 3:1.

The people of Paris and Strasbourg suffered starvation and bombardment. However, Bismarck limited his political ends, unlike Napoleon Bonaparte, who had threatened the very existence of his enemies.

1 Duped into declaring war by Bismarck, Napoleon III was told by his generals that the campaign could last 100 years and they wouldn't need so much as a gaiter button. The truth was sadly different: French organization was such an oxymoron that "muddling through" was a celebrated virtue. Their better-prepared opponents fielded an army twice the size, with breech-loading artillery that dominated the battlefields (map below).

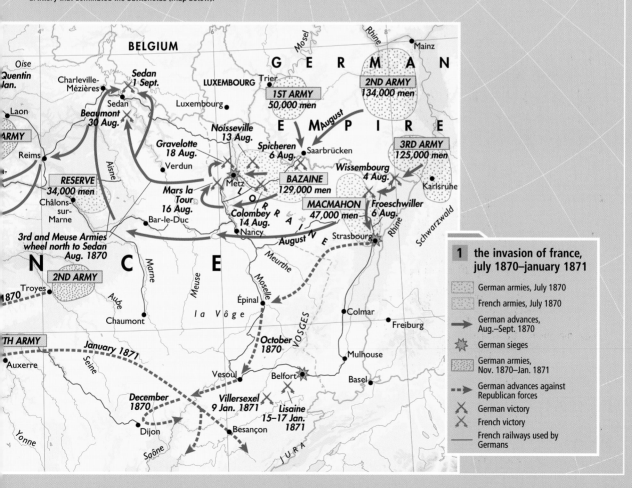

1 the invasion of france, july 1870–january 1871

German armies, July 1870
French armies, July 1870
German advances, Aug.–Sept. 1870
German sieges
German armies, Nov. 1870–Jan. 1871
German advances against Republican forces
German victory
French victory
French railways used by Germans

1861
Major Robert Anderson surrenders Fort Sumter (13 April); Confederate victory at Manassas (Bull Run) (21 July); blockade of South begins (July)

1862
Nashville falls to Union forces (25 February); Confederacy moves troops from Charleston, Mobile, and New Orleans to surprise Grant at Shiloh (6 April); "Stonewall" Jackson forces Union forces back across Potomac (May); Battle of Antietam (17 September); Confederate victory at Fredericksburg (11–15 December)

1863
Lee defeats Hooker at Battle of Chancellorsville (1–6 May); Grant's victorious Vicksburg campaign (May); Confederates defeated at Battle of Gettysburg (1–3 July)

The Civil War was an ideological conflict, releasing deep antagonisms on both sides, fought across vast distances with poor communications. The improvised armies had similar weapons and levels of training, so neither side had a qualitative edge. Tactical equality and the defensive power of modern weapons forced both sides to entrench as thoroughly as had the Romans. American infantry learned to fight in open order, and avoid frontal attacks.

2 General Robert E. Lee led the Army of Northern Virginia in 1862–65, seldom passing up an opportunity to attack despite his numerical inferiority (map below). Chancellorsville was his most impressive victory: Lee divided his already outnumbered army to strike Hooker's army in the flank and drive it from the field. Tragically, his brilliant subordinate "Stonewall" Jackson was killed at the moment of triumph, shot by mistake by a Confederate picquet.

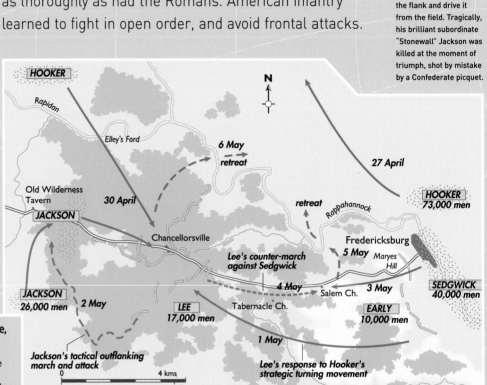

2 battle of chancellorsville, 1–6 may 1863

Confederate armies
Union armies
Confederate trenches
Union trenches

0   4 kms
0   4 miles

The Union outnumbered the Confederacy overall, but the rebels' interior position allowed them to concentrate their smaller forces against successive Union attacks. Railways were essential lines of communication in the undeveloped South, where roads did not exist, and the cotton/tobacco-based agriculture was unable to sustain large armies from local resources. Civil War generals used railways to mount strategic concentrations far more ambitious than those attempted in Europe. In 1862, the Confederacy succeeded in moving troops 500 miles from Charleston, Mobile, and New Orleans to surprise Grant at Shiloh.

The Battle of Chancellorsville (1–6 May 1863) epitomized Lee's methods. Although acting on the strategic defensive, Lee assumed the tactical offensive in response to Union advances on the Confederate capital Richmond, uncomfortably close to the front line. Always outnumbered, Lee made maximum use of the defensive superiority of entrenched riflemen to free sufficient forces for his offensive counter-moves. He could conceal his movements in the tangled woods of North Virginia, but the boldness of his plan bordered on the reckless. The collapse of the Union commander's morale shows how a battle lost is a battle believed to have been lost. When Hooker ordered his troops to retreat, Lee's advance was faltering, while Union troops at Fredericksburg had driven back the Confederate covering force. In the absence of wireless communications, the success of an enveloping maneuver depended on inspired cooperation, in this case between Lee and "Stonewal" Jackson. His death at Chancellorsville destroyed a battle-winning team, and may have cost the Confederacy the Battle of Gettysburg (1–3 July 1863).

The stalemate in the east was broken by General Ulysses S. Grant. Grant had shown a willingness to take risks in the Vicksburg campaign that baffled less able opponents. Against Lee, in the more confined spaces of North Virginia, Grant's tactics resulted in a series of bloody battles. In a month's fighting (3 May–3 June 1864), both armies lost half their strength. Grant then changed his line of operations, transferring his army across

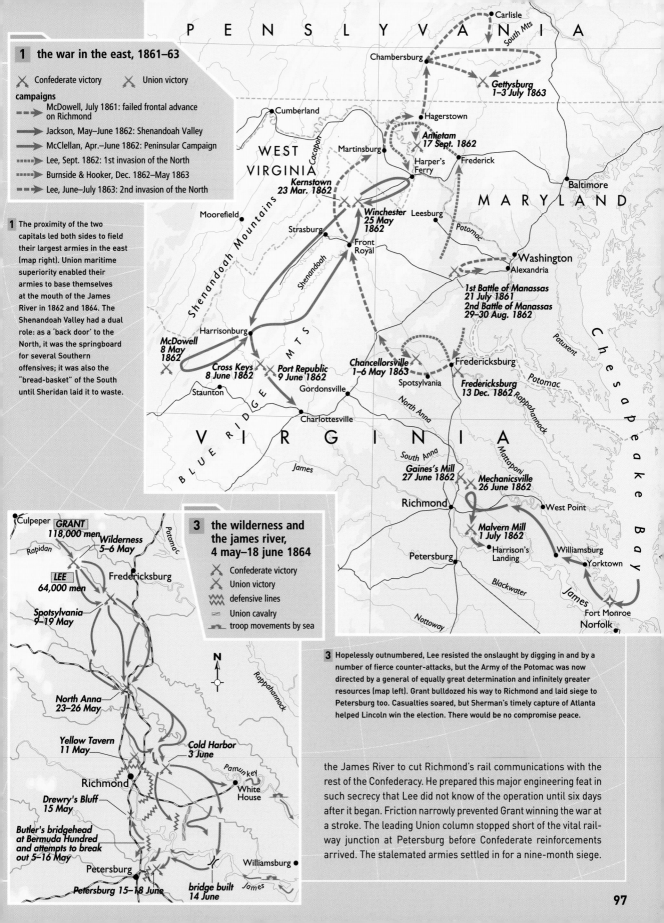

1 the war in the east, 1861–63

✕ Confederate victory   ✕ Union victory

campaigns

- → McDowell, July 1861: failed frontal advance on Richmond
- → Jackson, May–June 1862: Shenandoah Valley
- → McClellan, Apr.–June 1862: Peninsular Campaign
- ⋯▸ Lee, Sept. 1862: 1st invasion of the North
- ⋯▸ Burnside & Hooker, Dec. 1862–May 1863
- ⋯▸ Lee, June–July 1863: 2nd invasion of the North

1 The proximity of the two capitals led both sides to field their largest armies in the east (map right). Union maritime superiority enabled their armies to base themselves at the mouth of the James River in 1862 and 1864. The Shenandoah Valley had a dual role: as a 'back door' to the North, it was the springboard for several Southern offensives; it was also the "bread-basket" of the South until Sheridan laid it to waste.

3 the wilderness and the james river, 4 may–18 june 1864

✕ Confederate victory
✕ Union victory
〰 defensive lines
⌒ Union cavalry
▭ troop movements by sea

3 Hopelessly outnumbered, Lee resisted the onslaught by digging in and by a number of fierce counter-attacks, but the Army of the Potomac was now directed by a general of equally great determination and infinitely greater resources (map left). Grant bulldozed his way to Richmond and laid siege to Petersburg too. Casualties soared, but Sherman's timely capture of Atlanta helped Lincoln win the election. There would be no compromise peace.

the James River to cut Richmond's rail communications with the rest of the Confederacy. He prepared this major engineering feat in such secrecy that Lee did not know of the operation until six days after it began. Friction narrowly prevented Grant winning the war at a stroke. The leading Union column stopped short of the vital railway junction at Petersburg before Confederate reinforcements arrived. The stalemated armies settled in for a nine-month siege.

the **american civil war II**

1863
Battle of Chickamauga (19 September); Grant defeats Confederates at Chattanooga (23–25 November); siege of Knoxville (November–December)

1864
Grant's Wilderness Campaign (May); Battle of Cold Harbor (31 May–12 June); Battle of Mobile Bay (5 August); Sherman's Atlanta campaign (August); Atlanta surrenders (1 September); Sherman's March to the Sea (November)

1865
Sherman marches through South and North Carolina (February); Grant breaks through Confederate lines around Richmond (March); Lee evacuates Richmond (2 April); Army of Northern Virginia surrenders at Appomattox Courthouse (9 April)

By 1862 a third of the U.S. Army was acting as an occupation force. Like other belligerents unable to occupy enemy territory effectively, the U.S. army resorted to raids. The most spectacular was Sherman's march through Georgia to the sea. This not only inflicted economic damage on the areas traversed, but disrupted the railways that supplied Confederate armies.

Sherman realized he was fighting a hostile people, and deliberately made them feel the hard hand of war. Sherman's superior numbers and his willingness to feed them from the countryside achieved astonishing strategic mobility. He turned successive Confederate positions between Chattanooga and Atlanta, and by the end of the war had carried his army to Raleigh in North Carolina.

1 The Confederacy underwent a government-led industrial revolution during the war, but its economy was slowly strangled (map right). Imports were choked off as the U.S. Navy seized its ports and Union forces controlled the Mississippi. Internal communications relied on a ramshackle rail net that was soon exposed to Union cavalry raids and ultimately ripped up by Sherman's army on its march to the sea. Conversely, the Union war economy was so powerful it was exporting weapons and even building battleships for foreign countries during the war.

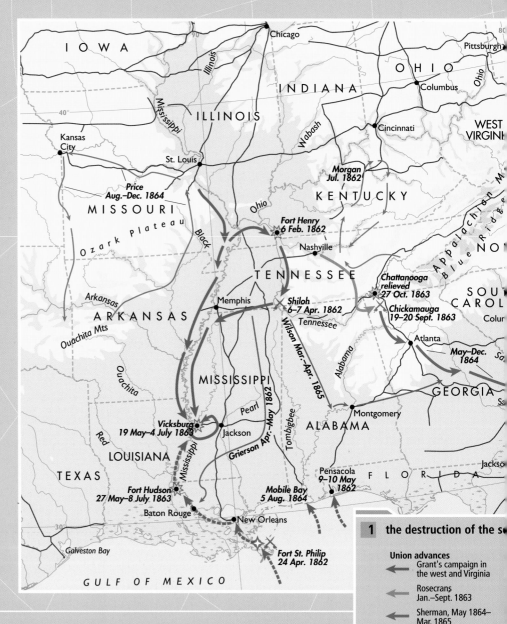

1 the destruction of the s

Union advances
← Grant's campaign in the west and Virginia
← Rosecrans Jan.–Sept. 1863
← Sherman, May 1864–Mar. 1865

2 The Confederates converted the hulk of the steam frigate *Merrimack* (also known as CSS *Virginia*) into an ironclad ram, intended to raise the blockade of Norfolk. Hopes that she might raid New York would never have been realized, her ancient powerplant and shallow freeboard restricting her to coastal waters, but she met her match in the bizarre shape of the *Monitor* off Hampton Roads on 9 March (map right). The *Merrimack*'s short life ended when Norfolk was abandoned by the Confederates: drawing too much water to escape up the James, she had to be blown up.

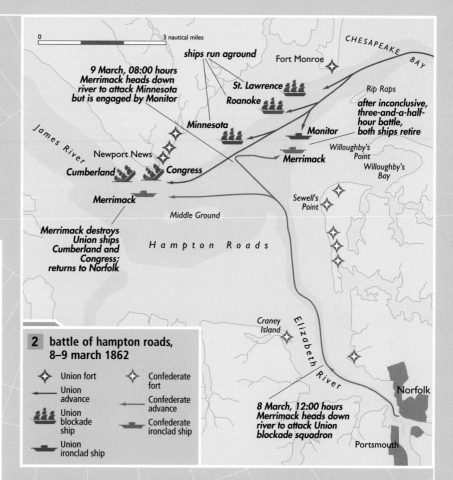

0 _____ 3 nautical miles

ships run aground

9 March, 08:00 hours
Merrimack heads down river to attack Minnesota but is engaged by Monitor

Fort Monroe

CHESAPEAKE BAY

St. Lawrence
Roanoke
Rip Raps

Minnesota

Monitor

after inconclusive, three-and-a-half-hour battle, both ships retire

James River

Newport News

Willoughby's Point

Merrimack

Willoughby's Bay

Cumberland   Congress

Merrimack

Sewell's Point

Middle Ground

Merrimack destroys Union ships Cumberland and Congress; returns to Norfolk

H a m p t o n   R o a d s

Craney Island

Elizabeth River

Norfolk

2 **battle of hampton roads, 8–9 march 1862**

◇ Union fort
← Union advance
🚢 Union blockade ship
▭ Union ironclad ship

◇ Confederate fort
← Confederate advance
▭ Confederate ironclad ship

8 March, 12:00 hours
Merrimack heads down river to attack Union blockade squadron

Portsmouth

VANIA   NEW JERSEY

MARYLAND   DELAWARE

Washington

Sheridan Aug.–Oct. 1864

Chesapeake Bay

VIRGINIA

Richmond

Hampton Roads 8–9 Mar. 1862

Petersburg June 1864–Apr 1865

...erate ...der ...omattox, 1865

Raleigh

Roanoke I. 1862

Fort Hatteras 1862

Fort Macon 26 Apr. 1862

...ROLINA

Fort Fisher 13–15 Jan. 1865

...ar. Wilmington

Fort Sumter 15 Jan. 1865 ...harleston

A T L A N T I C   O C E A N

...Pulaski ...v. 1861

11 Mar. 1862

St Augustine 9 Mar. 1862

The Confederacy was industrially weak, exchanging agricultural produce for foreign manufactured goods, including weapons. It was therefore vulnerable to naval blockade. Lack of roads and guerrilla raids on railways made rivers the most attractive lines of communication in the west.

Like the contemporary Royal Navy, The U.S. Navy had command of the sea, which it exploited by supporting land operations along the coast and great rivers, or strangling the Southern economy through blockade. The U.S. Navy carried Grant across the James River, linked up with Sherman at Savannah, and took the Atlantic coastal forts, to enforce the seaborne blockade. Significant naval actions arose from these activities. A Confederate attempt to lift the blockade of the James River led to the first clash between armored warships at Hampton Roads. One of them, the USS *Monitor*, mounted two big guns in a revolving turret, a revolutionary design giving a flexible arc of fire, independent of the vessel's movement. The Battle of Mobile Bay confirmed the difficulty of sinking armored ships by gunfire or ramming. The sinking of USS *Tecumseh* by a mine, however, suggested one antidote to armored ships.

Mobile Bay sealed off the last Southern port, not long before Sherman began his "March to the Sea," but the collapse of the Confederate armies in the field overtook the Union's economic strategy. Grant's efforts to turn Lee's flanks at Petersburg covered the front with 37 miles of trenches. When Grant broke through the attenuated Confederate lines in March 1865, Lee was unable to disengage. American cavalry had never aspired to a battlefield role, but adopted the rifle to pursue strategic raids and reconnaissance. Dismounted action by Sheridan's cavalry delayed Lee's retreat long enough for Union infantry to force the Army of Northern Virginia to surrender at Appomattox (9 April 1865).

←--- Union naval attacks
← Union raids
← Confederate raids
Savannah Confederate blockade-running ports
◇ Confederate fort

battles
✕ Union victory
✕ Confederate victory
sieges
● Union siege
✦ Confederate siege

the **russo-turkish** war

1877 to 1878

1877
Russia declares war on Ottoman Empire (24 April); 150,000 Russians cross the middle Danube (June); siege of Plevna (July–December)

1878
Unratified Treaty of San Stefano (March) gives Russians extensive gains, largely reversed by Treaty of Berlin (July)

Russia invaded the Turkish Empire in 1877 to protect Bulgaria's Christians against their Muslim rulers, but underestimated Turkish resistance. They mobilized insufficient forces, turning a peace-keeping operation into a major war.

Turkish command of the Black Sea since 1855 forced the Russians to advance inland, over the river Danube and the Balkan mountains. Communications were poor. The single-track Romanian railway system north of the Danube was useless for troop movements. Bulgaria was economically backward, with appalling roads. Nevertheless, the Russians crossed the middle Danube with 150,000 men in June 1877. The Russians believed that the mere appearance of their troops south of the Danube would terrify the sultan into giving up Bulgaria. Count Gourko led 30,000 men in a daring raid towards Adrianople, creating panic in Istanbul. Turkish armies on either flank of the Russian advance were undefeated, however, while reinforcements poured into Thrace by sea. When Osman Pasha marched from Vidin to Plevna (Pleven), threatening the Danube bridgeheads, he threw the whole Russian army on to the defensive. The Russians had occupied a huge salient, 180 miles across, its most advanced point at the Shipka Pass. They could not retreat without exposing Christian Bulgarians to unspeakable reprisals. The Russians' pursuit of geographical objectives with insufficient numbers had cost them the strategic initiative, and forced them to attack Osman in a position of his own choosing.

Defensive victories like those of Osman are rarely enough to end a war favorably. Osman failed to press his advantage, was shut up in Plevna, and starved out. The fall of Plevna in December 1877 released sufficient Russian troops to restore the momentum of their stalled advance. Crossing obscure Balkan passes on a wide front, the Russians surrounded 36,000 Turks at Shipka, and cut off their main army of 50,000 men from Istanbul. The mountains had proved a trap for their defenders. Sea power saved the Turks, moving the remains of their armies from Enez to Istanbul, covered by the guns of the British Mediterranean Fleet. Unwilling to provoke a European war, the exhausted Russians agreed to terms. The

2 The siege of Plevna anticipated some features of later wars, but the Russian tendency to attack superior numbers of entrenched Turks said as much about the need for reconnaissance as the advantages of field works (map below). With little artillery, and cavalry fit only for massacring civilians, the Turkish infantry was unable to exploit its victories or break through the Russian lines of investment when the food ran out.

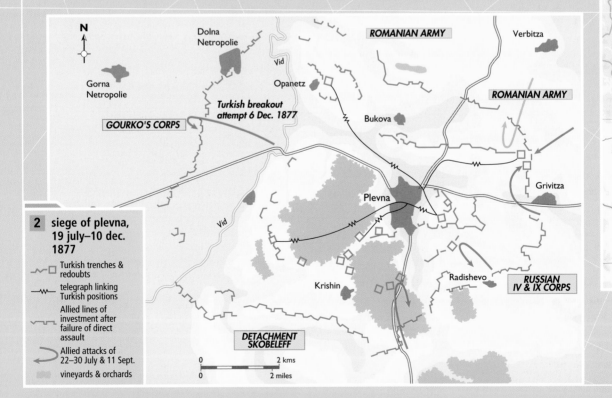

2 siege of plevna, 19 july–10 dec. 1877

- Turkish trenches & redoubts
- telegraph linking Turkish positions
- Allied lines of investment after failure of direct assault
- Allied attacks of 22–30 July & 11 Sept.
- vineyards & orchards

0   2 kms
0   2 miles

Russo-Turkish War underlined the tactical lessons of the Franco-Prussian and American Civil Wars. Turkish infantry dug themselves in, while Russian cavalry fought as mounted riflemen. Both sides used the latest breech-loading rifled artillery and small arms. More effective weapons increased absolute losses, but long-range firefights and larger armies led to lower-percentage casualties. The rifle became the main cause of wounds, reversing the Napoleonic dominance of artillery. Positions were no longer carried at bayonet point, but by developing superior fire to that of the defenders. Armies dispersed to reduce losses, and dominated larger areas with their longer-ranged weapons. The Russians held the 44-mile line around Plevna with 100,000 men, half the number of Germans needed for a similar front at Paris seven years earlier. To penetrate such a line was widely regarded as a purely theoretical possibility.

1 Making imaginative use of mounted infantry, the Russian army raced through Bulgaria to seize the Shipka Pass, but it was unable to advance south of the Balkan Mountains because a Turkish army had dug itself in at Plevna (map below). The campaign was marked by widespread atrocities; Turkish irregulars (the infamous Bashi-Bazouks) preyed on Bulgarian Christians who conducted some "ethnic cleansing" of their own against their Muslim neighbors, aided by the Cossacks.

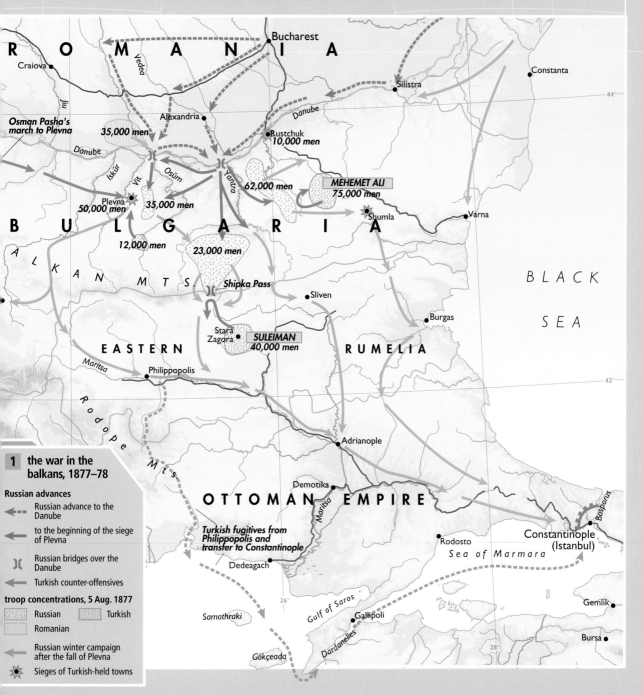

1 the war in the balkans, 1877–78

Russian advances

- - - →   Russian advance to the Danube

──→   to the beginning of the siege of Plevna

)(Russian bridges over the Danube

◄──   Turkish counter-offensives

troop concentrations, 5 Aug. 1877

▦ Russian   ▦ Turkish

▦ Romanian

──→   Russian winter campaign after the fall of Plevna

✦   Sieges of Turkish-held towns

colonial wars

1830 to 1902

From 1830
Algeria conquered by France

1842
hostile Afghan mountaineers destroy British army at Gandamak (13 January)

1874
Battle of Amoafu: the British campaign against the Asante (1 February)

1876
Americans defeated by Plains tribes at Battle of Little Big Horn

1880s
French overcome Vietnamese and Chinese forces

1885
Battle of Abu Klea, Sudan (17 January)

April–August 1898
Americans end Spanish rule in Cuba and the Philippines

1899–1902
Boer War

Colonial wars were the main source of military experience for the British, French, United States, and even Russian Armies in the 19th century. The colonial experience was at odds with 19th-century trends, encouraging recklessness and improvisation rather than professionalism and organization. Every colonial campaign was different. Western forces adapted to local conditions, or suffered catastrophic defeats.

Imperial forces could not match the mobility of their enemies. Operating in agriculturally undeveloped areas with poor roads or none, they had to bring their supplies with them, restricting strategic mobility. Difficulties of supply kept imperial forces small, and forced them to detach up to 90% of their strength to protect their supply lines. Western tactical superiority made it safe to take such risks against opponents unlikely to exploit the advantages of internal lines. A battle usually favored the imperial forces, so commanders preferred combat to maneuver. They needed a victory before disease, the weather, or supply problems forced them to withdraw.

The Boer War employed almost 500,000 British soldiers, many of them reservists. For all its imperial setting, the Boer War was a total war for the Transvaal and Orange Free State, who faced political annihilation if they lost. The war began with rapid advances by mounted Boer commandos, their mobility multiplying their initial numerical

1 The accelerating pace of military technology gave colonial powers an increasing advantage over irregular opponents. Formed armies that played the colonial forces at their own game came off worst: the Sikhs and Zulus were overcome, despite the occasional upset. Nomads, or the denizens of fever-stricken jungles, were harder to tame. European armies suffered heavy losses to tropical diseases, another reason to rely on locally recruited "native" regiments. Colonial "small wars" provided valuable experience for several European armies, but not every "lesson" would prove applicable to regular warfare, or even other colonial campaigns (map right).

1 the world impact of colonial empires to 1900

- British
- French
- Portuguese
- Italian
- German
- Spanish
- Dutch
- Russian
- USA
- Danish
- Belgian
- Japanese
- Ottoman
- other countries

ALASKA

DOMINION OF CANADA

NEWFOUNDLAND

GREEN

America's westward expansion doomed the Plains tribes, but the military forces employed over this vast area were very small. On one of the few occasions the tribes concentrated their forces, they inflicted the shock defeat of the Little Big Horn (1876).

UNITED STATES OF AMERICA

Algeria conquered by France in successive campaigns from the 1830s.

MEXICO

CUBA

Jamaica (Br.)

BRITISH HONDURAS

Spanish–American War; American forces invade Cuba in June 1898 in support of Cuban independence.

France's attempt to install a puppet regime in Mexico while the USA was torn with civil war led to a savage guerrilla campaign against Mexican insurgents. Napoleon III's marshals eventually concluded the war was unwinnable and Emperor Maximilian was abandoned to his fate.

VENEZUELA

BRITISH GUIANA
DUTCH GUIANA
FRENCH GUIANA

COLOMBIA

ECUADOR

Amoafu, 1874: The B campaign against the Asante place in dense jungle. Diseas greater enemy than the tribes

PERU **ACRE** **B R A Z I L**

BOLIVIA

PARAGUAY

C
H
I
L
E

A
R
G.

URUGUAY

The leading powers of South An established armies on the Europ pattern and used them in the sa manner to adjust their borders. Bolivia lost her coastline. Some modern navies too: by the 1880 had a larger and more modern than the USA.

advantage. British forces deployed too far forward, in a salient, making it easy to surround them. Fortunately for the British, the Boers failed to press on to seize the ports through which imperial re-inforcements would enter South Africa. The commandos sat down around Ladysmith and Kimberley (October 1899), blocking the only routes for British relief attempts: the railways. The British took four months to build up enough forces to break through the Boer lines.

Neither General Sir Redvers Buller nor Field Marshal Lord Roberts inflicted sufficient attrition on the Boers to defeat them outright. A hard core of "bitter-einders" fought on after the fall of the Boer capitals at Pretoria and Bloemfontein. Logistically independent of the towns, they drew food and remounts from their family farms, and replaced weapons and uniforms at the expense of the enemy. The British had too few

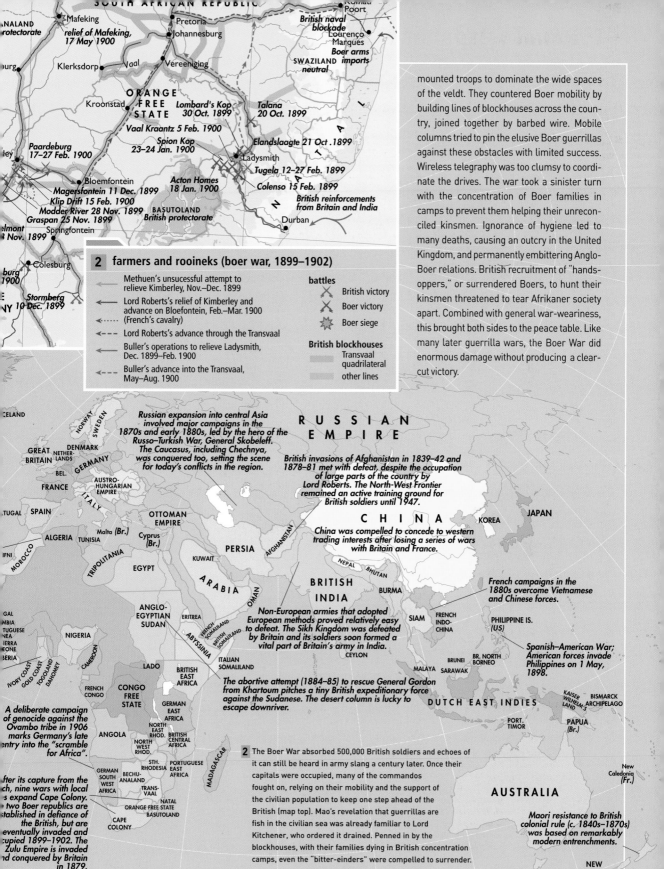

SOUTH AFRICAN REPUBLIC

Komati Poort

British naval blockade

Mafeking
relief of Mafeking, 17 May 1900
Pretoria
Johannesburg
Lourenço Marques
Boer arms imports

Klerksdorp
Vaal
Vereeniging
SWAZILAND
neutral

ORANGE FREE STATE
Kroonstad
Lombard's Kop 30 Oct. 1899
Talana 20 Oct. 1899
Vaal Kraantz 5 Feb. 1900
Spion Kop 23–24 Jan. 1900
Elandslaagte 21 Oct .1899
Paardeburg 17–27 Feb. 1900
Ladysmith
Tugela 12–27 Feb. 1899
Acton Homes 18 Jan. 1900
Colenso 15 Feb. 1899
Bloemfontein
Magersfontein 11 Dec. 1899
Klip Drift 15 Feb. 1900
British reinforcements from Britain and India
Modder River 28 Nov. 1899
Graspan 25 Nov. 1899
BASUTOLAND
British protectorate
Durban
Springfontein

Colesburg

Stormberg 10 Dec. 1899

2 farmers and rooineks (boer war, 1899–1902)

— Methuen's unsuccessful attempt to relieve Kimberley, Nov.–Dec. 1899
→ Lord Roberts's relief of Kimberley and advance on Bloefontein, Feb.–Mar. 1900
‹····· (French's cavalry)
‹--- Lord Roberts's advance through the Transvaal
→ Buller's operations to relieve Ladysmith, Dec. 1899–Feb. 1900
‹--- Buller's advance into the Transvaal, May–Aug. 1900

battles
✕ British victory
✕ Boer victory
✳ Boer siege

British blockhouses
Transvaal quadrilateral
other lines

mounted troops to dominate the wide spaces of the veldt. They countered Boer mobility by building lines of blockhouses across the country, joined together by barbed wire. Mobile columns tried to pin the elusive Boer guerrillas against these obstacles with limited success. Wireless telegraphy was too clumsy to coordinate the drives. The war took a sinister turn with the concentration of Boer families in camps to prevent them helping their unreconciled kinsmen. Ignorance of hygiene led to many deaths, causing an outcry in the United Kingdom, and permanently embittering Anglo-Boer relations. British recruitment of "hands-oppers," or surrendered Boers, to hunt their kinsmen threatened to tear Afrikaner society apart. Combined with general war-weariness, this brought both sides to the peace table. Like many later guerrilla wars, the Boer War did enormous damage without producing a clear-cut victory.

ICELAND
GREAT BRITAIN
NORWAY
SWEDEN
NETHER-LANDS
DENMARK
FRANCE
GERMANY
BEL.
AUSTRO-HUNGARIAN EMPIRE
ITALY
PORTUGAL
SPAIN
ALGERIA
TUNISIA
Malta (Br.)
OTTOMAN EMPIRE
Cyprus (Br.)
PERSIA
AFGHANISTAN
NEPAL
BHUTAN
KUWAIT
MOROCCO
TRIPOLITANIA
EGYPT
ARABIA
OMAN
BRITISH INDIA
BURMA
CHINA
KOREA
JAPAN
SIAM
FRENCH INDO-CHINA
PHILIPPINE IS. (US)
IFNI
SENEGAL
GAMBIA
PORTUGUESE GUINEA
SIERRA LEONE
LIBERIA
NIGERIA
ANGLO-EGYPTIAN SUDAN
ERITREA
FRENCH SOMALILAND
BRITISH SOMALILAND
ABYSSINIA
ITALIAN SOMALILAND
LADO
BRITISH EAST AFRICA
CEYLON
IVORY COAST
GOLD COAST
TOGOLAND
DAHOMEY
CAMEROON
FRENCH CONGO
CONGO FREE STATE
GERMAN EAST AFRICA
NORTH EAST RHOD.
BRITISH CENTRAL AFRICA
MALAYA
SARAWAK
BRUNEI
BR. NORTH BORNEO
DUTCH EAST INDIES
KAISER WILHELM'S LAND
BISMARCK ARCHIPELAGO
ANGOLA
NORTH WEST RHOD.
STH. RHODESIA
PORTUGUESE EAST AFRICA
MADAGASCAR
PORT. TIMOR
PAPUA (Br.)
GERMAN SOUTH WEST AFRICA
BECHUANALAND
TRANSVAAL
NATAL
ORANGE FREE STATE
BASUTOLAND
CAPE COLONY
New Caledonia (Fr.)
AUSTRALIA
NEW ZEALAND

RUSSIAN EMPIRE

Russian expansion into central Asia involved major campaigns in the 1870s and early 1880s, led by the hero of the Russo–Turkish War, General Skobeleff. The Caucasus, including Chechnya, was conquered too, setting the scene for today's conflicts in the region.

British invasions of Afghanistan in 1839–42 and 1878–81 met with defeat, despite the occupation of large parts of the country by Lord Roberts. The North-West Frontier remained an active training ground for British soldiers until 1947.

China was compelled to concede to western trading interests after losing a series of wars with Britain and France.

French campaigns in the 1880s overcome Vietnamese and Chinese forces.

Non-European armies that adopted European methods proved relatively easy to defeat. The Sikh Kingdom was defeated by Britain and its soldiers soon formed a vital part of Britain's army in India.

Spanish–American War; American forces invade Philippines on 1 May, 1898.

A deliberate campaign of genocide against the Ovambo tribe in 1906 marks Germany's late entry into the "scramble for Africa".

The abortive attempt (1884–85) to rescue General Gordon from Khartoum pitches a tiny British expeditionary force against the Sudanese. The desert column is lucky to escape downriver.

[Af]ter its capture from the [Dut]ch, nine wars with local [tribe]s expand Cape Colony. [The] two Boer republics are [est]ablished in defiance of the British, but are [ev]entually invaded and [oc]cupied 1899–1902. The [Z]ulu Empire is invaded [and] conquered by Britain in 1879.

2 The Boer War absorbed 500,000 British soldiers and echoes of it can still be heard in army slang a century later. Once their capitals were occupied, many of the commandos fought on, relying on their mobility and the support of the civilian population to keep one step ahead of the British (map top). Mao's revelation that guerrillas are fish in the civilian sea was already familiar to Lord Kitchener, who ordered it drained. Penned in by the blockhouses, with their families dying in British concentration camps, even the "bitter-einders" were compelled to surrender.

Maori resistance to British colonial rule (c. 1840s–1870s) was based on remarkably modern entrenchments.

the **russo-japanese** war

1 June 1904–
2 January 1905
siege of Port Arthur

19–24 August 1904
capture of 174 Meter Hill at cost
of 15,000 Japanese lives

5 December 1904
capture of 203 Meter Hill

21 February–
10 March 1905
Battle of Mukden

27–29 May 1905
Battle of Tsushima

The Russo-Japanese War was the first major conflict of the 20th century. The Japanese saw it as a war for national survival. They employed all the means at their disposal, showing how a small power can defeat a stronger but less-committed power.

The total destruction of the Russian fleet contrasted with the indecisive results of the war on land. The Japanese tipped the local balance of naval forces in their favor by a surprise torpedo-boat attack on Port Arthur (8 February 1904), followed by a close blockade by their battleships. The Japanese achieved strategic surprise by attacking without first declaring war, but found it difficult to follow up. Russian mine warfare, pursued in defiance of international law, sank two Japanese battleships, forcing them to abandon their close blockade.

The Japanese could not devote all their energies to Port Arthur. They had to cover the siege against Russian troops in Manchuria, who

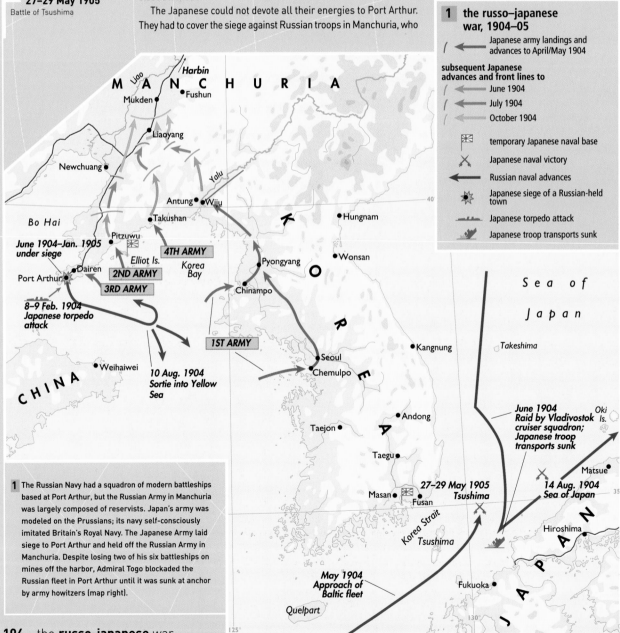

1 the russo–japanese war, 1904–05

Japanese army landings and advances to April/May 1904

subsequent Japanese advances and front lines to
— June 1904
— July 1904
— October 1904

temporary Japanese naval base

Japanese naval victory

Russian naval advances

Japanese siege of a Russian-held town

Japanese torpedo attack

Japanese troop transports sunk

1 The Russian Navy had a squadron of modern battleships based at Port Arthur, but the Russian Army in Manchuria was largely composed of reservists. Japan's army was modeled on the Prussians; its navy self-consciously imitated Britain's Royal Navy. The Japanese Army laid siege to Port Arthur and held off the Russian Army in Manchuria. Despite losing two of his six battleships on mines off the harbor, Admiral Togo blockaded the Russian fleet in Port Arthur until it was sunk at anchor by army howitzers (map right).

2 The tsar and his senior officers indulged in racist jokes at the expense of the Japanese when war was declared. But the unthinkable happened: the Russian field armies were defeated and a first-class naval squadron was destroyed at Port Arthur. A non-European power had overturned three centuries of unbroken European expansion. On the sprawling battlefields of Manchuria, cosmic levels of incompetence exposed the Russian Army as a "rubber lion" in the parlance of the German General Staff (map right). It was effectively downgraded in Germany's war plans for future conflict in Europe.

3 Russia's Baltic Fleet sailed from Petersburg to Japan only to meet with annihilating defeat at Tsushima (map below right). Gunnery seldom produces fast results in naval actions although some Russian battleships were so overloaded their main armor belts were submerged and their waterline protection consequently reduced. Japanese torpedo boats finished off damaged vessels and even laid mines in the path of escaping battleships, actions studied with grim interest by British and German naval officers.

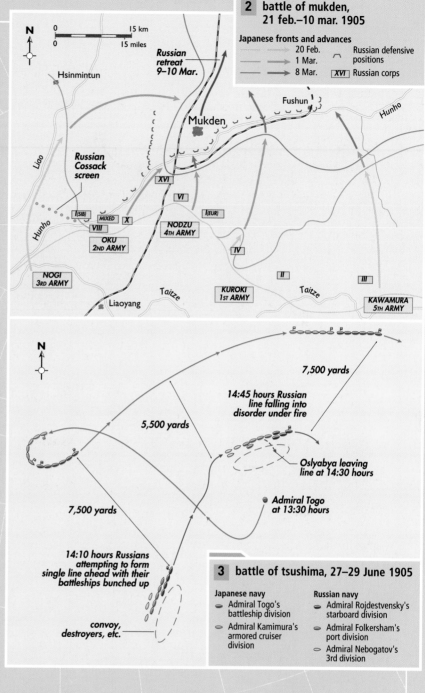

2 battle of mukden, 21 feb.–10 mar. 1905

Japanese fronts and advances
— 20 Feb.
— 1 Mar.
— 8 Mar.

Russian defensive positions

XVI Russian corps

0   15 km
0   15 miles

Hsinmintun

Russian retreat 9–10 Mar.

Mukden

Fushun

Hunho

Liao

Russian Cossack screen

XVI

VI

I (EUR)

Hunho

I (SIB)   MIXED   X

VIII

NODZU 4TH ARMY

OKU 2ND ARMY

IV

NOGI 3RD ARMY

Taitze

KUROKI 1ST ARMY

Taitze

II

III

KAWAMURA 5TH ARMY

Liaoyang

3 battle of tsushima, 27–29 June 1905

7,500 yards

14:45 hours Russian line falling into disorder under fire

5,500 yards

Oslyabya leaving line at 14:30 hours

Admiral Togo at 13:30 hours

7,500 yards

14:10 hours Russians attempting to form single line ahead with their battleships bunched up

convoy, destroyers, etc.

Japanese navy
— Admiral Togo's battleship division
— Admiral Kamimura's armored cruiser division

Russian navy
— Admiral Rojdestvensky's starboard division
— Admiral Folkersham's port division
— Admiral Nebogatov's 3rd division

were steadily reinforced by the Trans-Siberian Railway. Needing a quick victory, the Japanese began a converging advance against the main Russian army. The Russians retreated after tied battles at Liaoyang and the Sha-Ho (October 1904). Outnumbered 3:2, Marshal Oyama persisted with his double-envelopment strategy at Mukden, employing deception to even the odds. Troops released from the siege of Port Arthur massed behind the Japanese left, unknown to the Russians, while other troop movements on the other flank drew Kuropatkin's reserves away from the true point of attack. After two weeks' fighting, Kuropatkin's troops were in a pocket around Mukden. The Japanese advance had reached its culminating point at Mukden. They had committed every man available without decisively defeating the Russian army, which regrouped still further up the railway line. The war would be ended, as it had begun, at sea.

The naval Battle of Tsushima (27–29 May 1905) left the strategic situation unchanged, but dramatically confirmed Japanese command of the sea. Tsushima was the only fleet action fought to a finish by pre-dreadnought battleships. Tsushima was the product of decisively superior Japanese seamanship and gunnery, which allowed Admiral Togo, hailed as the Japanese Nelson, to take the same sort of risks as his predecessor. Japanese battleships made 15 knots against the Russian nine. Togo easily crossed the Russian "T," concentrating gunfire on the leading Russian ships. The big gun was still the dominant weapon at sea, despite mine and torpedo successes off Port Arthur. Tsushima's most significant lesson was psychological. It spelled the end of European supremacy at sea.

The Russo–Japanese War showed how easily a limited war might escalate. Both sides suffered enormous losses in week-long battles that made a mockery of distinctions between limited and absolute war. The Russians saw their fleet destroyed and revolution shake the tsar's government. Even the pursuit of limited objectives needs effective preparation and organization, without which superior resources remain unrealized potential and losses reach catastrophic levels.

the **war** in the **west**

The First World War was not the inevitable result of an arms race, nor was it an accident. It was the product of political choices, but military developments over the previous quarter of a century ensured a plentiful supply of inflammable material.

Armies doubled in size after the Franco-Prussian War, outpacing the rate of population growth. Only Great Britain, secure in its naval supremacy, still relied on volunteers. The great powers resembled mistrustful travelers, brought together in a carriage by chance. If one of them put his hand into his pocket, his neighbor would get his own revolver ready to fire the first shot. However, no one army had the qualitative advantage possessed by the Prussians over the ill-led French Gardes Mobiles of 1870.

Industrial growth provided new weapons for nations now truly in arms. Practical rates of field artillery fire rose to eight rounds a minute, compared with two previously. Gunners could remain near their gun as it fired, sheltered by bullet-proof shields. The flat trajectories of field guns were ineffective against trenches, so howitzers reappeared, lobbing a heavier round to a shorter range. Automatic machine guns epitomized the effect of industrialization on war. Easily mass-produced, they created a large volume of accurate fire with minimal effort. Machine guns added to the vulnera-

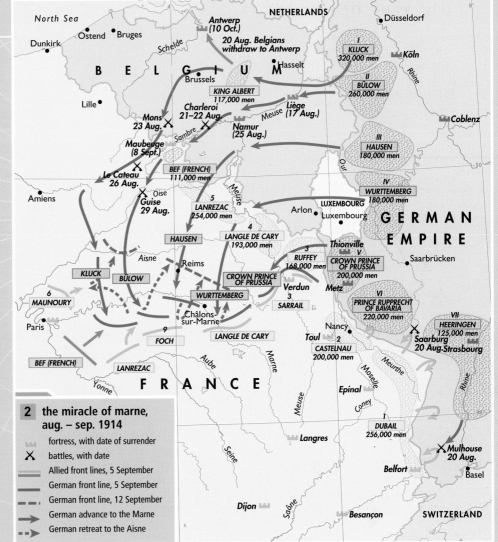
2 the miracle of marne, aug. – sep. 1914

- fortress, with date of surrender
- battles, with date
- Allied front lines, 5 September
- German front line, 5 September
- German front line, 12 September
- German advance to the Marne
- German retreat to the Aisne

1 the drift to war

- mobilizations, with date
- Entente powers at outbreak of war
- joined Entente powers during the war, with date
- Central Powers at outbreak of war
- joined Central Powers during the war, with date

troop concentrations, 1914
1 block per 100,000 combatants
- Entente and allies
- Central Powers and allies

naval bases
- Entente and allies
- Central Powers and allies

industrial strength
- 1 block per million tons of steel
- frontiers, 1914

bility of horsed cavalry, already at a disadvantage in Europe's enclosed countryside. Motor vehicles would restore a degree of mobility but, like wireless telegraphy and aircraft, were scarce and unreliable in 1914.

Absolute war had previously been moderated by political factors and the impossibility of a state deploying all its reserves at once. In 1914, offensive strategy, untempered by diplomacy, could deploy the whole of a nation's military resources instantaneously, by rail. Absolute war had become a realizable prospect, the only strategic aim the total defeat of the other side. With both sides prepared to make every effort to avoid such an outcome, wars would be long and hard-fought, leading to the ruin of both sides.

The technical forces that revolutionized military weaponry also applied at sea. Precision-made heavy guns could deliver accurate long-range fire, centrally controlled by mechanical computers and range finders. Tsushima prompted development of the all-big-gun battleship. HMS *Dreadnought* (1906), the first of the new type, gave a new twist to a naval race underway since the British Naval Defence Act of 1889. German Navy Laws of 1898 and 1900 refocused British naval concerns. Britain mended fences with France and Russia, and concentrated the Royal Navy in home waters, confirming German fears of encirclement. The British won the naval race, but the Agadir crisis confirmed Anglo–German hostility, entangling Great Britain in a European alliance for the first time in a century. The British Army was small, but the empire possessed enormous resources, capable of balancing the industrial power of Germany. Britain's adherence to the Entente made it likely that a renewed Franco-German war would be long.

the **eastern front I**

The German Army, the leading military power of Europe, was obsessed by fears of a two-front war against Russia and France. Count von Schlieffen, Chief of the General Staff 1893–1905, hoped to defeat France before Russia, hampered by its size, could mobilize. The Schlieffen Plan launched 90% of Germany's mobile forces through neutral Belgium. The war on the Eastern Front started with one of those brilliant maneuvers so noticeably absent in the west, the Battle of Tannenberg.

The Schlieffen Plan was crucially flawed by its assumption that the enemy would behave as planned. Instead Joffre, the French commander-in-chief, regrouped his forces and the enveloping force was pierced by British forces (the BEF) when aerial reconnaissance revealed a gap between the German armies. In frustrating the Schlieffen Plan, Joffre had won the decisive battle of the war, and perhaps of the century.

On the other hand, the Battle of Tannenberg was the most striking German victory of the war. General Paul von Hindenberg took over the Eighth Army after the unscripted German defeat at Gumbinnen (20 August 1914), with Erich Ludendorff as his chief of staff. German I Corps trapped a whole Russian army in a pocket near Tannenberg. Its commander shot himself, and 100,000 prisoners surrendered. However, Tannenberg was the result of Russian command failures, not innate backwardness. The subsequent Battle of the Masurian Lakes against the surviving Russian army in the north began well for the Germans, but bogged down by the end of September 1914. It cost the Eighth Army 100,000 casualties out of 250,000. Masurian Lakes, not Tannenberg, would be the pattern of the war in the east.

Germany was not Russia's only opponent. The Eastern Front formed a series of salients: Germany in East Prussia; Russia at Warsaw; Austria-Hungary in Galicia to the south. Pushed back into the Carpathians, Austria-Hungary appealed for German help. Hindenberg and Ludendorff flattened the Warsaw salient, but there were no more wholesale Russian surrenders. By year end, Russian gains in Galicia balanced losses in Poland.

The German General Staff had attacked France in order not to be caught out in Austria's quarrel with Serbia and Russia, thus turning the Balkan crisis into a world war. Their politically naïve invasion of Belgium placed Britain's economic and strategic potential at the disposal of the Entente. Germany faced a two-front war, with no clear idea of how to end it.

2 The Russian 1st and 2nd Armies failed to coordinate their invasion of East Prussia and, while Rennenkampf was bluffed into immobility, the Germans concentrated every man against Samsonov, who committed suicide when his surrounded army was compelled to surrender (map left).

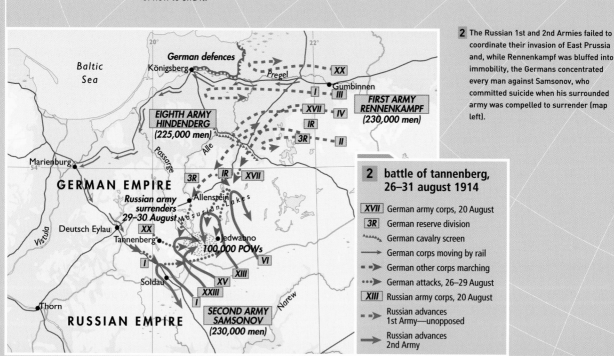

2 battle of tannenberg, 26–31 august 1914

XVII	German army corps, 20 August
3R	German reserve division
▲▲▲▲▲	German cavalry screen
→	German corps moving by rail
■-■-■	German other corps marching
••••	German attacks, 26–29 August
XIII	Russian army corps, 20 August
- - -	Russian advances 1st Army—unopposed
→	Russian advances 2nd Army

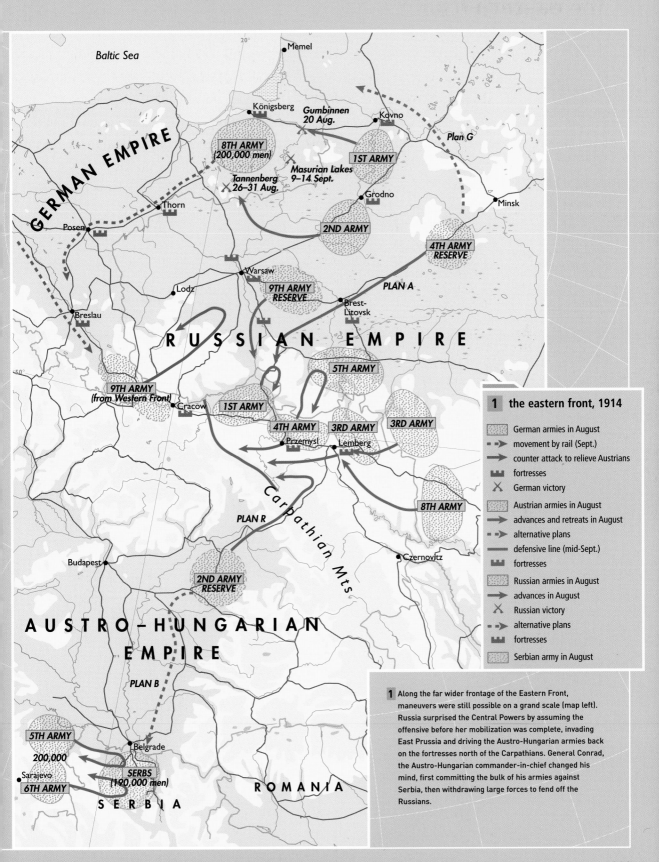

Baltic Sea

GERMAN EMPIRE

Memel

Königsberg

Gumbinnen
20 Aug.

Kovno

Plan G

8TH ARMY
(200,000 men)

1ST ARMY

Tannenberg
26–31 Aug.

Masurian Lakes
9–14 Sept.

Grodno

Minsk

Thorn

2ND ARMY

4TH ARMY
RESERVE

Posen

Warsaw

9TH ARMY
RESERVE

PLAN A

Lodz

Brest-
Litovsk

Breslau

R U S S I A N   E M P I R E

5TH ARMY

9TH ARMY
(from Western Front)

Cracow

1ST ARMY

4TH ARMY

3RD ARMY

3RD ARMY

Przemysl

Lembeng

8TH ARMY

Carpathian Mts

PLAN R

Czernovitz

Budapest

2ND ARMY
RESERVE

A U S T R O – H U N G A R I A N

E M P I R E

PLAN B

5TH ARMY

200,000

Belgrade

Sarajevo

SERBS
(190,000 men)

R O M A N I A

6TH ARMY

S E R B I A

1 the eastern front, 1914

German armies in August

-- ► movement by rail (Sept.)

──► counter attack to relieve Austrians

🏰 fortresses

✕ German victory

Austrian armies in August

──► advances and retreats in August

-- ► alternative plans

── defensive line (mid-Sept.)

🏰 fortresses

Russian armies in August

──► advances in August

✕ Russian victory

-- ► alternative plans

🏰 fortresses

Serbian army in August

1 Along the far wider frontage of the Eastern Front, maneuvers were still possible on a grand scale (map left). Russia surprised the Central Powers by assuming the offensive before her mobilization was complete, invading East Prussia and driving the Austro-Hungarian armies back on the fortresses north of the Carpathians. General Conrad, the Austro-Hungarian commander-in-chief changed his mind, first committing the bulk of his armies against Serbia, then withdrawing large forces to fend off the Russians.

trench warfare

1915

10–13 March 1915
Battle of Neuve Chapelle

22 April–25 May 1915
Second Battle of Ypres; Germans release chlorine gas at Ypres; first large-scale use of weapons of mass destruction

9 May 1915
General Pétain's 33rd Corps arrives at the top of Vimy Ridge

23 May 1915
Italy declares war on Austria–Hungary

25 September–early November 1915
Artois–Loos offensive

The development of trench warfare in late 1914 is less surprising than the war of movement it replaced. Twentieth-century firepower made it possible to hold long fronts with far fewer men than ever before. Armies had grown so large they could occupy the entire space available, creating an inviolable front without flanks. Only the Germans possessed large number of weapons appropriate to trench warfare: howitzers, grenades, signal rockets. The French had neglected howitzers, and hastily stripped their fortresses of heavy guns for the front line.

Joffre's tactics resembled those of d'Erlon at Waterloo. Massive columns advanced after concentrated artillery had blasted a path through the enemy position. The two regiments of each brigade followed each other in waves, so close together that 3,600 men formed a mass 1,300 yards wide and 185 yards deep. Surprisingly, the concept almost worked. Petain's 33rd Corps reached the top of Vimy Ridge on 9 May 1915, but machine-gun fire from fortified villages held up progress on the flanks. Joffre's September attacks were on a wider front: 22 divisions broke through on a 10-mile front in Champagne. The Germans

1 General Joffre conducted a succession of offensives in 1915, but hopes of a strategic breakthrough foundered against barbed wire, machine guns, and concealed artillery (map below). French losses were catastrophic, although one officer showed that a thoroughly prepared attack could succeed: General Pétain led his 33rd Corps to the top of Vimy Ridge in May 1915.

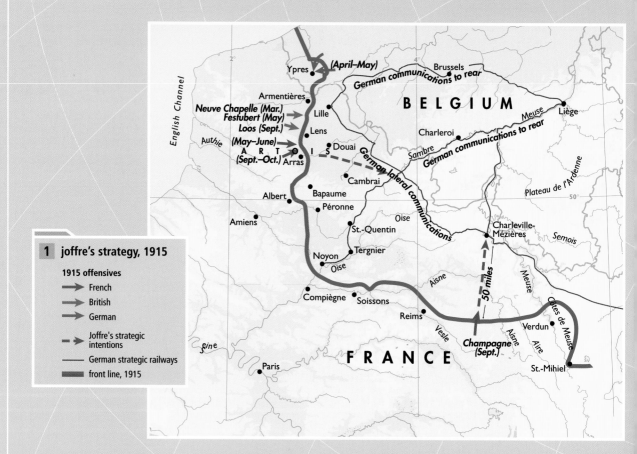

1 joffre's strategy, 1915

1915 offensives
→ French
→ British
→ German
---→ Joffre's strategic intentions
—— German strategic railways
━━ front line, 1915

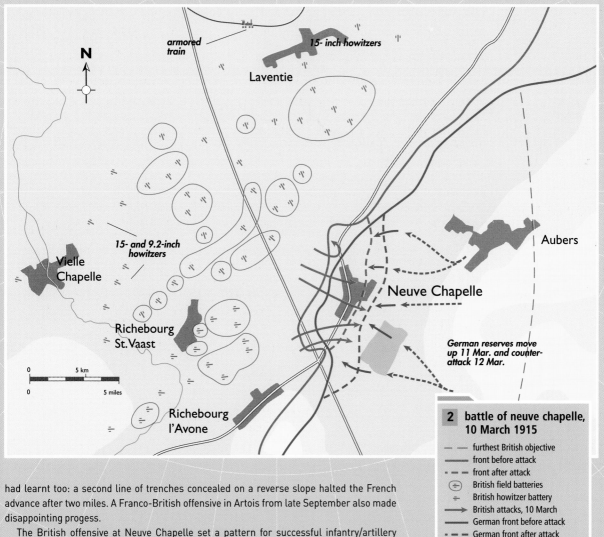

armored train

15- inch howitzers

N

Laventie

Vielle Chapelle

15- and 9.2-inch howitzers

Richebourg St. Vaast

Richebourg l'Avone

0   5 km
0   5 miles

Aubers

Neuve Chapelle

German reserves move up 11 Mar. and counter-attack 12 Mar.

2 battle of neuve chapelle, 10 March 1915

– – – furthest British objective
——— front before attack
- - - - front after attack
⊜ British field batteries
⊜ British howitzer battery
——➤ British attacks, 10 March
——— German front before attack
- - - - German front after attack

had learnt too: a second line of trenches concealed on a reverse slope halted the French advance after two miles. A Franco-British offensive in Artois from late September also made disappointing progess.

The British offensive at Neuve Chapelle set a pattern for successful infantry/artillery attacks. The BEF's leadership showed awareness of new tactical conditions, combining methodical preparation and surprise. An unprecedented whirlwind bombardment by 340 guns cut the wire and wrecked the German front line. Tactical novelties included aerial photography, an orchestrated fire plan, and first official use of the term "barrage." Neuve Chapelle, like Vimy Ridge, showed how the German front line might be penetrated, starting a debate among the high command. Some hoped better planning or more firepower would produce a decisive breakthrough. Others preferred to wear the Germans down by a "bite and hold" strategy, a strategy unacceptable to a public still expecting speedy victory.

The Germans launched only one significant offensive on the Western Front in 1915. They released clouds of chlorine gas at Ypres, in the first large-scale use of weapons of mass destruction. The Germans took half the Ypres salient, but suffered a resounding propaganda defeat. The unbelievable horror of a gas-cloud attack confirmed perceptions of Hun beastliness first inspired by atrocities against Belgian civilians. Gas masks transformed soldiers into dehumanized monsters, but human qualities of morale and training remained essential for troops to survive gas warfare.

2 British experience at Neuve Chapelle showed the German line could be penetrated, but the defender's reserves could plug the gap before the attacker could move fresh troops forward (map above). Until this conundrum was solved, no major breakthrough was possible. The last regular cadres of the BEF were expended in these assaults; larger British operations would have to wait until the volunteer Kitchener armies were equipped and trained.

gallipoli

The stalemate on the Western Front stimulated a search for alternative areas of operations. Over-optimistic expectations of what sea power could achieve inspired an Anglo-French amphibious attack on Turkey, which had joined the Central Powers in October 1914.

The failure of both sea and land operations at Gallipoli underlined the gulf between strategic vision and operational reality during the First World War. The scheme depended on makeshift expedients: obsolete ships officially regarded as expendable; civilian trawlers impressed as minesweepers; half-trained divisions with incomplete artillery and staffs. A purely naval attack on the Dardanelles flew in the face of experience going back to 1807, and begged the question of what to do if the Turks refused to surrender on the fleet's arrival at Istanbul. Pre-Dreadnought battleships were to silence the Turkish forts at the mouth of the Dardanelles, the straits leading to the Sea of Marmara and the Bosphorus. Trawlers would then clear the minefields for the battleships to engage forts inside the Narrows. Shore bombardment failed to silence Turkish forts permanently. Flat-trajectory naval guns were ineffective against the mobile howitzer batteries that hampered mine-clearing operations. When the fleet attempted to brazen it out on 18 March, unswept mines sank three old battleships and damaged another two, almost a third of the force. The underwater threat ended the purely naval phase of the campaign. Two months later a U-boat torpedoed two more pre-Dreadnoughts, confirming the dangers of traditional naval power projection in the face of mines and submarines.

The naval bombardments lost any chance of strategic surprise. The Turks held the April landings on the Cape Helles beaches, until nightfall. The red stain in the sea was visible from the air. The début of Australian and New Zealand Dominion forces at Anzac Cove was more successful but, once ashore, the troops became entangled in razor-backed hills and scrub not apparent from a small-scale map. Rifle, barbed wire, and spade dominated the battlefield as in the West, but at Gallipoli the Allies had no continuous line, no high ground for observation, no depth providing escape from enemy fire and no clean water. Over half the British and Dominion casualties, 145,000 out of 214,000, were from dysentery. The losses from disease associated with every 1914–18 "sideshow" condemn all of them as a way of winning the war on the cheap. The landings

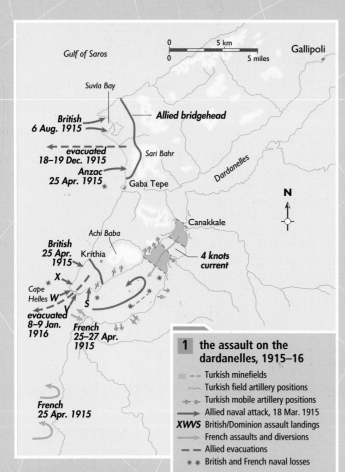

1 the assault on the dardanelles, 1915–16

- Turkish minefields
- Turkish field artillery positions
- Turkish mobile artillery positions
- Allied naval attack, 18 Mar. 1915
- **XWVS** British/Dominion assault landings
- French assaults and diversions
- Allied evacuations
- British and French naval losses

1 An unsupported naval attack in March gave notice of Allied intentions, so the improvised amphibious assault in April met with disaster. The attacking troops were shot down in the water; so much blood spilled it was visible from the air. Attempts to break out from the beachhead were defeated by the familiar combination of wire, machine guns, and concealed artillery (map left).

2 In November 1914 the Ottoman Empire joined the Austro-German alliance against the Allied powers in return for a promise that Macedonia would be restored to Turkish rule (map right). Early Turkish offensives were unsuccessful: an attack against Russia was repelled and ended with Russia seizing Armenia. Turkish efforts against the other Western allies fared better. The landing by British Empire forces at Gallipoli in April 1915 was repelled after nine months. In 1916 an Anglo-Indian force was captured at Kut trying to secure Middle Eastern oil supplies. Kut was finally retaken in 1917; Baghdad fell in March 1918. Meanwhile, with the aid of a widespread Arab revolt against Turkish rule, British Empire forces under Allenby had pushed through Sinai and on into Jerusalem. A combined Anglo-French force stationed at Salonica in October 1915 was bottled up there by Bulgarian and other Central Powers' forces until 1918.

Black Sea

RUSSIAN EMPIRE

BULGARIA

Constantinople

Gallipoli

Dardanelles

April 1915

Smyrna

Dodecanese to Italy

OTTOMAN

Angora

EMPIRE

Erzinjan

Batum

Kars

1916–18

Sept. 1918

ARMENIA

AZERBAIJAN

Baku

Tabriz

Caspian Sea

PERSIA

Teheran

Mosul

Nisibin

Kirkuk

Hamadan

Sultanabad

1916–17

Adana

Alexandretta

Aleppo

SYRIA

Cyprus annexed by Britain 1914

Oct. 1918

Oct. 1918

Homs

Oct. 1918

Beirut

Damascus

Samarra

Baghdad

MESOPOTAMIA

Kut el Amara

Amara

Apr. 1916

Jan.–Mar. 1917

Basra

Apr. 1916

Mediterranean Sea

Megiddo

Oct. 1918

Jerusalem

Gaza

PALESTINE

Amman

1917

Alexandria

Port Said

Cairo

1917

1914–15

El Akaba

Sinai

EGYPT

1914 British protectorate

ARABIA (NEJD)

KUWAIT

Kuwait

HASA annexed by Arabia 1913–14

Persian Gulf

QATAR

Red Sea

HEJAZ

Medina

Yenbo

Empty Quarter (Rub' al Khali)

Jedda

Mecca

Taif

ASIR

2 the war in the middle east, 1914–18

Entente powers

Central powers

Advances

→ British
- - → Arab
→ French

→ Russian
→ Ottoman

Offensives

—— area of Arab revolt against Ottomans

—— Ottoman front line at time of surrender, 30 Oct. 1918

------ railways

at Suvla in August once more showed the futility of amphibious assaults with untrained troops. Only the flawlessly planned and executed evacuation of December 1915/January 1916 showed the impressive capabilities of the staffs, when operating beyond the constraints of bullet, wire, and spade. The rapid technical response to the demands of modern amphibious operations suggests what more careful preparation might have achieved: small cheap monitors replaced battleships for fire support; modified destroyers took over minesweeping; motorized barges or "beetles" replaced the ships' boats traditionally used for landing troops. The British would not resolve the deeper problems of political/military relations that underlay the disaster until the Second World War.

1914 to 1918

28 August 1914
Battle of Heligoland Bight

1 November 1914
Battle of Coronel

8 December 1914
Battle of Falkland Islands

24 January 1915
Battle of Dogger Bank

31 May–1 June 1916
Battle of Jutland

9 January 1917
Unrestricted submarine warfare adopted by Germans; campaign beings 1 Feb.

Events at sea were crucial to the outcome of the war. The Royal Navy possessed significant material and geographical advantages over the Imperial German Navy.

The British had 50% more Dreadnoughts, with numerous cruisers, to blockade German ports, protect British commerce, and escort expeditionary forces. The British Isles physically obstructed German access to the Atlantic, except via the easily blocked Dover Straits, or the Iceland–Faroes Gap. The Grand Fleet's concentration confined the German High Seas Fleet to the North Sea. Wireless permitted steam warships to concentrate independent of the weather, in response to enemy initiatives, while signal intercepts provided early warning of German intentions.

Like other outnumbered fleets, the High Seas Fleet remained in harbor, inspiring the first air attack on warships in harbor, by RNAS seaplanes on Christmas Day 1914. German cruisers bombarded civilian targets along the east coast of Great Britain in attempts to draw out part of the Grand Fleet. One raid brought on the first action between Dreadnoughts at the Dogger Bank. The refusal of the stricken German cruiser *Blücher* to surrender marked a return to the obstinate savagery of earlier naval wars.

The Battle of Jutland, the only fleet action between Dreadnoughts, resulted from a complex German plan, combining U-boats and zeppelins, to trap part of the Grand Fleet. But the Grand Fleet was forewarned of the German moves by signals intelligence. Only nightfall and two very smart 180-degree turns saved the High Seas Fleet. Jutland was almost the last fleet action in the old style, the combatants in view of one another. Meanwhile, German maritime trade was subject to a blockade of increasing rigor. A patrol line of cruisers and armed merchantmen intercepted ships passing between Iceland and Scotland, and redirected those carrying "contraband" to British ports. Although the Admiralty had been planning economic warfare since 1906, there was no pre-concerted plan to starve Germany out. Food was not declared contraband until 1915, after the first unrestricted U-boat campaign began. The military effects of the blockade are unclear, although it has been blamed for the deaths of 750,000 German civilians.

2 Most U-boat sinkings were achieved in coastal waters, the submarines lying off familiar landfalls just like 18th-century privateers (map left). Many attacks were carried out by gun, to save torpedoes, but the advent of "Q" ships led most captains to make their attacks from underwater.

2 u-boat sinkings in the western approaches, 1917–18

• ships sunk by submarines, May 1917
• ships sunk by submarines, May 1918

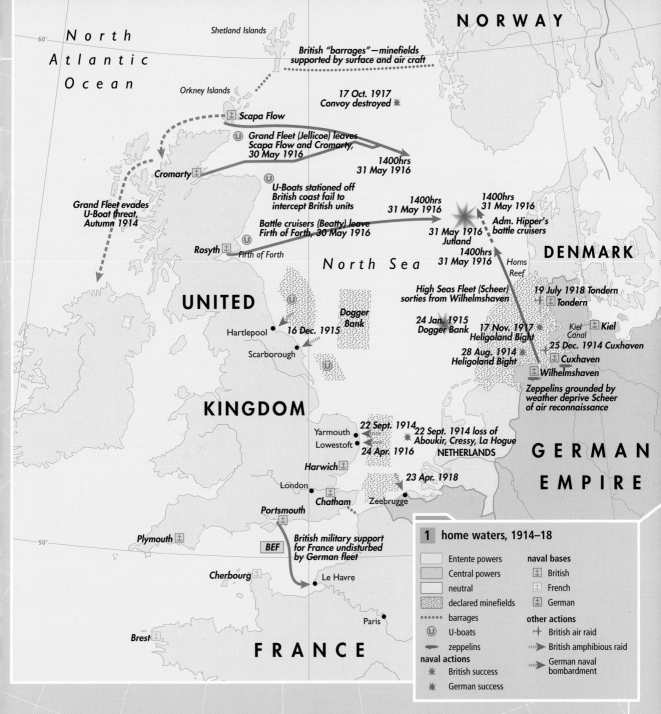

home waters, 1914–18

North Atlantic Ocean

Shetland Islands

British "barrages"—minefields supported by surface and air craft

Orkney Islands

NORWAY

17 Oct. 1917 Convoy destroyed *

Scapa Flow

Grand Fleet (Jellicoe) leaves Scapa Flow and Cromarty, 30 May 1916

1400hrs 31 May 1916

Cromarty

U-Boats stationed off British coast fail to intercept British units

Grand Fleet evades U-Boat threat, Autumn 1914

Battle cruisers (Beatty) leave Firth of Forth, 30 May 1916

1400hrs 31 May 1916

1400hrs 31 May 1916

Adm. Hipper's battle cruisers

Rosyth

Firth of Forth

31 May 1916 Jutland

1400hrs 31 May 1916

DENMARK

Horns Reef

North Sea

High Seas Fleet (Scheer) sorties from Wilhelmshaven

19 July 1918 Tondern
Tondern

UNITED

Dogger Bank

24 Jan. 1915 Dogger Bank

17 Nov. 1917 Heligoland Bight

Kiel Canal

Kiel

Hartlepool

16 Dec. 1915

28 Aug. 1914 Heligoland Bight

25 Dec. 1914 Cuxhaven

Scarborough

Cuxhaven

Wilhelmshaven

Zeppelins grounded by weather deprive Scheer of air reconnaissance

KINGDOM

GERMAN

Yarmouth
Lowestoft

22 Sept. 1914

24 Apr. 1916

22 Sept. 1914 loss of Aboukir, Cressy, La Hogue

NETHERLANDS

EMPIRE

Harwich

London

Chatham

Zeebrugge

23 Apr. 1918

Portsmouth

Plymouth

BEF

British military support for France undisturbed by German fleet

Cherbourg

Le Havre

Paris

Brest

FRANCE

1   home waters, 1914–18

Entente powers	**naval bases**
Central powers	British
neutral	French
declared minefields	German
•••••• barrages	**other actions**
Ⓤ U-boats	⊦ British air raid
zeppelins	British amphibious raid
naval actions	German naval bombardment
✳ British success	
✴ German success	

In January 1917, German naval and military leaders agreed they could not win the war by conventional means, and insisted on a resumption of unrestricted submarine warfare. This tactic brought Great Britain to the brink of ruin in April 1917, the only month when U-boats sank the target of 600,000 tons. The carnage prompted the Allies to re-allocate shipping, ration civilian food supplies, and introduce convoys. Convoy escorts, transferred from futile seek-and-destroy missions, found targets for their new hydrophones and depth charges. Of 88,000 ships convoyed by 11 November 1918, only 436 were lost. Convoys with air cover lost no ships to U-boats at all. The Germans, on the other hand, lost half their submarine flotilla, with the pick of their crews. The losses contributed to morale problems in the High Seas Fleet, whose mutiny precipitated Germany's political collapse in 1918.

1 Public opinion in Britain expected the German fleet to be annihilated in a 20th-century Trafalgar, but the Kaiser forbade his battleships to risk themselves at sea. From its bleak anchorage at Scapa Flow, the British Grand Fleet dominated the North Sea, ensuring an economic blockade of German ports that denied her war economy key resources (map above). The Germans tried to trick the British on to minefields or submarine ambushes preparatory to an engagement. This tactic failed and at Jutland in 1916 the Germans had to turn and escape.

the **eastern front II**

1915
Russians evacuate East Prussia (January); Battle of Gorlice-Tarnow; Austrians break Russian line (2–13 May); Russian forces pull out of Poland (July); Germans capture Brest-Litovsk (26 August); Serbia falls to German and Austrian forces (November)

1916
Brusilov offensive (4 June–17 October) shatters Austrian defensive line; Romania declares war on Central Powers (27 August); Bucharest falls to Central Powers (6 December)

1917
February Revolution in Russia; Tsar Nicholas II abdicates; Kerensky counter-offensive by Russia (26 June–19July); Germans take Riga (3 September); Bolsheviks seize power in Russia (7 November)

1918
Treaty of Brest-Litovsk

Falkenhayn, chief of the German General Staff since the failure of the Schlieffen Plan, believed Russia was too large to defeat in a single offensive. He wanted a limited campaign of attrition; the Gorlice-Tarnow offensive of May 1915 was to be a victory for firepower and organization, not manoeuvre.

Falkenhayn transferred eight divisions from France to the Carpathian front, deploying 700 guns, one to every 60 yards of front. This sufficed to smash the shallow Russian front line in a four-hour bombardment. No-man's-land was two miles across, much wider than in France, allowing German infantry to approach the Russian trenches unseen and capture the shell-shocked defenders. For the first time, aircraft strafed headquarters and billets in the Russian rear. In a fortnight the Germans advanced almost 100 miles. Falkenhayn exploited north and then east, cutting the Russians' lateral railway through Brest-Litovsk. The offensive petered out in the autumn mud, as the Russians slipped away eastwards. Events had justified Falkenhayn's skepticism about achieving a strategic decision against a numerically stronger enemy prepared to retreat into Russia's endless wastes.

Falkenhayn had not crippled Russia's offensive strength as he hoped. Winter 1915/16 provided a breathing space for Russian industry to make up shortages in rifles and munitions. Material deficiencies persuaded some Russian commanders to seek subtle alternatives to simply piling up masses of shells and men. In June 1916 General Brusilov achieved surprise by attacking on a wide front, with no apparent preparations to alert the enemy. After a 24-hour bombardment, Russian infantry patrols tested the defenses. Often the Russians surprised Austrian defenders in their dugouts. The Brusilov offensive finished the Austro-Hungarian army, which never recovered from losing a

1 Timed to coincide with the Anglo–French offensive on the Somme, General Brusilov's attack led to a widespread collapse of the Austro–Hungarian front. German troops had to be integrated with the dual monarchy's enfeebled divisions.

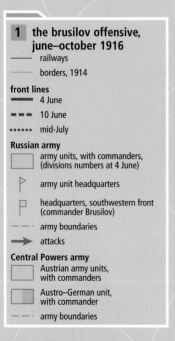

1 the brusilov offensive, june–october 1916
— railways
— borders, 1914
front lines
— 4 June
--- 10 June
•••• mid-July
Russian army
army units, with commanders, (divisions numbers at 4 June)
army unit headquarters
headquarters, southwestern front (commander Brusilov)
--- army boundaries
→ attacks
Central Powers army
Austrian army units, with commanders
Austro–German unit, with commander
--- army boundaries

1 the dictated peace – the treaty of brest-litovsk

- ———— western border of Russian territory, 1914
- [ ] Central Powers territory in 1914
- ———— frontline at Armistice, 15 Dec. 1917
- ———— furthest extent of Central Powers occupation, 9 Jan. 1918
- area of Russia occupied by Central Powers at armistice, 15 Dec. 1917
- area of Russia occupied by Central Powers at peace treaty, 3 Mar. 1918
- area of Russia independent after Dec. 1917
- ✊ serious Russian mutinies in Aug. 1917
- ● principal towns where Bolsheviks took power, Nov. 1917–Feb. 1918

2 The harsh terms of the peace treaty dictated to Russia by the victorious Germans in 1918 suggest how ghastly the consequences might have been for Western Europe had the Kaiser's armies met with victory there. Ironically, the Germans toyed with removing Lenin and his regime, but eventually supported the revolutionaries who were prepared to make peace on any terms.

Map labels:

SWEDEN · FINLAND · independence of Finland recognized Dec. 1917 · Abo · Stockholm · Helsingfors · return of Lenin from exile · Reval · Lake Onega · Petrozavodsk · Lake Ladoga · Petrograd 7 Nov. 1917 · Novgorod · Vologda · Baltic Sea · Riga · Pskov · German drive on Petrograd forces Bolsheviks to sign peace treaty at Brest-Litovsk 3 Mar. 1918 · Dvinsk · Government moved from Petrograd Mar. 1918 · Moscow 15 Nov. 1917 · Yaroslavl · Kostroma · Ivanovo · Nizhniy Novgorod · Danzig · Königsberg · GERMAN EMPIRE · Vilna · Vitebsk · Tver · Smolensk · Kaluga · Minsk · Mogilev · Tula · RUSSIA · Warsaw · POLAND · Lodz · Brest-Litovsk · Orel · Penza · Vistula · Gomel · Tambov · Cracow · 42 Austro-German divisions left as occupation forces exposed to Bolshevik subversion · Kursk · Voronezh · Don · Kassa · Lemberg · Zhitomir · Kiev · AUSTRO-HUNGARIAN · Vinnitsa · grain supplies from Ukraine prevent starvation in Vienna · Dniester · Poltava · Dnieper · Kharkov · Tsaritsyn · Debrecen · EMPIRE · Kolozsvár · Yekaterinoslav · Don · Volga · Temesvár · Jassy · Kishinev · Nikolayev · Novocherkassk · Brassó · Odessa · Rostov · Astrakhan · ROMANIA · Sea of Azov · Kuma · SERBIA · Bucharest · Simferopol · Danube · Ruse · Novorossiysk · Sofia · Sevastopol · BULGARIA · Varna · Black Sea · Plovdiv · Burgas · Adrianople · Caucasus · Salonica · Constantinople · Tiflis · GREECE · OTTOMAN EMPIRE · GEORGIA

third of its total manpower in a week. The Germans had to stabilize the front with more divisions from the west, despite the Battle of the Somme. Hindenberg and Ludendorff replaced Falkenhayn, completing the military subordination of Germany's political leadership.

The Brusilov offensive cost the Russians a million casualties, but led nowhere strategically. Another million Russian soldiers deserted. Military failure, however, was not the immediate cause of Russia's leaving the war. There were still 6.5 million troops at the front when Russia's internal collapse justified pre-war claims that protracted war was economically unsustainable. Wartime inflation had eroded the price paid to Russian grain producers. Peasants refused to market their corn, causing hunger and revolutionary disturbances in the towns. The Germans quietly allowed the Russian Army to disintegrate from within, returning exiled dissidents, such as Lenin, to hasten the process. Peace was essential to the Central Powers, particularly Austria-Hungary, but unlike the Russians they still had an army capable of imposing a "peace of violence." The Treaty of Brest-Litovsk was an example to Germany's other enemies of what they might expect, if forced to sue for peace.

verdun and the somme

21 February–December 1916
Battle of Verdun

July–November 1916
Battle of the Somme

15 September 1916
first use of tanks, by British at Flers-Courcelette

24 October 1916
Recapture of Fort Douaumont

February 1917
Germans withdraw to Hindenburg line

Falkenhayn needed to end the war in the west before the Allied blockade or the new British armies became effective. Verdun was the strategic hinge of the Allied line.

The Germans had 14 railways against a single narrow-gauge railway on the French side. Tactically Verdun was vulnerable to converging artillery fire, its woods and steep ravines concealing offensive preparations. Falkenhayn was relying on an unprecedented bombardment of two million shells to destroy not just the front line, but the whole zone under attack. German air superiority and the absence of the usual advanced trenches ensured surprise, while the short bombardment left no time for French reserves to react. German troops advanced inexorably, seizing the outlying fort at Douaumont. For a few hours they held open the way to Verdun.

Lacking railways, the French passed lorries full of troops and stores along La Voie Sacrée from Bar-le-Duc to Verdun, at 14-second intervals, while battalions of territorials continually shoveled gravel into the potholes. For the first time, a great battle depended entirely on the internal combustion engine. The British relieved the French Tenth Army at Arras, releasing fresh divisions to be rotated through the mincing machine at Verdun. Falkenhayn could not halt the offensive, lest the 550,000 French troops drawn to Verdun launched a counter-attack.

German infantry attacks suffered heavy losses for little gain, as they tried to end the battle before the anticipated Allied offensive on the Somme. Its opening bombardment in June forced Falkenhayn to close down operations at Verdun. However, German positions on the Somme were particularly strong.

The British in 1916 possessed unprecedented material and mechanical resources, which may have dulled their tactical ingenuity. Organization of the rear areas, however, was a logistical masterpiece, including three broad-gauge railways, water and accommodation for 400,000 men and 100,000 transport animals, and 7,000 miles of telephone cable to control 1,500 guns. Allied air superiority ensured the preparations remained secret.

The disastrous failure of the initial British attacks on 1 July was tactical in origin. The BEF suffered the heaviest casualties ever suffered by one army in a single day's fighting. Contributory factors included a late start and the infantrymen's excessive load. However, many British soldiers were shot down as they went over the top, implying the enemy was waiting for them. Almost two million shells were fired during a seven-day bombardment, but one in three failed to explode. There were too few heavy guns. The British had no gas shells and infantry–artillery cooperation was poor.

The first day of the Somme showed the difficulty of piercing the German line, but the balance of losses shifted against the defenders as the BEF learned its trade. German commanders unwillingly accepted the need for a less rigid defense, after they had destroyed the last of the peace-trained German infantry in repeated counter-attacks. In February 1917 the Germans withdrew to the Hindenberg Line to spare their infantry another Somme battle.

1 The initial assault failed to take Verdun, but did capture Fort Douaumont. The offensive widened to take in the left bank of the Meuse, but the French line held and a battle of attrition ensued. A final German offensive took Fort Vaux, but with the Brusilov offensive and Somme battles under way, no more troops could be spared to prosecute the offensive. French counter-attacks continued into December 1916, returning the front to where it had been in February.

---

first use by Germans of improved flame throwers

0 — 5 km
0 — 5 miles

VII CORPS

I LANDWEHR CORPS   Consenvoye

XVIII CORPS

III CORPS

Montfaucon •   • Brabant

72 DIV

XV CORPS

IV RESERVE CORPS

▲ **67 DIV**
Hill 304 ▲   Hill 295
Mort Homme

51 DIV

Etain •

✖ *Ft. Douaumont*

29 DIV
Avocourt

✖ *Ft. Vaux*

10 DIV

Ft. Souville   ✖   *first use by Germans of phosgene gas 22 June*

VERDUN

II CORPS

main railway cut by German artillery

Clermont

La Voie Sacrée — the only road link with Verdun

2 battle of verdun, 1916

front line at start of offensive, 21 Feb. 1916

✖   French forts

narrow-gauge Chemin de fer Meusien — the only rail link with Verdun

III CORPS   German assault corps

French corps in reserve (at Bar-le-Duc, 50 miles from Verdun)

Souilly

II DIV   French formations

↓ *I + XX DIV CORPS*

2 Popular British attitudes to the First World War remain dominated by the first day of the Somme offensive, when 57,000 casualties were suffered for negligible gains. Yet the battle went on for another 141 days and German generals described it as the "muddy grave of the German Army." A night attack two weeks later captured several key positions, British tactics improved, and tanks spearheaded later battles in September.

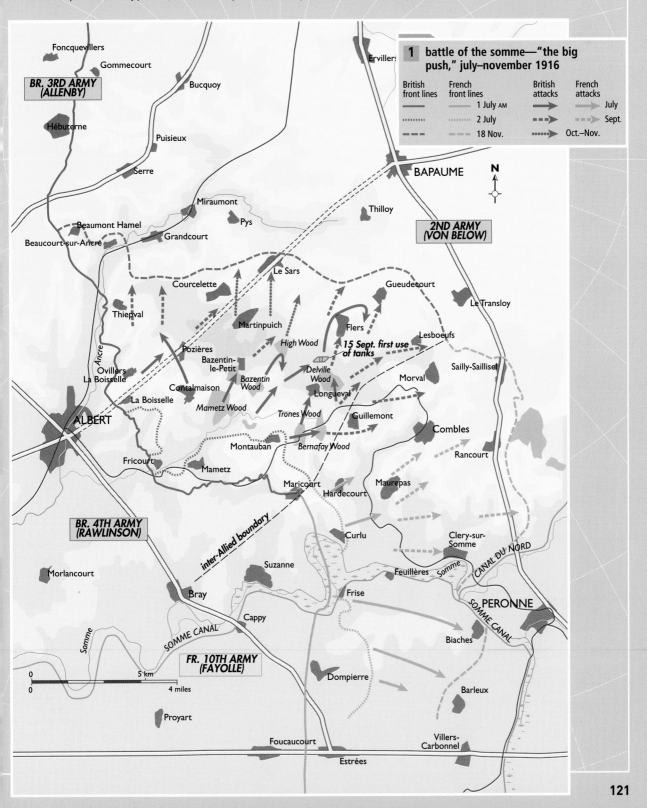

1 battle of the somme—"the big push," july–november 1916

British front lines	French front lines		British attacks	French attacks	
———	———	1 July AM	➤	➤	July
·········	·········	2 July	▸▸▸	▸▸▸	Sept.
— — —	— — —	18 Nov.	••••	••••	Oct.–Nov.

BR. 3RD ARMY (ALLENBY)

Foncquevillers
Gommecourt
Bucquoy
Hébuterne
Puisieux
Serre
Beaumont Hamel
Beaucourt-sur-Ancre
Grandcourt
Miraumont
Pys
Ervillers
BAPAUME
Thilloy
2ND ARMY (VON BELOW)

N

Le Sars
Courcelette
Gueudecourt
Le Transloy
Thiepval
Martinpuich
Flers
Lesboeufs
High Wood
Pozières
Bazentin-le-Petit
15 Sept. first use of tanks
Sailly-Saillisel
Ovillers
La Boisselle
Contalmaison
Bazentin Wood
Delville Wood
Longueval
Morval
Mametz Wood
La Boiselle
Trones Wood
Guillemont
Combles
ALBERT
Montauban
Bernafay Wood
Rancourt
Fricourt
Mametz
Maurepas
Maricourt
Hardecourt
Curlu
Clery-sur-Somme
Ancre

BR. 4TH ARMY (RAWLINSON)

inter-Allied boundary

Morlancourt
Suzanne
Feuillères
Somme
CANAL DU NORD
Bray
Frise
PERONNE
Cappy
Biaches
SOMME CANAL
Somme
Dompierre
Barleux
FR. 10TH ARMY (FAYOLLE)
SOMME CANAL
Proyart
Villers-Carbonnel
Foucaucourt
Estrées

0   5 km
0   4 miles

1917

The Third Battle of Ypres—the British Army's offensive in Belgium in the summer and autumn of 1917—was in many ways the epitome of 20th-century land combat. Third Ypres was the battle of the mud sea, where heavy rains running down slopes denuded of vegetation turned much of the low-lying areas into quagmire. It is important because it has since defined what people thought about the Great War and, in the years since, the myths have been used to legitimize political, cultural, and societal changes.

The offensive arose from a desire to capture the German submarine bases on the Belgian coast, to cover for the weakened and mutinous French Army, and to crack a German Army that was thought to be reeling from its losses. The bombardment opened on 18 July and continued until zero hour on 31 July. Strong German defenses and incessant counter-attacks limited British gains in a series of attacks through September. After regrouping and a change in battlefield command, the British resumed the offensive on 20 September with a series of systematic, limited blows. By October, the new attacks had inflicted heavy losses on the Germans, but torrential rains and the need to rush reserves to the Italian Front prevented any lasting success. With Passchendaele Ridge finally taken by the Canadian Corps in November, Third Ypres petered out.

An earlier British plan for a raid with massed tanks through German defenses to the railhead town of Cambrai was revived as Third Ypres failed to yield a breakthrough. The massing of tanks and troops was carried out while still retaining some element of surprise. On the morning of 20 November, the artillery fired a short but intense barrage and the tanks went forward, with seven infantry divisions. The German defenses were blown wide open. The cavalry divisions even came forward, seeing their long-awaited chance to exploit the breakthrough.

Rapidly arriving German reserves, heavy combat losses, and mechanical breakdowns to the tanks, combined with a lack of reserve infantry divisions to follow up, meant that the British never made it to Cambrai, the objective that was so close on 20 November. After bitter fighting for Bourlon Wood, the Germans were able to bring up reserves.

On 30 November, the German counter-attack hit the British flanks after a brief, intense artillery barrage, mainly with gas shells. The infantry advanced. They included what the Germans styled *Stosstruppen*, specialist assault troops used to infiltrate and bypass enemy strongpoints. The Germans soon took back most of their losses and even penetrated the British front line in a demonstration of their offensive power.

Cambrai was to shape debates on the use of tanks for decades thereafter. The lessons were read very differently then, but as 1917 closed and more German troops arrived in the west from the Eastern Front, the Germans believed they had managed to forge a solution that could bring victory on the modern battlefield. The British did as well and, unlike the Germans, they had the matériel to make it yield victory.

2 Cambrai saw the British Army first coming to grips with the need for tanks and infantry to fight as a combined arms team (map below). This has been, in practice, one of the hardest elements of modern operations and tactics to get right, and was to be responsible for many British defeats in 1941–42.

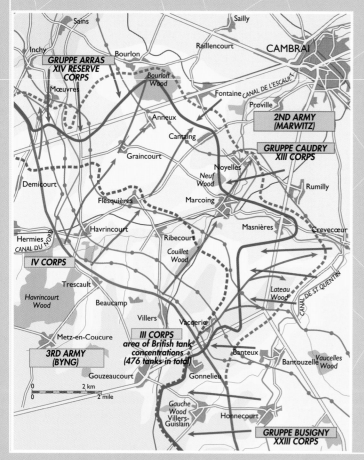

2 battle of cambrai, nov.–dec. 1917

⎯⎯⎯ front line before British attack, Nov. 20
•–•–• German defense lines
⬅ British advances
------ front line, Nov. 29
⬅ German counter-attacks
⎯⎯⎯ front line after German counter-attacks, Dec. 3
▪▪▪▪ front line after British withdrawal, Dec. 5

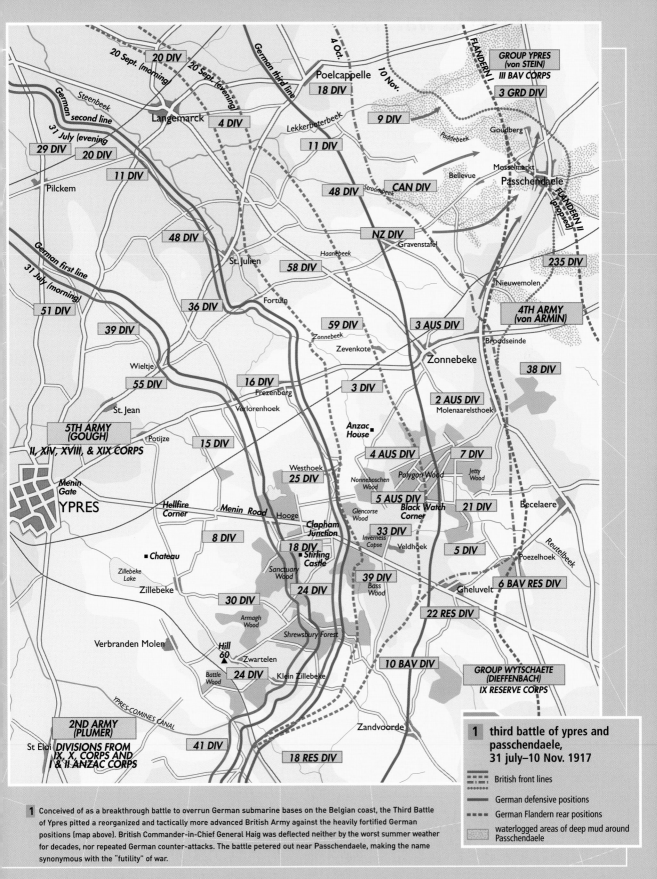

20 Sept. (morning)
20 Sept. (evening)
German third line
4 Oct.
10 Nov.
FLANDERN I
20 DIV
German second line
Steenbeek
Langemarck
4 DIV
Poelcappelle
18 DIV
Lekkerboterbeek
9 DIV
Paddebeek
GROUP YPRES (von STEIN)
III BAV CORPS
3 GRD DIV
Goudberg
31 July (evening)
29 DIV
20 DIV
11 DIV
Pilckem
11 DIV
Stroombeek
48 DIV
CAN DIV
Bellevue
Mosselmarkt
Passchendaele
FLANDERN II (proposed)
48 DIV
German first line
St. Julien
Haanebeek
NZ DIV
Gravenstafel
235 DIV
31 July (morning)
51 DIV
58 DIV
Nieuwemolen
39 DIV
36 DIV
Fortuin
Zonnebeek
59 DIV
Zevenkote
3 AUS DIV
Broodseinde
4TH ARMY (von ARMIN)
Wieltje
55 DIV
St. Jean
16 DIV
Frezenberg
Verlorenhoek
3 DIV
Zonnebeke
38 DIV
5TH ARMY (GOUGH)
II, XIV, XVIII, & XIX CORPS
Potijze
15 DIV
Anzac House
2 AUS DIV
Molenaarelsthoek
Menin Gate
YPRES
Hellfire Corner
Menin Road
Hooge
Westhoek
25 DIV
4 AUS DIV
Nonneboschen Wood
Polygon Wood
Jetty Wood
7 DIV
5 AUS DIV
Glencorse Wood
Black Watch Corner
21 DIV
Becelaere
Reutelbeek
Chateau
Zillebeke Lake
Zillebeke
8 DIV
Sanctuary Wood
18 DIV
Stirling Castle
Clapham Junction
33 DIV
Inverness Copse
Veldhoek
5 DIV
Poezelhoek
Gheluvelt
6 BAV RES DIV
30 DIV
24 DIV
39 DIV
Bass Wood
22 RES DIV
Verbranden Molen
Armagh Wood
Shrewsbury Forest
Hill 60
Zwartelen
10 BAV DIV
GROUP WYTSCHAETE (DIEFFENBACH)
IX RESERVE CORPS
Battle Wood
24 DIV
Klein Zillebeke
YPRES-COMINES CANAL
2ND ARMY (PLUMER)
St Eloi DIVISIONS FROM IX, X, CORPS AND I & II ANZAC CORPS
Zandvoorde
41 DIV
18 RES DIV

1 third battle of ypres and passchendaele, 31 july–10 Nov. 1917

British front lines

German defensive positions

German Flandern rear positions

waterlogged areas of deep mud around Passchendaele

1 Conceived of as a breakthrough battle to overrun German submarine bases on the Belgian coast, the Third Battle of Ypres pitted a reorganized and tactically more advanced British Army against the heavily fortified German positions (map above). British Commander-in-Chief General Haig was deflected neither by the worst summer weather for decades, nor repeated German counter-attacks. The battle petered out near Passchendaele, making the name synonymous with the "futility" of war.

the **first world war** 1918

1918

21 March 1918
Ludendorff's first offensive begins

9 April and 27 May 1918
two further Geman offensives are less successful

July 1918
French and American troops attack Germans on the Marne

8 August 1918
British troops crack the German front near Amiens with 400 tanks. German troops surrender in droves

September– November 1918
Germans retreat all along the front

1 The U.S. declared war in 1917 but the U.S. Army needed at least 18 months to expand and re-equip for operations in Europe. Germany had one final chance to win the war before the correlation of forces became impossible. In March 1918, reinforced by divisions released from Russia, General Ludendorff began a series of offensives that drove back the British and French, but cost the German Army nearly a million casualties (map right). New weapons and tactics were restoring mobility, but the new warfare would be no less deadly.

For Germany, there was no option but to launch one final blow at the Western Allies before the United States Army could make its weight felt on the Western Front.

Ludendorff planned five successive but basically uncoordinated offensives. The first and largest opened on 21 March, hitting the southernmost part of the British line. The Germans made tremendous gains in the first day and followed this up by a week of advance towards Amiens that brought the Germans forward over much of the ground given up after the Somme in 1916. But after a week, heavy casualties, diminishing supplies, and the inability to bring the heavy artillery forward brought the offensive to a halt. An attempt to resume the drive, against Arras, was stopped in its tracks.

Ludendorff then launched his second offensive on 9 April, aimed at cutting off the southern flank of the Ypres salient that the British had expanded at such cost in 1917. By the end of April, this offensive had also sputtered out, having failed to achieve its goals.

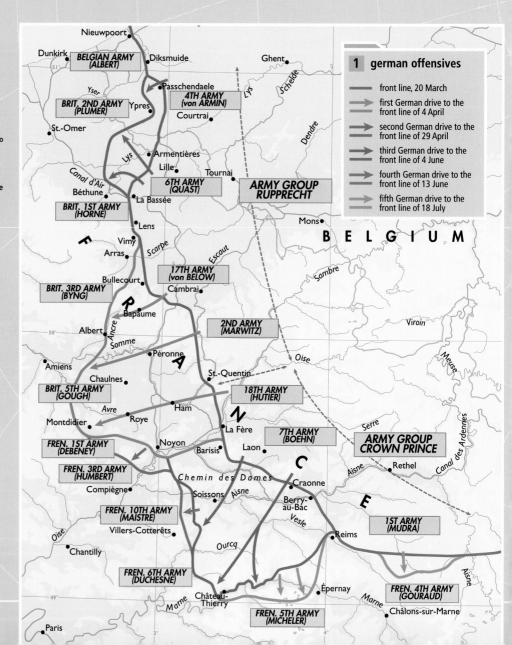

1 german offensives

— front line, 20 March
→ first German drive to the front line of 4 April
→ second German drive to the front line of 29 April
→ third German drive to the front line of 4 June
→ fourth German drive to the front line of 13 June
→ fifth German drive to the front line of 18 July

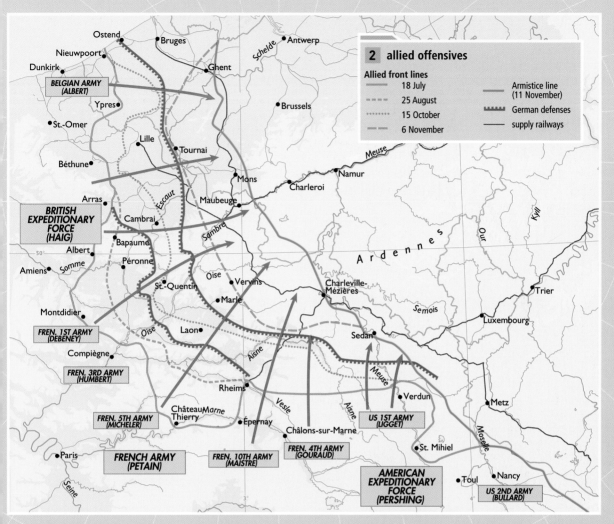

2 allied offensives

Allied front lines

—— 18 July	—— Armistice line (11 November)
---- 25 August	▪▪▪▪ German defenses
···· 15 October	—— supply railways
– – 6 November	

The third offensive hit the French lines in the Chemin des Dames along the Aisne on 27 May. This was the fastest and deepest drive of all: 13 miles gained the first day, then Soissons taken and German spearheads were back on the Marne. The next offensive, opening 9 June on the Noyon-Montdidier sector of the French line to the north, soon ground to a halt. The last offensive, an attempt to push over the Marne on 15 July, gained a sizeable bridgehead across the river but soon hit strong Franco-American resistance and, as reserves arrived, was halted within days.

Germany's offensives failed because they lacked the resources of their opponents and because, in the absence of strong planning and coordination, the Germans' tactical strengths could not be translated to operational success. They also lacked the logistics infrastructure to bring supplies or reserves forward to exploit their successes.

Unlike the German plan, the Allied solution worked, in large part because they had more resources but also because they had worked out a system that was better able to translate tactical victories into operational gains that could open up the enemy defenses. Despite the terrible losses inflicted by the German offensives, the Allied divisions of 1918 were far from the hapless infantry of 1914–16. Tanks, heavy guns, aircraft, combined arms, thorough planning, and logistics support all made the success possible.

The French and Americans attacked the German penetrations in the Marne in July, within days of the German offensive starting, while the main British blow, on 8 August, with over 400 tanks, cracked the German front near Amiens. After that, Foch ordered *"tout le monde à la bataille"* ("everyone to war") and there followed a repeated series of blows on a broad front. There was nothing left for the Germans but retreat until, on 11 November, the political collapse at home that had followed the mutiny of the German Navy, joined by troops and workers, led to the Armistice.

2 As the German spring offensives petered out, the Allies counter-attacked with equal tactical skill but greater resources (map above). The German army was never able to stabilize its front as in previous years: successive Allied attacks ruptured its defenses and systematically drove the invader from French and Belgian territory. The German high command accepted defeat and demanded Germany's politicians make peace before the Allied armies crossed the Rhine.

the **russian revolution**

The Great War's legacy of the fall of the empires of central and eastern Europe and the rise of ideological states, first the Soviet Union, followed by Fascist Italy and Nazi Germany, had a direct impact on the evolution of war-fighting. Ideology would, in the Second World War, help bring about a return to savagery not seen in Europe since the Thirty Years War.

Ideologically oriented countries also had as one of their characteristics the mobilization of all potential resources within the state, much as Ludendorff had tried to do with wartime Germany.

Revolutions present their own form of military requirements, which, like everything else in war-fighting, had changed with the Industrial Revolution. The dynamics of Petrograd in 1917 differed from Paris in 1789—the model so many expected it to follow—because of the impact of the railway and the telegraph. The Leninist concept of the élite mobilizing revolutionary vanguard could be realized in military terms because modern weaponry allowed such a group to implement its policies by force of arms. The organizational development of the modern state allowed the secret police of the Soviet Union broader and deeper reach than that of Napoleonic France.

Militarily, the wars in the east did not offer the preview of future operations and tactics that the Western Front of 1918 did. But they were tremendously important for what they led to. The Soviet Union emerged, with both a supranational communist ideology and the potential for superpower status that had been Russia's for decades. The events also shaped the Soviet way of war—the need for mobile combat, for operations over widely dispersed fronts—in ways that would endure as long as that country. The multinational intervention by the Allies along the periphery of the Russian Empire, first to continue the war, then to support those fighting the Bolsheviks, was militarily limited. There were few resources available while the Germans were still fighting and, after the Armistice, little spirit for a new conflict.

The end of great wars, like the end of great empires, creates more wars. Once the issue of who would control centralized state power in the former Russian Empire was settled, the next effort was to bring back under its control those peripheral, non-Russian areas that had asserted independence. Poland, with support from France, was able to prevent its re-absorption and check the spread of Bolshevism via the Red Army in its victory in the Russo-Polish War. Elsewhere, the process of military exertion of central authority led to fighting in central Asia during the 1920s and paved the way for its consolidation through the Stalinist terror of the 1930s.

2 the transcaucasus, 1918–23

- frontiers, 1914
- to the Ottoman Empire under Treaty of Brest-Litovsk, Mar. 1918
- Transcaucasian SSR at declaration of independence, Apr. 1918
- to the Ottoman Empire under Treaty of Batum, June 1918
- Batum–Baku railway; under British control, Nov. 1918–Aug. 1919
- controlled by Armenia, Azerbaijan, Georgia, and British forces, May 1919
- disputed between Armenia and Azerbaijan, July 1919–Aug. 1920
- northern frontier of Turkey under Treaty of Kars, Oct. 1921
- Transcaucasian SSR, Mar. 1922
- Ottoman advances, with dates
- Red Army advances, with dates

2 After the fall of the tsar, a Transcaucasian Federal Republic was set up independent of Russia (map left). It was invaded and occupied by the Turks until May 1918, when Georgia, Armenia and Azerbaijan set up separate independent states under British and French protection. When the British left in December 1919, the Bolshevik armies began the slow reconquest of the region.

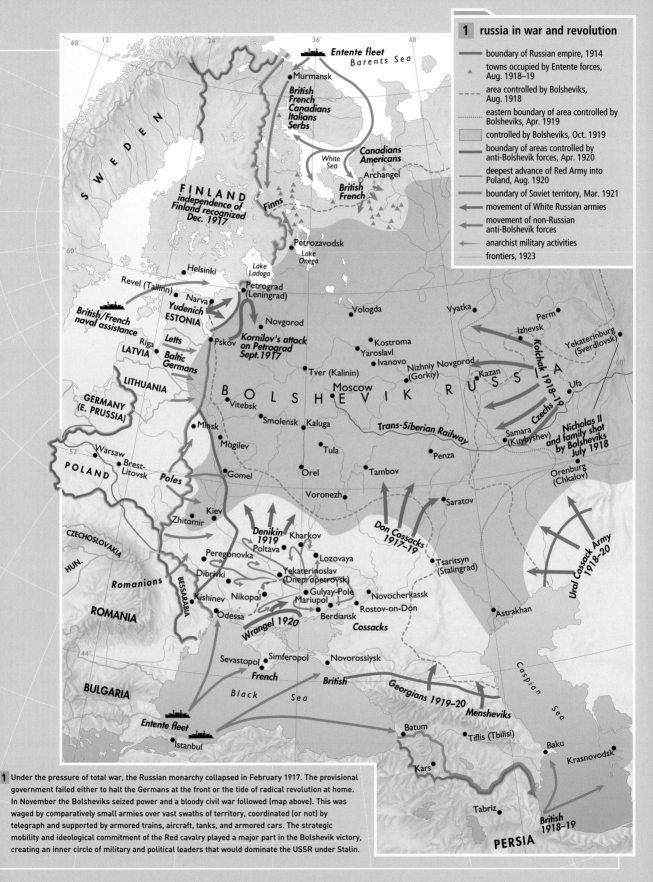

1 russia in war and revolution

- ———— boundary of Russian empire, 1914
- ▲ towns occupied by Entente forces, Aug. 1918–19
- ------ area controlled by Bolsheviks, Aug. 1918
- ·········· eastern boundary of area controlled by Bolsheviks, Apr. 1919
- controlled by Bolsheviks, Oct. 1919
- ———— boundary of areas controlled by anti-Bolshevik forces, Apr. 1920
- ———— deepest advance of Red Army into Poland, Aug. 1920
- ———— boundary of Soviet territory, Mar. 1921
- ⟵ movement of White Russian armies
- ⟵ movement of non-Russian anti-Bolshevik forces
- ⟵ anarchist military activities
- ———— frontiers, 1923

Entente fleet
Barents Sea

Murmansk

British French Canadians Italians Serbs

White Sea

Canadians Americans

Archangel

British French

SWEDEN

FINLAND
independence of
Finland recognized
Dec. 1917

Finns

Petrozavodsk

Lake Onega

Helsinki

Lake Ladoga

Revel (Tallinn)

Narva

Petrograd (Leningrad)

Yudenich
ESTONIA

Novgorod

Vologda

Vyatka

Perm

Izhevsk

Yekaterinburg (Sverdlovsk)

British/French naval assistance

Riga

LATVIA

Letts

Baltic Germans

Pskov

Kornilov's attack
on Petrograd
Sept. 1917

Kostroma

Yaroslavl

Ivanovo

Nizhniy Novgorod (Gorkiy)

Kazan

Ufa

Kolchak 1918–19

LITHUANIA

Tver (Kalinin)

B O L S H E V I K R U S S I A

GERMANY
(E. PRUSSIA)

Vitebsk

Smolensk

Kaluga

Moscow

Trans-Siberian Railway

Czechs

Samara (Kuybyshev)

**Nicholas II
and family shot
by Bolsheviks
July 1918**

Minsk

Mogilev

Tula

Penza

Warsaw

Brest-Litovsk

Poles

Gomel

Orel

Tambov

Voronezh

Saratov

Orenburg (Chkalov)

POLAND

Zhitomir

Kiev

Denikin 1919

Kharkov

Don Cossacks 1917–19

Ural Cossack Army 1918–20

CZECHOSLOVAKIA

HUN.

Peregonovka

Poltava

Lozovaya

Tsaritsyn (Stalingrad)

Dibrivki

Yekaterinoslav (Dnepropetrovsk)

Gulyay-Pole

Novocherkassk

Astrakhan

Romanians

BESSARABIA

Kishinev

Nikopol

Mariupol

Rostov-on-Don

Berdiansk

Cossacks

ROMANIA

Odessa

Wrangel 1920

Sevastopol

Simferopol

Novorossiysk

Caspian Sea

BULGARIA

French

British

Georgians 1919–20

Black Sea

Mensheviks

Batum

Tiflis (Tbilisi)

Baku

Krasnovodsk

Entente fleet

Istanbul

Kars

Tabriz

British 1918–19

PERSIA

1 Under the pressure of total war, the Russian monarchy collapsed in February 1917. The provisional government failed either to halt the Germans at the front or the tide of radical revolution at home. In November the Bolsheviks seized power and a bloody civil war followed (map above). This was waged by comparatively small armies over vast swaths of territory, coordinated (or not) by telegraph and supported by armored trains, aircraft, tanks, and armored cars. The strategic mobility and ideological commitment of the Red cavalry played a major part in the Bolshevik victory, creating an inner circle of military and political leaders that would dominate the USSR under Stalin.

the **sino-japanese** wars

1931
Mukden Incident (18 September); Japanese occupy Manchuria

1932
Shanghai Riots (28 January); Japanese take control of city

1933
Japanese occupy China north of Great Wall; puppet state of Manchukuo established by Japanese

1937
Japanese begin invasion of rest of China (July); Japanese seize Peking (28 July); the "Rape of Nanking" (December)

1938
Japanese install puppet government in Nanking; capture of Canton (October)

1944
Operation *Ichi-go*—last major Japanese offensive in China

1945
Japanese surrender in China signed (9 September)

1 Japan's occupation of Manchuria in 1931 shattered the cosy belief that the League of Nations could prevent the use of war as an instrument of state policy (map right). No amount of international condemnation stopped the Japanese Army in its subsequent invasion of China. Its military operations were conducted with bestial savagery epitomized by the mass slaughter of civilians at Nanking.

By 1914, it had already become apparent that the military history of the world was no longer equivalent to that of just Europe, even though European wars had been fought out on a global stage over the two preceding centuries. Now came Japan's industrialization and entry on the world stage as a military power as a result of the Sino-Japanese and Russo-Japanese Wars.

By 1931, Japan was looking for a solution to its problems and thought it lay in the use of armed force. Japan felt itself a have-not power, with a combination of Western imperialism, closed markets, and racist exclusion preventing it from the type of imperial expansion that the West had carried out in the preceding century and that was now

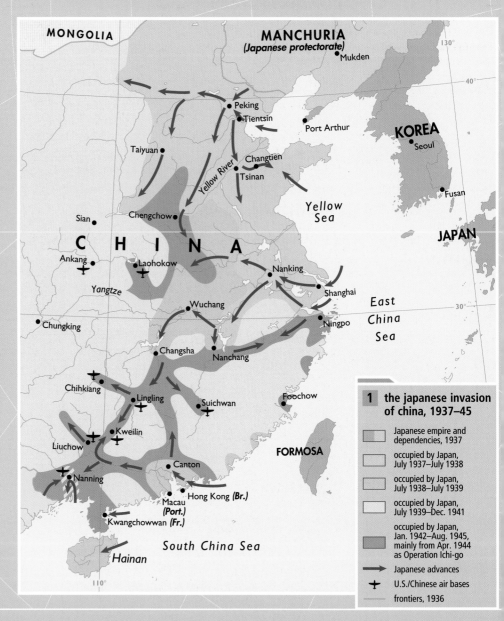

1 the japanese invasion of china, 1937–45

- Japanese empire and dependencies, 1937
- occupied by Japan, July 1937–July 1938
- occupied by Japan, July 1938–July 1939
- occupied by Japan, July 1939–Dec. 1941
- occupied by Japan, Jan. 1942–Aug. 1945, mainly from Apr. 1944 as Operation Ichi-go
- → Japanese advances
- ✛ U.S./Chinese air bases
- frontiers, 1936

proving increasingly difficult to sustain. The lessons of the Great War had shown that national power was affected by natural resources, and Japan remained resource-poor. Compounding this was the rise of the political power of the Japanese military and an ethos of militarization of society.

This armed force was first applied in the occupation of Manchuria in 1931 (dealing a body blow to another potential "solution" to the problems of modern statecraft, the League of Nations). It was followed by a war against the rest of China, starting in 1937, in which Japan used its superior sea power to occupy ports and coastal areas. Moving inland from these and from Manchuria, the Japanese soon defeated the Chinese armed forces, weak from decades of internal instability. Militarily, perhaps the most significant threat to the Japanese came from guerrilla warfare, most notably practiced by the Communist Eighth Route Army.

The Western powers had long opposed the Japanese expansion in China. This led to increasing US support for China in the years before Pearl Harbor. But, despite reinforcements of US air power, the Japanese were still able to launch successful offensives in China well into 1944, reflecting in part the Chinese emphasis on preparing for their upcoming civil war rather than devoting resources to defeating Japan.

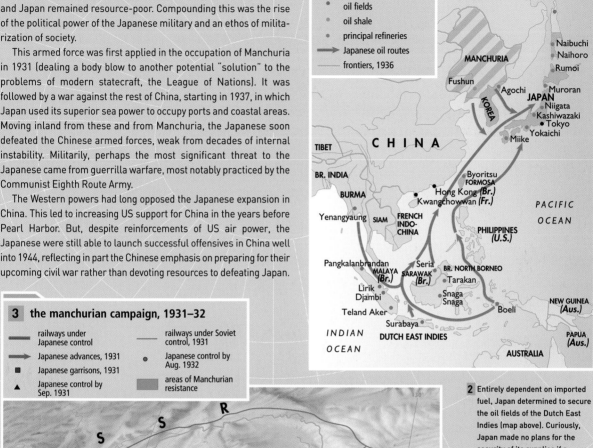

2 japan's oil sources, 1936–41

- Japanese empire, 1936
- oil fields
- oil shale
- principal refineries
- Japanese oil routes
- frontiers, 1936

3 the manchurian campaign, 1931–32

- railways under Japanese control
- railways under Soviet control, 1931
- Japanese advances, 1931
- Japanese garrisons, 1931
- Japanese control by Aug. 1932
- Japanese control by Sep. 1931
- areas of Manchurian resistance

2 Entirely dependent on imported fuel, Japan determined to secure the oil fields of the Dutch East Indies (map above). Curiously, Japan made no plans for the security of its supplies if a prolonged war resulted: she had sufficient oil tankers, but few naval escorts and no operational plans for convoying them. The oil fields would be overrun in 1941–42, but U.S. submarines would send Japan's tanker fleet to the bottom by 1944.

3 On 18 September 1931, Japanese soldiers of the Manchurian Kwantung Army blew up a short stretch on the South Manchurian Railway near Mukden, run by Japan. The "incident" was taken as the opportunity to extend Japanese control over an area rich in mineral resources. Japan struck north into Manchuria, establishing a puppet government and eventually a new land border with Russia (map left).

the **spanish civil war**

1936

Popular Front wins national elections in Spain (February); military uprisings in Spanish Morocco (July); Franco takes command of army in Morocco (19 July); first International Brigade volunteers arrive in Spain (August)

1937

Nationalists start major offensive against Madrid (February); Battle of Guadalajara (March); Guernica bombed (April); Bilbao taken by Nationalists (June)

1938

Republican offensive splits Nationalist territory in two (April); Battle of Ebro (July) leads to collapse of Republican army

1939

Barcelona falls to Nationalists (January); Madrid surrenders (March)

The Spanish Civil War was, first and foremost, the result of currents in Spanish politics, history, and culture that had endured since the French invasion of 1808. Since then, Spain had been seen as increasingly peripheral to the European power system. The loss of most of its colonial empire and its late and limited industrialization compounded this perception.

When, in 1936, Spaniard started to fight Spaniard, the place of armed conflict in the European power system ensured that this would have wider ramifications. The Nationalist rebels were identified ideologically with the Fascist states in Italy and Germany, while the Republican government had the Soviet Union as its prime external patron. The weakness of the non-ideological powers and the League of Nations underlined that, at the highest level, ideology might be part of the solution of the end of the old order in the Great War.

At the operational and tactical levels, other solutions, more developed versions of those seen in 1918, were brought into play. In most cases, this was the result of technological intervention by outside powers, while the bulk of the fighting was Spaniard against Spaniard using older technologies and tactics. Tanks were used in significant numbers but, where not supported by combined arms tactics, they often failed against anti-tank guns or even stalwart infantry, as in 1917–18. Bombers—including the accurate German Stukas—proved important and strategic bombing advocates stressed their efficacy. Anti-aircraft guns—including the German 88mm— were as important in countering the bomber threat. Overall, the lessons of Spain were distorted and mythologized, not only by ideologists but also by advocates for military change.

1 In 1936 the Spanish army under General Francisco Franco rebelled against the republic established in 1931. The result was a bitter and sanguinary civil war between the nationalist right and the liberal and socialist left, which came to symbolize the wider struggle between fascism and communism (map right). It began with the first strategic airlift in history: German transport aircraft shuttled Franco's Army of Africa to the mainland where it spearheaded the Nationalist revolt. Although aircraft and tanks were employed by both sides, the fighting was reminiscent of the First World War and many pundits, not least the British commentator Basil Liddell-Hart, published articles basing their prognosis for the future on the persistence of static warfare, a view that would be overturned by the advent of Blitzkrieg in 1939.

with Nationalists:
75,000 Italian,
20,000 Portuguese and
17,000 German soldiers

with Republicans:
500 Russian soldiers,
40,000 foreign
volunteers

from Hamburg

El Ferrol
La Coruña
GALICIA
Santiago de Compostela
Vigo
Oporto
PORTUGAL
40°
Tag
Các
Lisbon
Badaj
H
Atlantic Ocean

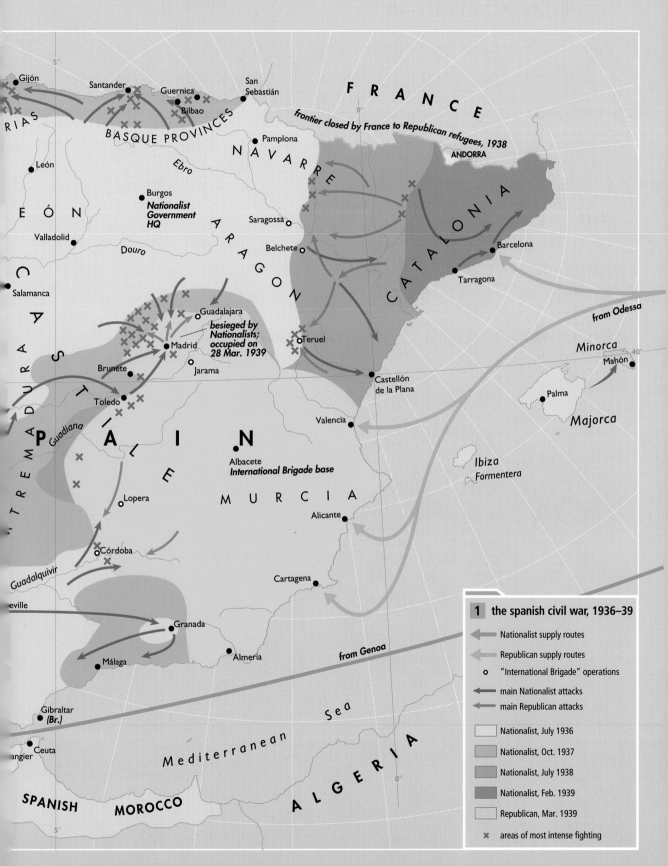

Gijón

Santander
Guernica
Bilbao
San Sebastián

BASQUE PROVINCES
Pamplona
NAVARRE
frontier closed by France to Republican refugees, 1938

F R A N C E

ANDORRA

RIAS

León

LEÓN

Valladolid

Burgos
**Nationalist
Government
HQ**

Ebro

ARAGON

Saragossa

Belchete

CATALONIA

Barcelona

Tarragona

Salamanca

CAS

Douro

Guadalajara
**besieged by
Nationalists;
occupied on
28 Mar. 1939**

Teruel

from Odessa

Minorca

Mahón

40°

Madrid
Brunete
Jarama

Toledo

Castellón
de la Plana

Palma

Majorca

Guadiana

EMADURAS

P   A   I   N

E

Valencia

Albacete
International Brigade base

Ibiza

Formentera

Lopera

M U R C I A

Alicante

Córdoba

Guadalquivir

Cartagena

from Genoa

eville

Granada

Almería

Málaga

Gibraltar
(Br.)

angier
Ceuta

SPAIN

MOROCCO

M e d i t e r r a n e a n   Sea

A L G E R I A

0°

5°

1939 to 1941

1939
Germany invades Poland (1 September)

April 1940
Germans occupy Denmark and invade Norway (9th)

May 1940
Germany attacks Holland, Belgium, and Luxembourg (10th); Holland surrenders (15th); Belgian Army capitulates (27th)

June 1940
Norway surrenders (10th); Dunkirk evacuation of British Army (26 May–3 June); German Army reaches Paris (14th); Franco–German Armistice (22nd)

September 1940
climax of Battle of Britain

The years between the two world wars saw the greatest transformation of the modern era in society and war over the shortest period of time. The internal combustion engine and the wireless could now take their role at the center of the enabling technologies of war-fighting. The wireless's offspring, radar, ensured that the pre-war belief that "the bomber will always get through" was misplaced. Its undersea acoustic counterpart, sonar, did much the same for war at sea. By the end of the Second World War, technologies scarcely anticipated before its outbreak were introduced: the jet aircraft, the ballistic missile, and the atomic bomb.

The Second World War was politically, in many ways, a continuation of the First. The failure of the international system to put in place a stable replacement for the old order that had perished by 1917 became apparent as the transition from a post-war to a pre-war world unfolded. The German campaigns in Europe from September 1939 to June 1941 represented the most complete use of military power to reshape the world since Napoleon.

Those victories demonstrated the quality of the new German armed forces, built for a short war rather than the attritional battles of the previous war. The key element was combined-arms panzer divisions. While the quality of German tanks (and their ground weapons in general) was not greatly superior to their enemies' (and most of the German Army still relied on the railroad and horse transport as in 1914), they had mastered the new technologies and the operational level of war far better than any of their opponents.

The Germans were also fortunate in their opponents. Poland was in a strategically indefensible position even before the Hitler–Stalin pact of 1939. The only militarily significant opponents were the French and the British. In 1940, they had, in most areas, numerical superiority over the Germans. Where they failed was in two decisive areas. The first was air power. The Luftwaffe was able to

1 German plans for an invasion of England were improvised in the wake of the French victory. They depended on winning air supremacy, but the integrated air defense of the UK proved impossible to overcome before autumn weather ruled out a sea crossing.

2 Thanks to the skills of her armed forces rather than numerical superiority, between 1939 and 1941 Germany conquered much of continental Europe (map right). Mastery of what opponents dubbed "Blitzkrieg" (lightning war) allowed Germany to defeat Poland in two weeks, and to overcome Belgium, Luxembourg, Holland, France, Denmark, and Norway in six weeks. The invasion of the USSR in 1941 seemed set to presage Hitler's greatest triumph as German forces swept aside a feeble Red Army.

1 battle of britain, 1940

HQ Fighter Command headquarters

G group headquarters — group boundaries

△ sector command post — ▲ fighter bases

high-level radar station — low-level radar station

• observer centers — Luftflotte HQ

• Luftwaffe bomber base

The Blitz
※ 1–5 major raids (100 tons+) — ✹ 6–10 major raids
— ✸ more than 10 major raids

Glasgow 1,329 tons
Galashiels
Fighter Command 13 Group
Carlisle
Newcastle 152 tons
Durham
G R E A T
Lancaster
York
Leeds
Hull 593 tons
Liverpool/Birkenhead 1,957 tons
Manchester 578 tons
Sheffield 355 tons
Lincoln
Wrexham
Nottingham 137 tons
Derby
Shewsbury
Fighter Command 12 Group
Norwich
B R I T A I N
Birmingham 1852 tons
Coventry 818 tons
Bedford
Cambridge
Gloucester
Oxford
Stanmore
Colchester
Ipswich
Uxbridge
Cardiff 115 tons
Bath
London 18,800 tons
Bristol/Avonmouth 919 tons
Fighter Command 11 Group
Fighter Command 10 Group
Southampton 647 tons
Portsmouth 687 tons
Exeter
Brussels
Luftflotte 2 HQ
BELGIUM
Calais
Lille
Plymouth/Devonport 1,228 tons

maximum effective range of low-level radar: minimum detection altitude c. 150 m.

maximum effective range of high-level radar: minimum detection altitude c. 4,570 m.

English Channel

North Sea

Cherbourg
Rouen
Laon
Beauvais
Caen
F R A N C E
Evreux
Paris **Luftflotte 3 HQ**
St. André-de-l'Eure
Orly
Dreux
Etampes
Melun
Chartres
Brest
Dinard

seize air superiority and serve as a powerful force multiplier for the ground forces. The second was in the type of combined-arms mechanized formations represented by the panzer divisions. The French and British lacked the tactics, and organization to be as effective as the Germans. Even though the British Expeditionary Force had its infantry divisions motorized, the lack of reliable armored formations limited its operational maneuverability.

But the German war machine's limitations became apparent in the months after its greatest triumph, the fall of France. Then, in the Battle of Britain, the Luftwaffe found itself unable to defeat the Royal Air Force. The RAF demonstrated that it was more than equal to the Luftwaffe in the use of technology, using aircraft on a par with any in the world as part of an integrated air defence system, a new British creation, made possible by a British invention, radar. The first decisive campaign fought between air forces ensured that Germany's successes would not solve its fundamental strategic problems.

2 **The axis advance, 1939–41**

Axis territory, 1 Sep. 1939
Axis co-belligerents by 1941
occupied by Axis after Sep. 1939
Vichy France and territories
Soviet annexed territory, 1939–41
neutral powers
frontiers, 1 Sep. 1939

→ Axis advances, 1939
→ Axis advances, 1940
→ Axis advances, 1941
⚓ Axis airborne landings
→ Allied forces
→ Soviet advances, 1939–40
⤍ Allied retreat and withdrawal
🏙 major cities severely damaged by bombing

the **war** in **north africa**

1940
Italians invade Egypt (September); British capture Sidi Barrani (11 December)

1941
Tobruk falls to British (22 January); Germans capture Benghazi (4 April); siege of Tobruk raised (10–11 December); British retake Benghazi (25 December)

1942
Germans take Tobruk (20–21 June); Second Battle of El Alamein (23 Oct.–4 Nov.); Operation **Torch**, U.S. invasion of North Africa begins (8 November)

1943
British capture Tripoli (23 January); Allies enter Tunisia (February); German surrender in North Africa (12 May)

The war in North Africa and, indeed, the Mediterranean as a whole, started off as a sideshow to the ill-fated Italian offensives in 1940. It ended up as the major campaign in the West in 1940–43, attracting Britain's strategic reserve.

The initial 1940–41 campaign saw the defeat of non-mechanized Italian forces, which had invaded Egypt from the Italian colony of Libya. They were defeated by a mechanized British force, permanently reducing Italy to the status of a dependent partner on its German ally and leading to the commitment of German land, sea, and air forces, although their numbers remained relatively small until just before their final defeat in Tunisia in 1943.

The war in North Africa was part of a larger Mediterranean campaign that, previewed in the Norwegian campaign of 1940, integrated naval, air, and ground forces in a new type of warfare. It included Malta-based British air, sea, and submarine forces interdicting the Axis supply routes to North Africa while, in

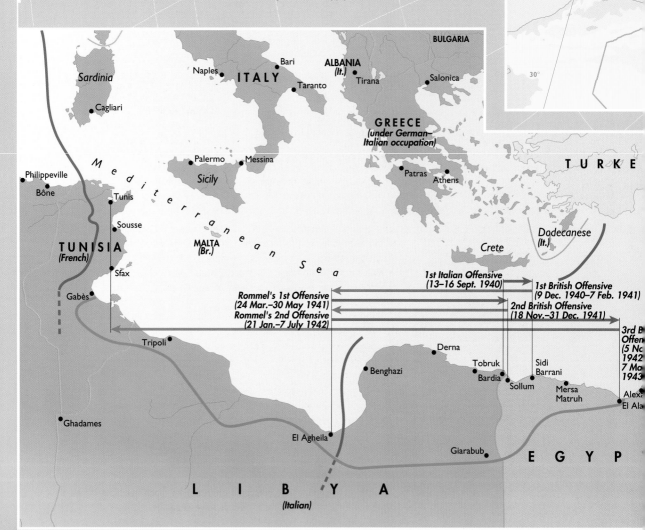

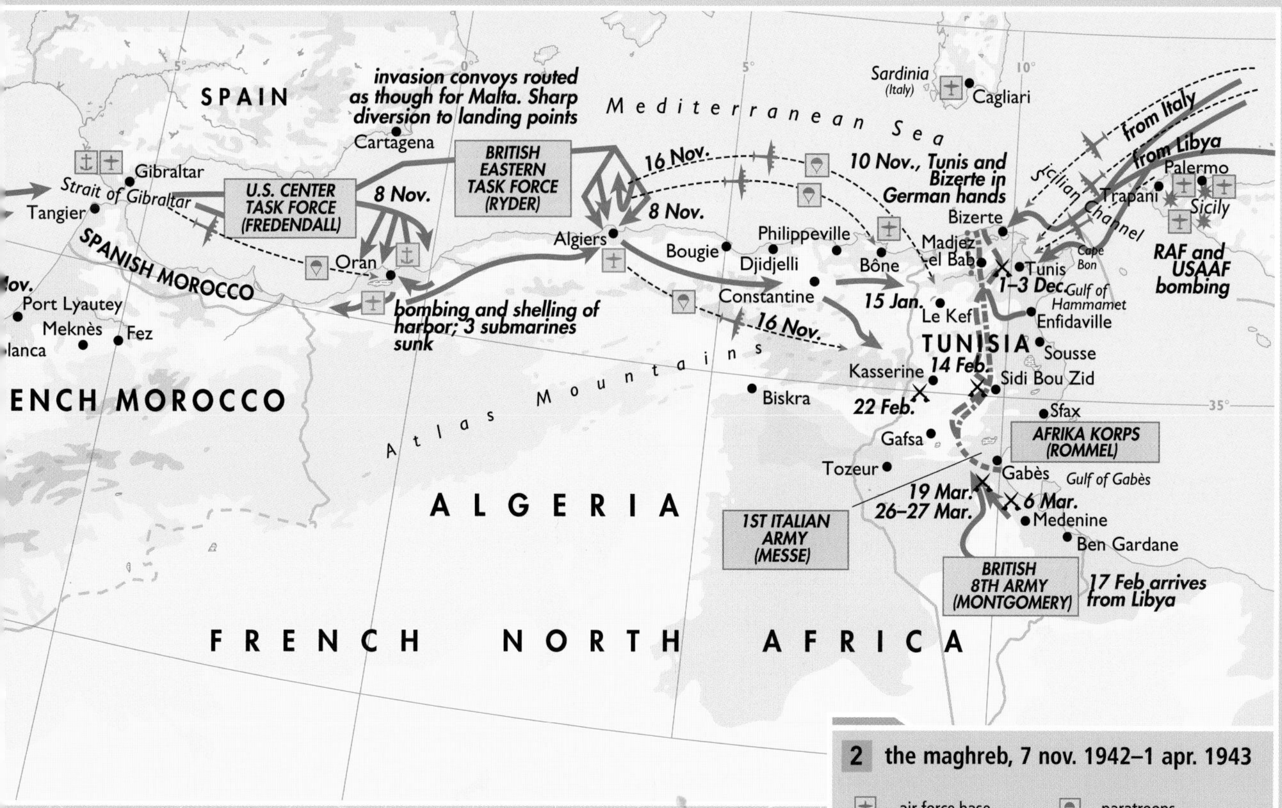
SPAIN
invasion convoys routed as though for Malta. Sharp diversion to landing points
Cartagena
Mediterranean Sea
Sardinia (Italy)
Cagliari
Gibraltar
Strait of Gibraltar
Tangier
U.S. CENTER TASK FORCE (FREDENDALL)
8 Nov.
BRITISH EASTERN TASK FORCE (RYDER)
16 Nov.
8 Nov.
10 Nov., Tunis and Bizerte in German hands
from Italy
from Libya
Sicilian Channel
Palermo
Trapani
Sicily
SPANISH MOROCCO
Oran
Algiers
Bougie
Philippeville
Djidjelli
Bône
Bizerte
Madjez-el Bab
Tunis
1–3 Dec.
Cape Bon
Gulf of Hammamet
RAF and USAAF bombing
Port Lyautey
Meknès
Fez
bombing and shelling of harbor; 3 submarines sunk
Constantine
15 Jan.
Le Kef
16 Nov.
Enfidaville
TUNISIA
Sousse
Kasserine
14 Feb.
Sidi Bou Zid
22 Feb.
Atlas Mountains
Biskra
Sfax
FRENCH MOROCCO
Gafsa
AFRIKA KORPS (ROMMEL)
Tozeur
Gabès
Gulf of Gabès
19 Mar.
26–27 Mar.
6 Mar.
Medenine
ALGERIA
1ST ITALIAN ARMY (MESSE)
Ben Gardane
BRITISH 8TH ARMY (MONTGOMERY)
17 Feb arrives from Libya
FRENCH NORTH AFRICA

2 the maghreb, 7 nov. 1942–1 apr. 1943

- air force base
- naval base
- paratroops
- air raid

Allied front lines

- 30 November 1942
- 1 January 1943
- 14 February 1943
- 22 April 1943
- 31 March 1943

2 The Axis presence in North Africa was doomed by "Operation Torch," an amphibious invasion of Morocco and Algeria for which a large contingent sailed directly from the USA. The signal failure of Germany's submarines to check this onslaught did not augur well for the future of Hitler's European empire. Once ashore, the Allies ground down the Axis army in Tunisia, capturing some 250,000 men in a campaign dubbed "Tunisgrad" by jaded German officers (map above).

Nicosia
RUS
r.)
Port Said
Suez
Asyut

1 The back-and-forth movement of the front line in North Africa was dubbed the "Benghazi handicap" by Eighth Army cynics, the war raging across Libya and into Egypt as the inspired leadership of General Erwin Rommel compensated for superior British resources (map left). German forces were superbly coordinated, and their commander an indisputable master of modern war.

1 the war in north africa, 1940–43

- Axis control, Oct. 1941 (including Vichy France)
- British control, Oct. 1941
- Axis advances in the desert war, with details
- Allied advances in the desert war, with details
- Allied landings, with date
- southern limit of major operations of the desert war
- limit of Axis control, 23 Nov. 1942
- frontiers, 1942

turn, the convoys required to keep Malta fighting in the face of intense air bombardment resulted in some of the most intense air–sea battles of the war. This larger Mediterranean dimension was critical to the war, shaping it at its start by the diversion of British forces to Greece and, at its end, presenting the Allies with the problem of how to use their hard-won conquest of the North Africa littoral as a trans-Mediterranean springboard against Axis-occupied Europe.

The campaign in North Africa in 1941–43 was dominated by the skill of Erwin Rommel, commander of the German Afrika Korps. But his charisma only compounded the superiority in combined-arms mechanized operations and tactics that the Germans had over the British. Once the initial force that had defeated the Italians was dispersed, the British had to learn the business of combined-arms mechanized combat—the model for future operations—in action. By their victory at the Second Battle of El Alamein in 1942, they had learned well enough.

The outcome in North Africa was shaped by two factors that did not easily show up in the orders of battle: logistics and intelligence. Logistics decided the outcome on the battlefield to a greater extent than the most brilliant tactical maneuvers. British Ultra decrypts of German secure communications, when available, provided excellent intelligence but could often not be made available to the war-fighters in time to be of decisive value.

the **german** invasion of **russia**

1941

June 1941
Germany invades USSR (22nd); Germans capture Minsk (28th)

July 1941
Germans capture Riga (1st); capture of Smolensk (15th)

August 1941
Germans surround Leningrad (19th)

September 1941
Germans occupy Estonia (5th); first snows slow German advance (12th); Germans take Kiev (19th)

October 1941
Odessa falls to Germans (16th); Germans take Kharkov (24th)

November 1941
Germans capture Kursk (3rd), Kerch (16th); German attack on Moscow, panzers within 20 miles of city (25th)

December 1941
Germans abandon attack on Moscow (5th)

The War in the East represented the largest-scale combat operations of the Second World War and many of the most intense. The Soviets long distinguished it as a separate conflict—the Great Patriotic War—from the Second World War of which it was a part. While for decades after 1945 Western historians tended to focus on their countries' own combat actions, the German Army suffered some 80% of its total casualties in the East.

The German 1941 invasion of the Soviet Union again reflected the increased importance of strategic surprise that resulted from techno-logical change. Aircraft and mechanized forces could inflict lasting damage swiftly, before the shock effect had worn off. It also showed that the increasing significance and sophistication of intelligence as a counter to surprise—the rise of the wireless meant that signals intelligence and cryptology were now a crucial element of war-fighting—meant nothing if the decision makers chose to believe their own preconceptions. Hitler was the only man Stalin ever trusted.

The initial months of the invasion saw tremendous advances and volumes of prisoners but, as the summer came to an end, increasingly savage if disorganized Soviet resistance and Hitler's shifting of objectives prevented the rapier thrust to Moscow that was thought necessary to bring down the Soviet Union. The Blitzkrieg forces intended to win a quick, limited-liability conflict now found themselves faced by a conflict for which Germany's lack of thorough industrial mobilization had not prepared them. The Soviets were able to evacuate much of their industrial base to the Urals, assuring that future forces could be supported even while those in the field in 1941 were destroyed.

The destruction of the pre-war Soviet forces in the western military districts did not win the campaign. Military improvisation, the arrival of the Soviet strategic reserve from Siberia and the Far East, and the over-stretch of the few German motorized units when the Russian autumn and then winter arrived brought the advance to a halt.

At the end, the German spearheads actually could see the spires of the Kremlin. But it was too late. In December, the Soviets launched their first major counter-attack. Their losses were heavy, but in the end the Germans were forced to give ground in front of Moscow. They would never come as close to the prize again.

1 the german assault on the ussr, june–sept. 1941

Germany and her allies, 22 June 1939

Stalin line

German attacks

occupied by Germany and her allies by 9 June 1941

frontline, 1 Sept. 1941

occupied by Germany and her allies by 30 Sept. 1941

under Soviet control on 30 Sept. 1941

trapped Soviet pockets

frontiers, early 1941

NORTH-WEST FRONT (VOROSHILOV) Soviet army groups

1 On 22 June 1941 Germany launched an attack against the Soviet Union on a front of almost 1,000 miles with three million troops (map right). In three months German armies, supported by troops from Romania, Finland, Hungary, and Italy, almost reached Moscow and Leningrad. By December the advance was halted and the Red Army began the counter-offensive that saved the Soviet capital.

FINLAND

Turku

Helsinki

Hangö

Stockholm

Baltic Sea

Vyborg

Lake Ladoga

Leningrad

Tallinn

NORTH-WEST FRONT (VOROSHILOV)

Pskov

Moscow

Ríga

ARMY GROUP NORTH (LEEB)

Duinsk

Vilnius

Vitebsk

Smolensk

Tula

USSR

WEST FRONT (TIMOSHENKO)

Königsberg

Danzig

Minsk

Don

ARMY GROUP CENTER (BOCK)

Vistula

Pripet

Marshes

Kursk

Warsaw

Brest

SOUTH-WEST FRONT (BUDENNY)

GERMAN

Lodz

EMPIRE

GENERAL GOVERNMENT

Kiev

Kharkov

Cracow

L'vov

Dnieper

Dniester

Vinnitsa

Dnepropetrovsk

SLOVAKIA

Kassa

ARMY GROUP SOUTH (RUNDSTEDT)

Budapest

Debrecen

HUNGARY

Kolozsvár

Jassy

Kishinev

Odessa

Pécs

Szeged

Timisoara

Braïov

ROMANIA

Novi Sad

Belgrade

Bucharest

Sevastopol

YUGOSLAVIA

under Axis occupation

Sarajevo

Danube

Ruse

Black Sea

January–August 1942

Russians recapture Kiev (13 January); Russian offensive in Crimea (March); Germans recapture Kerch Peninsula (20 May); Germans take Sevastopol (3 July); Germans cross river Don (31 July); Germans capture Krasnodar and Maikop (9 August)

September 1942

Fierce fighting around Stalingrad (1st); "final" German offensive at Stalingrad (13th)

October 1942

second "final" offensive at Stalingrad (14th)

November 1942

Russian counter-attack at Stalingrad begins (19th); German 6th Army surrounded (23rd); Russian offensive on central front (28th)

January 1943

Germans begin withdrawal from Caucasus (3rd); siege of Leningrad raised (18th); Russians capture airfield supplying Stalingrad (21st); General Paulus surrenders 6th Army at Stalingrad (31st)

The Germans did not put their weight into renewing the drive on Moscow that had come so close to success in 1941, although in many ways the 1942 campaign opened as a continuation of the year before. The Germans were still able to use their superior capability at combined-arms mechanized operations to defeat numerically superior Soviet forces. Increasing German industrial mobilization provided more resources.

The Soviet spring 1942 offensives largely failed, especially at Kharkov, and the Germans were able to follow this up with a planned thrust to Rostov and into the oil-rich Caucasus, an improvised switch to attempting a resource-based strategy. This would require blocking the River Volga's north–south communications at the city of Stalingrad. As in 1941, operational skill and mobility led to many victories and large numbers of prisoners. But even as the Germans swept down the north shore of the Black Sea to the northern slopes of the Caucasus, they lacked the forces and resources to consolidate these gains against increasing Soviet strength.

2 In Stalingrad, German armies drove the Soviet defenders to the very edge of the River Volga in the factory district and the city center. In November 1942, German forces were encircled and two months later capitulated with a total loss of 200,000 men.

2 the siege of stalingrad, sept.–nov. 1942

→ German advances
━━ German front line, 13 Sep.

Soviet frontlines
━━━━ 13 Sept.   ━ ━ ━ 3 Oct.
━━━━ 27 Sept.   ▪ ▪ ▪ 12 Nov.

The battle for Stalingrad negated the German advantages as dogged Soviet resistance created a massive house-to-house battle of attrition. While the Germans fed more forces into Stalingrad, without achieving ultimate success, the Soviets began to plan a counter-attack that would cut off both the forces in Stalingrad and those in the Caucasus.

The value of surprise was again demonstrated. Despite excellent reconnaissance and intelligence capabilities, aircraft, and signal intercepts, the power of self-delusion was too strong. The Germans were convinced there was no threat to the vulnerable flanks of the forces committed to Stalingrad. The Soviets put in place an effective deception plan—the first of many—to make sure they remained undisturbed until, on 19 November, the blow fell on weakened forces holding the flanks, many from Germany's poorly equipped client states. Stalingrad was encircled. The forces in the Caucasus escaped the same fate through withdrawal.

Thanks to German indecision and the inability to sustain Stalingrad by airlift, the Soviets were able to defeat attempts to relieve the besieged German forces. The 1942 campaign ended on 31 January 1943 with the surrender of the German headquarters in the Stalingrad pocket.

1 No longer strong enough to attack across the width of the Russian front, the German strategy for 1942 was to drive across the south, its target the oil wells of the Caucasus (map below). Stalingrad was a subsidiary objective; its occupation would block Soviet use of the River Volga, a vital strategic artery.

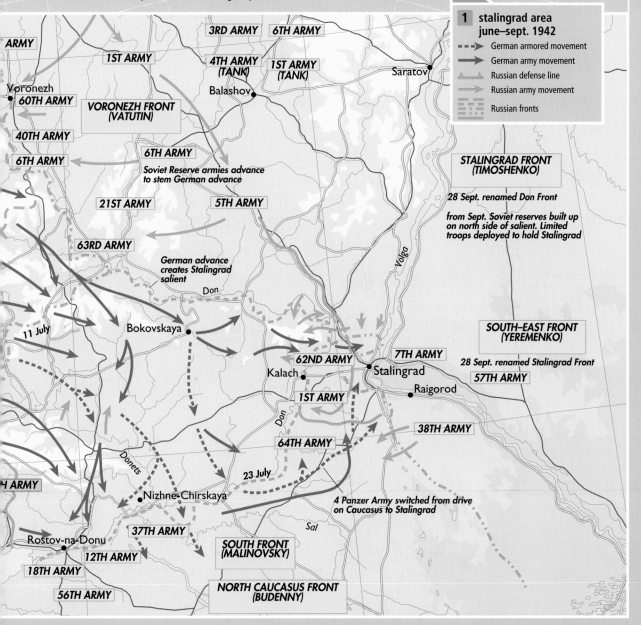

1 stalingrad area june–sept. 1942

- - - → German armored movement
── → German army movement
⌒ Russian defense line
→ Russian army movement
▦ Russian fronts

ARMY

1ST ARMY

3RD ARMY   6TH ARMY

4TH ARMY (TANK)

1ST ARMY (TANK)

Balashov

Saratov

Voronezh
60TH ARMY

VORONEZH FRONT (VATUTIN)

40TH ARMY

6TH ARMY

6TH ARMY

Soviet Reserve armies advance to stem German advance

21ST ARMY

5TH ARMY

STALINGRAD FRONT (TIMOSHENKO)

28 Sept. renamed Don Front

from Sept. Soviet reserves built up on north side of salient. Limited troops deployed to hold Stalingrad

63RD ARMY

German advance creates Stalingrad salient

Don

Volga

11 July

Bokovskaya

SOUTH–EAST FRONT (YEREMENKO)

62ND ARMY

7TH ARMY

Kalach

Stalingrad

28 Sept. renamed Stalingrad Front

57TH ARMY

Raigorod

1ST ARMY

Don

38TH ARMY

64TH ARMY

Donets

23 July

4 Panzer Army switched from drive on Caucasus to Stalingrad

H ARMY

Nizhne-Chirskaya

Sal

37TH ARMY

Rostov-na-Donu

12TH ARMY

SOUTH FRONT (MALINOVSKY)

18TH ARMY

56TH ARMY

NORTH CAUCASUS FRONT (BUDENNY)

the **battle** of the **atlantic**

1939 to 1945

1939
Graf Spee sinks first ship (30 September); Battle of River Plate (13 December)

1940
Allied shipping losses reach 585,000 tons in a month (June); Convoy SC-7 loses 21 of 30 ships to U-boats (17–19 October); Sunderland flying boat detects U-boat by using radar for first time (November)

1941
U.S. Navy begins to patrol West Atlantic; *Bismarck* sunk (27 May)

1942
Beginning of U.S. convoy system (1 April); Allied shipping losses reaches 834,200 tons in June

1943
Biggest convoy battle of war, 22 Allied ships sunk (5–20 March); Battle of Convoy ONS-5, 7 U-boats sunk (28 April); Dönitz suspends U-boat operations in North Atlantic (22 May); wolf-pack raids resume in North Atlantic (September); Germans abandon U-boat operations in Atlantic (15 November)

Germany's strategic warfare relied primarily on its submarine force, the U-boats. In 1939, the Royal Navy believed that, between the use of the convoy system and the introduction of ASDIC (now known as sonar), the U-boats would not prove the menace they had been in 1917.

The Germans had devised what they believed to be a counter to both the convoy and ASDIC. The U-boats were to operate not singly, like their Great War predecessors, but in a coordinated wolf pack. U-boats would be called in by others or by aircraft. This put a premium on radio communication. Thus, the British ability to decrypt these signals for much of the war was instrumental to eventual success. Still, the Germans also had success with decrypts and on a number of occasions throughout 1940–43 were able to inflict painful losses on merchant shipping, but they were never able to sever the Atlantic lifelines.

As in the First World War, the German surface navy was unable to defeat the Royal Navy in a major surface engagement. After its role in the invasion of Norway in 1940, its primary mission became commerce raiding. But while the Germans had originally emphasized surface ships rather than U-boats, they proved a less effective investment despite a number of victories, notably the sinking of HMS *Hood* by the *Bismarck* and the scattering of Convoy PQ 17 to North Russia by the threat of the *Tirpitz*.

The tide turned in the Battle of the Atlantic in 1943. The Allied victory resulted from many of the same elements as their ultimate victory in the war: a coalition effort, the superior numbers made possible by industrial and material strength, superior technology, and adaptive tactics employed by increasingly effective forces, all enabled by intelligence.

2 | **battle of the atlantic**
- • areas of merchant ship sinkings
- – – – maximum extent of air cover

sept. 1939–dec 1941

jan. 1942–july 1942

2 Until the U.S. entered the war, the bulk of U-boat sinkings occurred in the North Atlantic, although long-range Type IX U-boats had some success off West Africa (maps right). Insufficient aircraft were allotted to anti-submarine patrol by the British, and even if they found a U-boat, only a single attack resulted in a kill during this period. From summer 1942 to spring 1943 the U-boats were defeated in the Atlantic. Allied airpower covered progressively wider areas and aerial attacks became lethally effective. There were sufficient escort vessels to spare some for dedicated "hunter-killer" groups and the Allies had won the electronic battle with better radar and sonar.

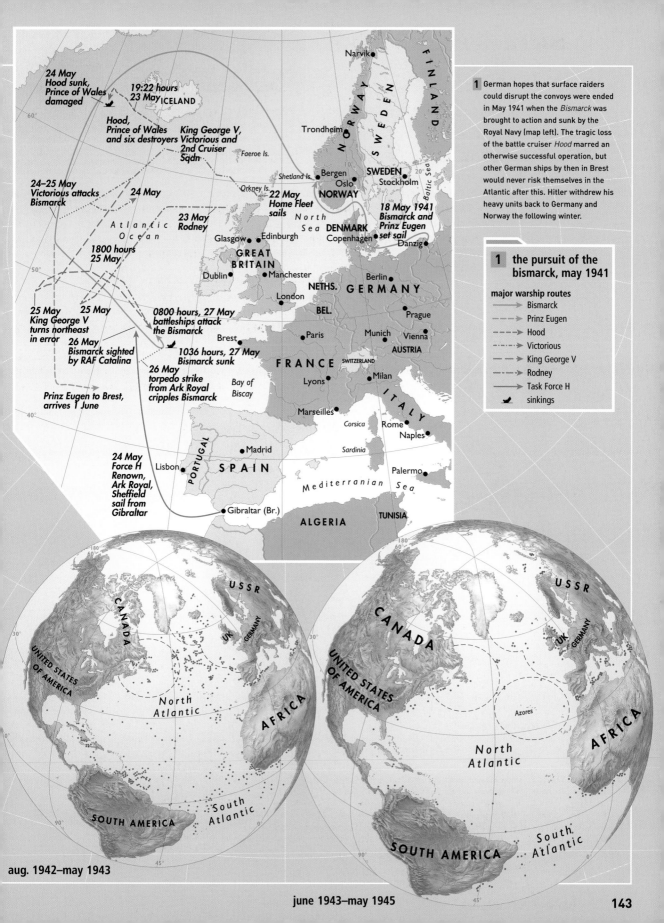

24 May
Hood sunk,
Prince of Wales
damaged

19:22 hours
23 May ICELAND

Hood,
Prince of Wales
and six destroyers

King George V,
Victorious and
2nd Cruiser
Sqdn

24–25 May
Victorious attacks
Bismarck

24 May

23 May
Rodney

Atlantic
Ocean

1800 hours
25 May

25 May
King George V
turns northeast
in error

25 May

26 May
Bismarck sighted
by RAF Catalina

0800 hours, 27 May
battleships attack
the Bismarck

Brest

1036 hours, 27 May
Bismarck sunk

26 May
torpedo strike
from Ark Royal
cripples Bismarck

Prinz Eugen to Brest,
arrives 1 June

Bay of
Biscay

24 May
Force H
Renown,
Ark Royal,
Sheffield
sail from
Gibraltar

Lisbon

Gibraltar (Br.)

Narvik

Trondheim

Bergen
Oslo

SWEDEN
Stockholm

Shetland Is.

NORWAY

Faeroe Is.

Orkney Is.

22 May
Home Fleet
sails

North
Sea

18 May 1941
Bismarck and
Prinz Eugen
set sail

FINLAND

SWEDEN

Baltic Sea

DENMARK
Copenhagen

Danzig

Glasgow
Edinburgh

GREAT
BRITAIN

Dublin
Manchester

NETHS.
London
BEL.

Berlin

GERMANY

Prague

Paris
Munich

Vienna
AUSTRIA

FRANCE
SWITZERLAND

Lyons
Milan

ITALY

Marseilles

Corsica
Rome
Naples

Madrid

PORTUGAL
SPAIN

Sardinia

Mediterranean Sea

Palermo

ALGERIA
TUNISIA

1 German hopes that surface raiders could disrupt the convoys were ended in May 1941 when the *Bismarck* was brought to action and sunk by the Royal Navy (map left). The tragic loss of the battle cruiser *Hood* marred an otherwise successful operation, but other German ships by then in Brest would never risk themselves in the Atlantic after this. Hitler withdrew his heavy units back to Germany and Norway the following winter.

1 the pursuit of the
bismarck, may 1941

major warship routes
→ Bismarck
→ Prinz Eugen
→ Hood
→ Victorious
→ King George V
→ Rodney
→ Task Force H
sinkings

CANADA

USSR

UK
GERMANY

UNITED STATES
OF AMERICA

North
Atlantic

AFRICA

SOUTH AMERICA

South
Atlantic

CANADA

USSR

UK
GERMANY

UNITED STATES
OF AMERICA

Azores

North
Atlantic

AFRICA

SOUTH AMERICA

South
Atlantic

aug. 1942–may 1943

june 1943–may 1945

the **war** in **italy**

1943
Operation Husky, main Allied landings on Sicily (10 July); Americans capture Palermo (23 July); Mussolini resigns (25 July); Allies take Messina (17 August); Armistice signed with Italy, Allies land in Calabria (3 September); Allies land at Salerno (9 September); Allied landings at Bari (14 September); 8th Army takes Ortona (28 December)

1944
Allied landing at Anzio (21 January); attack on Monte Cassino begins (15 March); Poles capture Monastery Hill at Monte Cassino (18 May); Allies enter Rome (4 June); Perugia falls to Allies (20 June); 8th Army enters Florence (4 August); 8th Army attacks Gothic line (31 August); Gothic line breached (8 September); Allies reach Forlì (10 November)

1945
Allied offensive in Po Valley (14 April); German armies in Italy surrender (2 May)

The Italian campaign of 1943–45 was the direct result of the Allied victory in North Africa. The invasion of Sicily—bigger than D-Day the following year—was the next step and was seen as required to open the Mediterranean to shipping.

Churchill advocated the invasion of Italy as providing a way into the "soft underbelly" of occupied Europe. This was opposed by the U.S., which saw it as a diversion of resources away from the coming climactic invasion of France. In the end, the Italian campaign emerged as a strategic compromise. The way it was treated reflected greatly on decision making within democracies and between democracies, issues in modern-era strategy that Clausewitz never foresaw.

The Italian campaign proved highly frustrating. It was marked by the hard-fought Salerno invasion and repeated attacks on fortified German positions, most notably that of Monte Cassino. The largest attempt to use Allied amphibious mobility capabilities, the Anzio invasion, failed due to Allied tactical deficiencies. The skilled German defensive tactics and the Italian terrain and weather made sure that the Allies had great difficulty applying the advantages of their superiority in numbers, material, and air power. Indeed, the secondary status of the Italian front made sure this superiority would be limited. It demonstrated how a low-investment strategy, such as that waged by the Germans through most of the campaign, can use operational and tactical skills to negate a stronger opponent.

British interest in the "soft underbelly" applied also to the Balkans. There, the Yugoslav partisan movement represented the largest national rising of the conflict. However, its lack of equipment and preoccupation with establishing post-war political control meant that the Germans were able to keep the lid on the Balkans with a minimum-force, minimum-cost approach. It was the advance of the Soviet army in 1944 that finally forced the German withdrawal, allowing Greece and Yugoslavia to get on with internal conflicts.

2 The Italian Navy (chart right) was thrown into the scales against the Allies in June 1940. It suffered a damaging air attack at Taranto in November 1940 and was constantly harassed by British submarines, surface ships, and aircraft. By 1943 two-thirds of Italian shipping had been sunk.

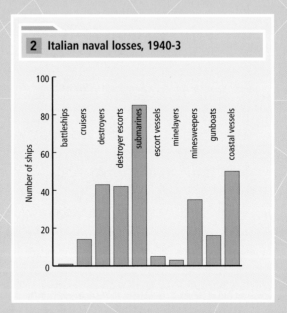

2 Italian naval losses, 1940-3

Number of ships — battleships, cruisers, destroyers, destroyer escorts, submarines, escort vessels, minelayers, minesweepers, gunboats, coastal vessels

SWITZERLAND

ARMY GROUP C (KESSELRING/VIETINGHOFF)

Alpine line

advance to cut Brenner Pass road

...ce to clear ... and Turin

Milan

...crossed using Fantails and Duplex drive tanks

14TH ARMY (LEMELSEN)

Verona

Venice

...rin

10TH ARMY

Po

Adige (Venetian) line

...g. 8 extra divisions (4 from Russian front) designated for defense of Gothic line

76TH PANZER CORPS

...RIA ARMY (...AZZIANI)

Genoa

ARMY GROUP SOUTHWEST (KESSELRING)

1ST AIRBORNE CORPS

Modena

...crossed by marine boat squadron 9 Apr. 1945

Genghis Khan line

51ST AIRBORNE CORPS

14TH PANZER CORPS

27 Oct. 1944

Gothic line

Jan.– Mar. 1945 front line

LIGURIAN SEA

25 Aug.

19 July

2ND & 4TH CORPS

2ND CORPS

Pisa

Florence

5TH, 10TH & 13TH CORPS

8TH ARMY (McCREERY)

Ancona

19 July 1944

15TH ARMY GROUP (CLARK)

A D R I A T I C

...Aug. German forces blow up all but one bridge in Florence and withdraw to N. bank of Arno

5TH ARMY (TRUSCOTT)

Arno

10TH ARMY

51ST MTN CORPS

21 June 1944

14TH PANZER CORPS

76TH CORPS

10TH CORPS

13TH CORPS

2ND CORPS

1ST CORPS

1ST AIRBORNE CORPS

13TH CORPS

20 June 1944

FRENCH EXP. CORPS

Trasimene line

Tiber

5 June 1944

4TH CORPS

Viterbo line

5 June 1944

13TH CORPS

5 June 1944

Ortona

X 20–28 Dec. 1943

R. Sangro 27 Nov.–2 Dec. 1943

Rome

4 June 1944

76TH CORPS

5TH CORPS

1ST AIRBORNE CORPS

14TH PANZER CORPS

13TH CORPS

X Monte Cassino 24 Jan.–18 May 1944

Anzio 21 Jan. 1944

Gustav line

8TH ARMY (MONTGOMERY)

6TH CORPS

15 Jan. 1944

10TH CORPS

2ND CORPS

Bari 14 Sept. 1943

25 Sept. 1943

6TH CORPS (LUCAS)

Napoli (Naples)

U.S. 5TH ARMY (CLARK)

Taranto

9 Sept. 1943

10TH CORPS (McCREERY)

Salerno 9–16 Sept. 1943

15 Sept. 1943

U.S. 5TH ARMY (CLARK)

6TH CORPS (DAWLEY)

13 Sept. 1943

T Y R R H E N I A N

8 Sept. 1943

10 Sept. 1943

14TH PANZER CORPS (HUBE)

I O N I A N

S E A

San Stefano line 23 July 1943

San Frantello line

Messina 17 Aug. 1943

SEA

Palermo

14TH PANZER CORPS (HUBE)

16 Aug. 1943

S E A

6TH ARMY (GUZZONI)

11 July 1943

13 July 1943

10 July 1943

10 July 1943

7TH ARMY (PATTON)

15TH ARMY GROUP (ALEXANDER)

10 July 1943

1 italy, 1943–45

Allied advance

Allied fronts

Axis fronts

battle

U.S.

British

Canadian

Polish

German

Italian

1 The "soft underbelly" of the Axis proved nothing of the sort once the Germans occupied Italy after the Italian surrender in September 1943. Allied amphibious assaults at Salerno and Anzio failed to break the deadlock as fierce German counter-attacks and lackluster Allied leadership confined the invasion forces to their beachheads. Both sides believed they were forcing the enemy to devote disproportionate resources to the Italian campaign.

the **german retreat** in **russia**

1943 to 1944

- **February 1943**
  Russians take Kursk (8th), Rostov (14th), Kharkov (16th)

- **March 1943**
  Germans retake Kharkov (15th)

- **July 1943**
  largest tank battle in history at Kursk (12th)

- **August 1943**
  Russians take Orel (5th), Kharkov (23rd)

- **September 1943**
  Germans begin evacuation of Ukraine (7th); Russians take Smolensk (25th)

- **November 1943**
  Russians take Kiev (6th)

Despite Stalingrad, as 1943 opened the Germans could point to a number of battlefield successes that could suggest—especially to Hitler but also to senior military commanders—that Germany could regain the offensive initiative. These successes included the halting of a number of Soviet attacks in front of Moscow. One major offensive, Operation Mars, went so poorly that it was retrospectively downgraded to a diversion for Stalingrad. More important was General von Manstein's halting of the Soviet advance that threatened to capitalize on their victory at Stalingrad, one of the best-executed maneuver defenses of the war. In the battles in the Donetz basin and around Kharkov in January–February, Manstein restored stability to the front.

The Germans decided in the summer of 1943 that they would restart the Blitzkrieg by cutting off the Soviet-held salient near Kursk. This time, there was no operational surprise. The Germans delayed the opening of the offensive until July, bringing up new Tiger and Panther tanks, but this gave the Soviets time to dig in their defensive forces—with improved tactics learned over the past two years—and carefully plan the commitment of armored reserves.

In the resulting week-long climax of the Battle of Kursk, the Blitzkrieg, for the first time in summer, was stopped. It was unable to penetrate into the depths of the Soviet forces as it had in previous years. Where the Germans bludgeoned their way through defensive belts, Soviet tank counter-attacks—most notably at Prokhorovka—stopped them.

The Soviets immediately went over to the offensive, which they continued through the summer and autumn. Kiev was liberated and, as winter set in, bridgeheads were pushed over the Dnieper. Manstein tried to recreate his successes of the previous winter but failed; his forces were much weaker, the Soviets stronger and more adept. The Soviet war machine was no longer a struggling giant.

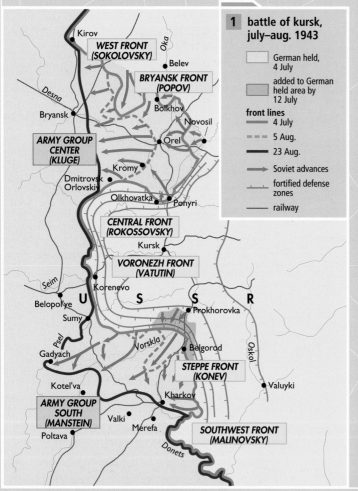

1 battle of kursk, july–aug. 1943

- German held, 4 July
- added to German held area by 12 July

front lines
- 4 July
- 5 Aug.
- 23 Aug.
- Soviet advances
- fortified defense zones
- railway

1 The Red Army had never yet succeeded in stopping a full-scale German summer attack short of the strategic depths. With good intelligence of German intentions, the Russians fortified the Kursk salient and, optimistically, prepared offensives of their own to take place once they had absorbed the German blow (map left). The blunting of the German offensive was duly followed by a Soviet onslaught that liberated Orel and ultimately most of the Ukraine.

2 The collapse of German ambitions in the Caucasus and the loss of the Sixth Army at Stalingrad was followed by a Soviet offensive that briefly recaptured Kharkov (map right). By spring 1943 the Germans had recovered and the army high command urged a third summer offensive in Russia, this time aimed at the Kursk salient.

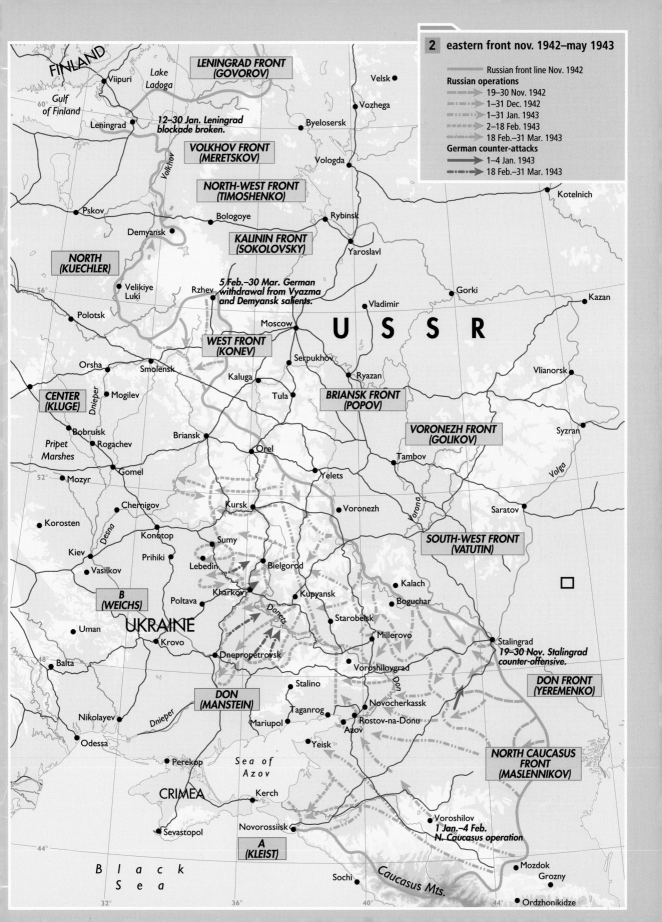

FINLAND

Gulf of Finland

Lake Ladoga

LENINGRAD FRONT (GOVOROV)

Viipuri

Leningrad

12–30 Jan. Leningrad blockade broken.

Velsk

Vozhega

Byelosersk

VOLKHOV FRONT (MERETSKOV)

Vologda

NORTH-WEST FRONT (TIMOSHENKO)

Pskov

Bologoye

Rybinsk

Kotelnich

Demyansk

KALININ FRONT (SOKOLOVSKY)

Yaroslavl

NORTH (KUECHLER)

Velikiye Luki

Rzhev

5 Feb.–30 Mar. German withdrawal from Vyazma and Demyansk salients.

Gorki

Vladimir

Kazan

Polotsk

U S S R

Orsha

Smolensk

Moscow

Serpukhov

Vlianorsk

Mogilev

WEST FRONT (KONEV)

Kaluga

Ryazan

Syzran

Dnieper

Bobruisk

Tula

BRIANSK FRONT (POPOV)

CENTER (KLUGE)

Rogachev

Briansk

VORONEZH FRONT (GOLIKOV)

Pripet Marshes

Gomel

Orel

Tambov

Mozyr

Yelets

Volga

Chernigov

Kursk

Voronezh

Saratov

Korosten

Konotop

Sumy

SOUTH-WEST FRONT (VATUTIN)

Kiev

Prihiki

Lebedin

Bielgorod

Vasilkov

Kharkov

Kupyansk

Kalach

B (WEICHS)

Poltava

Donets

Starobelsk

Boguchar

UKRAINE

Uman

Krovo

Millerovo

Stalingrad

Dnepropetrovsk

19–30 Nov. Stalingrad counter-offensive.

Balta

Voroshiloygrad

Don

DON FRONT (YEREMENKO)

DON (MANSTEIN)

Stalino

Novocherkassk

Nikolayev

Dnieper

Taganrog

Rostov-na-Donu

Mariupol

Azov

Odessa

Yeisk

NORTH CAUCASUS FRONT (MASLENNIKOV)

Perekop

Sea of Azov

CRIMEA

Kerch

Voroshilov

1 Jan.–4 Feb. N. Caucasus operation

Sevastopol

Novorossiisk

A (KLEIST)

B l a c k S e a

Sochi

Caucasus Mts.

Mozdok

Grozny

Ordzhonikidze

the **normandy** landings

1944

June 1944
D-Day landings (6th); all Normandy landing zones linked up (12th); Americans capture Cherbourg (27th)

July 1944
Caen falls to Allies (9th); Operation Goodwood begun by Allies (18th)

August 1944
Nantes falls to Allies (6th); Operation Anvil/Dragoon begins, Allied 7th Army invades southern France (15th); Canadians surround Falaise (16th); Allies liberate Paris (25th); Marseilles and Toulon fall to Allies (28th); British 1st Army reaches Amiens (31st)

September 1944
Dieppe and Rouen fall to Allies (1st); Antwerp and Brussels liberated (3rd–4th); U.S. 1st Army enters Germany (12th); Operation **Market Garden** ends in destruction of Allied airborne forces (17th–25th); Calais surrenders (28th)

October 1944
Germans surrender Aachen (21st)

November 1944
U.S. 3rd Army crosses Moselle (9th); French take Strasbourg (24th)

December 1944
Battle of the Bulge begins (16th); U.S. 3rd Army relieves Bastogne (26th)

The D-Day landings were a triumph of planning and organization, with follow-up support including two artificial harbors to be towed across the English Channel and an underwater pipeline. Air superiority was assured; only two German fighters made it over the beachhead on D-Day.

The execution was less than smooth. On Omaha, one of the U.S. beaches, reinforced German defenses threatened to halt the invasion until resolute U.S. infantry action took them inland. Opposition on the other beaches, while strong, was less and yet despite, the dropping of three divisions of paratroops, the invasion force was unable to seize its first day's objectives, most significantly the city of Caen. Taking it would now require many weeks of hard fighting.

The subsequent Normandy campaign ashore was bitter and frustrating, with the German Army demonstrating its defensive tactics, honed in the east, among the hedgerows. The Allies had planned the invasion itself splendidly, but had left the key operational issue of how to win the battle of Normandy to improvisation.

When the breakout from Normandy finally came, the Allies missed the chance of encircling the German forces opposing them. The manpower, if not their equipment, escaped through the Falaise Gap. As the Allies pursued, liberating much of France, logistics now became the great determinant. The Allies seized ports such as Antwerp (through a long campaign for the Schelde estuary) and Marseilles (through the invasion of southern France), but lines of communication became seriously stretched and it was a great tribute to Allied logistics capability that they did not break.

A last grab at victory in the west in 1944 came in September, with Operation Market Garden. Three airborne divisions, seizing key bridges, would open a highway across the Rhine for a British armored corps. Hastily improvised, the plan failed when the Germans defeated the British airborne bridgehead at Arnhem.

Bitter fighting on the German frontier at Aachen, the Hürtgen Forest, in Lorraine and Alsace showed that the logistical limitations of the rapid advance and stiffening of German resistance meant there was still much hard fighting ahead.

1 The greatest amphibious invasion in history, the Normandy landings were preceded by a successful deception campaign that diverted major German forces to the defense of the Calais area. The initial beachhead was not as deep as anticipated, but German counter-attacks were too little and too late to drive the invaders into the sea. The ensuing battle of attrition in the Normandy bocage could have only one ending (map right).

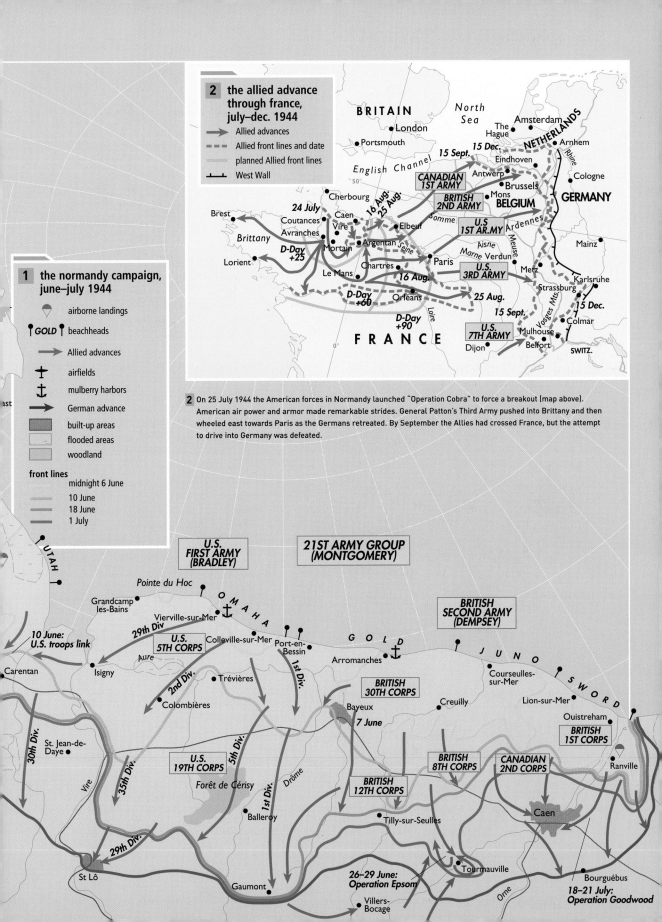

the **german defeat** in the **east**

1944 to 1945

January 1944
Leningrad relieved after 900-day siege

May 1944
Russians capture Sevastopol

June 1944
Russian offensive in Belorussia; Dnieper crossed (27 June)

August 1944
Russians take Bucharest

January 1945
Russians take Warsaw (17th), liberate Auschwitz (26th)

April 1945
Russians take Vienna (7th–13th), enter Berlin (23rd). U.S. 1st Army and Russian patrols meet at Torgau (26th)

May 1945
battle for Berlin ends (2nd); Russians occupy Prague (9th)

The 1944 fighting in the east saw the Germans driven from the banks of the Dnieper to the Oder River in front of Berlin.

Winter and spring offensives by the Soviets liberated the Ukraine and raised the three-year siege of Leningrad. The most significant of the many Soviet offensives that rippled from north to south in June–August was Operation Bagration, which effectively destroyed the German Army Group Center in the salient it was holding at Hitler's insistence, pushing the Germans out of Belorussia and to the banks of the Vistula.

The Soviets next looked to clear their flanks, attacking to clear the Ukraine and then, as Romania and Bulgaria changed sides, into the Balkans. In the north, the surviving German forces were pushed into the Courland Peninsula as the Soviets advanced into East Prussia. Finland switched sides: only Hungary would be made to fight to the end. Repeated offensives against the German center then followed: the hammer blows of the Vistula–Oder operation, and the assault on East Prussia. By February 1945, the Soviets were on the Oder.

The Soviets were now short of manpower due to massive losses, but their industrial production—with Western aid—increased while that of their opponents weakened. Never as tactically adept as the Germans, the Soviets were able to prevail by mastering the operational level of war. The great breakthroughs of 1944 were made possible not by overwhelming numbers but by massing force at the decisive spot, an approach made possible by intelligence and deception.

The war in the east was on a massive scale. Battles in which the Soviets suffered hundreds of thousands of casualties were simply never discussed, lost in the "noise" of the clash not only of armies but also of ideologies. The Soviets had realized since 1941 that the Germans' racial ideology meant that defeat would lead to utter collapse, preventing Germany from using the national and political fissures in the Soviet Union against Moscow. Now, the Soviets made sure of the political consolidation of the areas they occupied.

Germany's ability to shift and reorganize troops, along with the breathing space provided by the failure of Market Garden and the need to clear ports and build up supplies, gave Hitler the chance for a last counter-attack in the west. This, along with the V1 and V2 missile attacks, was seen as having given Germany a chance for successes that might divide the Allies.

The resulting offensive, the Battle of the Bulge, achieved some early success, but was soon halted and forced back. Allied offensive operations continued and, with the weather and logistics situations improving, they resumed the offensive. In the spring, a final drive over the Rhine led to resistance crumbling. By 1945, the Western Allies and the Soviet Union had widely differing military forces that represented widely different solutions to the problem of waging modern industrial war. These forces not only gained the final victory in the Second World War but shaped those that followed over subsequent decades.

The Soviets continued to attack, in Hungary (site of the last German counter-offensive at Lake Balaton in March 1945), East Prussia, Silesia, Yugoslavia, and Czechoslovakia, driving to Vienna by April. But the main Soviet goal was planning and bringing up supplies for the final drive across the Oder to Berlin. This opened in April and, after strong early resistance, the German defenses gave way. Berlin was encircled and then reduced, Hitler committing suicide. Soviet spearheads moved west.

The Soviets met U.S. forces on the Elbe, but already the political landscape was being set for another conflict of a different type. Civil wars were in progress in Greece and Yugoslavia. Germany was divided into what would, in the following decade, emerge as the western Federal Republic and eastern Democratic Republic.

PORTUGAL

SPAI

40

Nov. 1942

30

1 Hitler's failure to defeat Britain by bombing and the Atlantic submarine campaign, coupled with the reverse of German fortunes at Stalingrad, left Germany fighting a two-front war (map right). While the German Army in the east was worn down by Soviet forces in a series of gigantic battles, Anglo–American armies invaded North Africa in 1942, Italy in 1943, and France in 1944. Western air forces undermined the German war effort through bombing, while partisans and resistance movements challenged German occupation. The Allies' insistence on unconditional surrender was never to be tested by a credible peace offer from Germany. The minority of military officers opposed to Hitler fantasized that they could make a separate peace with the Western powers, but none of their assassination plans worked. In consequence, the German Army resisted to the end, fighting with diabolical efficiency until 1945.

1 the defeat of germany

- ▭ Grossdeutches Reich, 1942
- ⟵ Axis attacks
- ⟵ --- Axis withdrawals
- ⟵ Allied attacks
- ☁ major cities under heavy air attack
- ✶ major battle, with date
- ✊ partisan/resistance movements
- ● commando raids
- ╲ V1 launching sites
- ◣ V2 launching sites
- ···· frontiers, 1942

UNION OF SOVIET SOCIALIST REPUBLICS

Kirkenes
Petsamo
1944
Murmansk
1944
1944
1944
1944
1944

Archangel

Shetland Is.
Orkney Is.

NORWAY
1940–45

Oslo

SWEDEN

FINLAND

Lake Ladoga
1944
1944
Helsinki
Leningrad
Narva
1941–42
Novgorod

Stockholm

Gorkiy
Volga

North Sea

Copenhagen
Flensburg
1940–45
Lübeck
Hamburg
Bremen
HOLLAND
Sept. 1944
Hanover
Arnhem

Baltic Sea

Memel
Riga
ESTONIA
LATVIA
LITHUANIA
Feb.–Apr. 1945
Königsberg
Kaunas
E. PRUSSIA
1944
Białystok
June–Aug. 1944
Minsk
1943–44

Velikiye Luki
Vyazma
Smolensk
Mogilev
Bryansk
Gomel
July–Aug. 1943

Rzhev
Dec. 1941
Moscow
1942–43
Tula
1941–42
Orel
Kursk
Don
Voronezh
Saratov
Volga

GREAT BRITAIN
London
June–July 1944
Rotterdam
Calais
Antwerp
BEL.
Brussels
Dieppe
Dec. 1944
St. Lô
Caen
Rheims
Cherbourg

ENGLAND

1944–45
Düsseldorf
Cologne
GERMANY
Berlin
May 1945
Torgau
Dresden
Frankfurt
Prague
May 1945
Mannheim
Stuttgart
Munich

Stettin
Oder
POLAND
Vistula
Warsaw
Jan. 1945
1941–44
Lemberg
Tarnopol

Kiev
Nov.–Dec. 1943
Dnieper
1942–43
UKRAINE
Stalino
Krivoy Rog
1942–43

Kharkov
Stalingrad
Nov. 1942–Feb. 1943
Rostov
1942–43

Paris
1944

FRANCE
1942–44
Nazaire

Metz
Rhine

Lyon
VICHY FRANCE
1943–45
Marseilles
Toulon
Aug. 1944

SWITZERLAND
Linz
Vienna
Apr. 1945
Danube
ALPS
Milan
Po
1944–45
Genoa
Livorno
Rimini
Florence
ITALY
Zara
Jan.–Mar. 1944

AUSTRIA
Budapest
1944–45
HUNGARY
Zagreb
1945
CROATIA
Belgrade
SERBIA
1941–45
Sarajevo
Danube
1941–45

SLOVAKIA
1944
Debrecen
Dniester
Jassy
Transnistria
Prut
Odessa
ROMANIA
Ploești
Bucharest
Danube
Sofia
BULGARIA
1944

Sevastopol
Crimea
Yalta
Kerch
Caucasus

Black Sea

Batum

Corsica
Rome taken June 1944
Anzio
Cassino
Naples
Salerno
Sept. 1943
Jan.–Mar. 1944
Bari
Taranto
Kotor
MONTENEGRO
ALBANIA
1944

Istanbul
Ankara

TURKEY

SYRIA

Balearic Is.

Sardinia

July 1943

Nov. 1942

Messina
Sicily
1943
July 1943
Pantelleria
Malta

Salonika
GREECE
1941–45
Oct. 1944
Athens
Aegean Sea
Leros
Kos
Rhodes
Crete
1941–45
Cyprus

LEBANON

1942
Nov. 1942
Algiers
Bougie
Bizerta
Tunis
April–May 1943
Feb.–May 1943

ALGERIA
TUNISIA
Tripoli

Mediterranean Sea

PALESTINE
TRANS/JORDAN

LIBYA
Benghazi
Cyrenaica
Jan.–June 1942
El Agheila
EGYPT
July–Sept. 1942
Tobruk
Bardia
23 Oct. 1942 British offensive
El Alamein
Alexandria
Cairo

war in the pacific

December 1941
Japanese bomb Pearl Harbor (7th); Japanese land in Siam and Malaysia (8th); Japanese land on Luzon (10th), in North Borneo (17th); Hong Kong falls to Japanese (25th)

1942
Japanese occupy Manila (2 January); Japanese take Kuala Lumpur (11 January); Japanese land in Solomon Is. (26 January); British surrender Singapore (15 February); Japanese invade Bali (19 February); Battle of Java Sea (27 February); Japanese land on Dutch New Guinea (1 April); Battle of the Coral Sea (4–8 May); Battle of Midway (4 June), 4 Japanese carriers sunk; U.S. Marines land on Guadalcanal (7 August)

The opening stages of the Second World War in the Pacific demonstrated many of the themes seen throughout the era: resource war, anti-imperialism, surprise, intelligence, transoceanic warfare (largely unique to this theater on such a massive scale), and the rise of air warfare.

The origins of the conflict included the demands of industrial-age material war. Japan needed the resources of Southeast Asia to generate and sustain the forces needed to prevail in its war against China, let alone implement its larger expansionist goals. Japan's shortage of currency, Allied action, and U.S. embargoes had cut off access to these resources.

Despite its own repressive occupations of Korea and China, Japan sought to legitimize its actions in anti-imperialist terms, and indeed Western rule in Asia never recovered from the military defeats Japan inflicted on it in the first six months of the war in the Pacific. The late modern-era "barbarization of warfare" was also apparent in Japanese treatment of Asians and Allied prisoners of war alike.

The importance of surprise in late modern warfare was seldom better demonstrated than in the Japanese attack on Pearl Harbor: "the day that will live in infamy," 7 December 1941. Japan's leaders had counted on the initial, surprise-generated success to provide six months of victory, and then they would dig in and hold their defensive perimeter, the Greater East Asia Co-Prosperity Sphere. Only when the "victory disease" led them to attack outside the perimeter was their advance decisively halted at the battles of the Coral Sea and Midway. U.S. intelligence failure made possible the Japanese success at Pearl Harbor as much as intelligence success was responsible for the later victories.

The geography of the Pacific meant that navies would be the primary war-fighting assets, but the opening months of the war soon reinforced that aircraft—land- or, more importantly, carrier-based—made naval movement possible. Coral Sea and Midway were the first fleet actions in which opposing surface warships never sighted each other, relying on aircraft to attack and for much of their defense as well.

2 | **battle of midway, 0400–0830 hours 4 June 1942**

✈ U.S. air and naval forces

✈ Japanese air and naval forces

2 Japan's run of victories came to an abrupt halt in June 1942 when all four fleet carriers escorting the Midway Island invasion force were sunk in action with the U.S. Navy (maps below). U.S. signals intelligence provided timely warning, while Japanese overconfidence led them to disperse their superior forces.

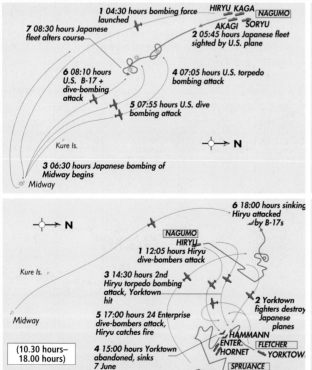

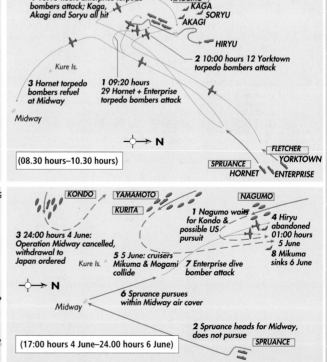

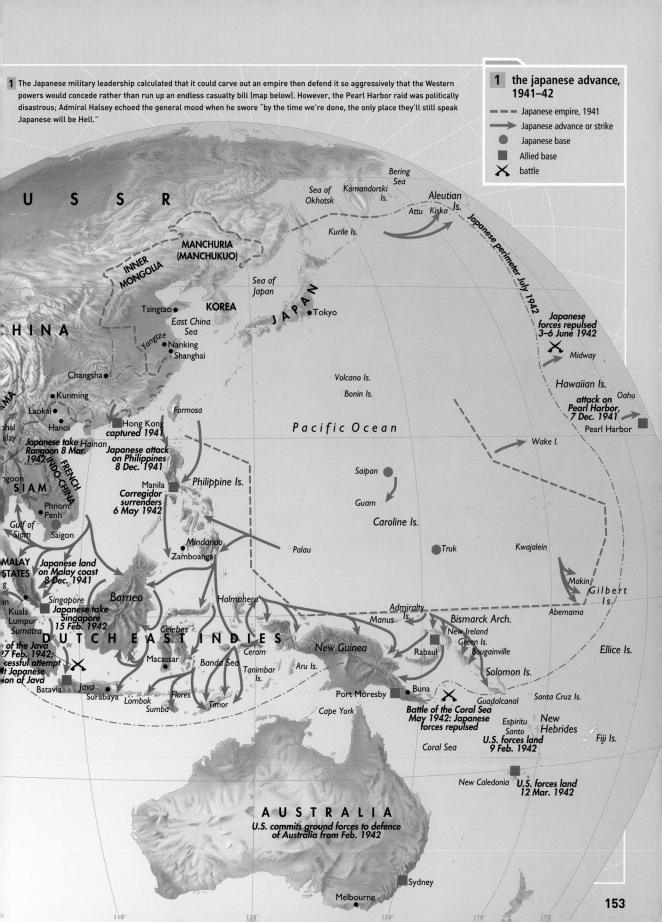

1 The Japanese military leadership calculated that it could carve out an empire then defend it so aggressively that the Western powers would concede rather than run up an endless casualty bill (map below). However, the Pearl Harbor raid was politically disastrous; Admiral Halsey echoed the general mood when he swore "by the time we're done, the only place they'll still speak Japanese will be Hell."

1 the japanese advance, 1941–42

- – – – Japanese empire, 1941
- → Japanese advance or strike
- ● Japanese base
- ■ Allied base
- ✕ battle

U S S R

MANCHURIA (MANCHUKUO)

INNER MONGOLIA

Bering Sea

Sea of Okhotsk

Komandorski Is.

Aleutian Is.

Attu Kiska

Kurile Is.

Japanese perimeter July 1942

CHINA

Sea of Japan

KOREA

Tsingtao

East China Sea

JAPAN

Tokyo

Yangtze
Nanking
Shanghai

Changsha

Kunming

Laokai

Hanoi

Formosa

Hong Kong captured 1941

Japanese take Hainan Rangoon 8 Mar. 1942

Japanese attack on Philippines 8 Dec. 1941

FRENCH INDO-CHINA

SIAM

Phnom Penh

Gulf of Siam

Saigon

Manila
Corregidor surrenders 6 May 1942

Philippine Is.

Volcano Is.

Bonin Is.

Pacific Ocean

Japanese forces repulsed 3–6 June 1942

Midway

Hawaiian Is.

attack on Pearl Harbor, 7 Dec. 1941

Oahu

Pearl Harbor

Wake I.

Saipan

Guam

Caroline Is.

Truk

Kwajalein

Makin

Gilbert Is.

Abemama

MALAY STATES

Japanese land on Malay coast 8 Dec. 1941

Kuala Lumpur

Singapore
Japanese take Singapore 15 Feb. 1942

Borneo

Sumatra

of the Java 27 Feb. 1942; cessful attempt t Japanese ion of Java

Batavia

Java

Surabaya

Lombok

Sumba

Flores

Celebes

Macassar

Ceram

Banda Sea

Tanimbar Is.

Timor

Mindanao
Zamboanga

Palau

Halmahera

Admiralty Is.
Manus

New Guinea

Aru Is.

Port Moresby

Buna

Battle of the Coral Sea May 1942: Japanese forces repulsed

Cape York

Coral Sea

DUTCH EAST INDIES

Bismarck Arch.

New Ireland Green Is.

Rabaul

Bougainville

Solomon Is.

Guadalcanal

Santa Cruz Is.

Ellice Is.

Espiritu Santo

New Hebrides

Fiji Is.

U.S. forces land 9 Feb. 1942

New Caledonia

U.S. forces land 12 Mar. 1942

A U S T R A L I A
U.S. commits ground forces to defence of Australia from Feb. 1942

Sydney

Melbourne

110°   130°   150°   170°   170°

153

burma and malaysia

1942
Japanese enter Rangoon (8 March); Japanese cut Burma Road (29 April); British and Indian forces advance into Burma (21 December)

1943
first Chindit raids (8 February); Japanese occupy Maungdaw (14 May); Burma–Siam "Death Railway" completed (25 October)

1944
British recapture Maungdaw (9 January); Japanese offensive in Arakan starts (4 February); Japanese attacks on Imphal and Kohima defeated after long siege (4 Apr.–22 June); last Japanese resistance in India ends (16 August); Allies take Kalewa (24 December)

1945
Burma Road reopened (22 January); Japanese evacuate Mandalay (19 March); Allies capture Rangoon (3 May); Japanese surrender in Burma signed (13 September)

2 The British 14th Army absorbed the Japanese 1944 offensive at Imphal and Kohima, then launched the most brilliantly conducted offensive conducted by Commonwealth forces in the war (map far right). The Japanese were wrong-footed by the British advance, and the long overdue employment of substantial air and armored forces in Burma. The race was on to take Rangoon before the monsoon rains turned the roads to liquid mud.

1 The Burma campaign followed the Japanese occupation of French Indochina (despite the authorities' loyalty to the Vichy regime) and their entry into Thailand (map right). The Japanese leadership toyed with an invasion of India, and formed a nationalist Indian army, but by the time the Imphal–Kohima offensive began, Japan was losing the war in the Pacific.

The Japanese advance into Burma in 1942 represented, like the advance into New Guinea at the other end of their would-be empire, a continuation of the offensive tidal wave. The Japanese were able to overcome the initial British resistance of the 1942 campaign.

Their victory was assured, despite British reinforcement and even in the absence of strategic surprise, given Japanese air superiority and the tactical superiority of an army experienced in China and in hard training against second-line garrison forces. A major naval raid into the Indian Ocean made an invasion of India appear imminent.

But the mountains and jungles of the Northeast Frontier of India proved an effective barrier, along with Japanese logistics limitations. The Burma front was a low priority for resource allocation on both sides. The British rebuilt their forces and attempted several limited offensives, with varying degrees of success. The Japanese tactical superiority was only slowly countered, through a combination of training a new, predominantly Indian army for the liberation of Burma and the capabilities provided by new technologies, most notably air resupply. This made possible the Chindit operations behind Japanese lines.

These operations led to the Japanese allocating resources—brought forward over the infamous Burma Railway, built across Thailand by prisoners—to a 1944 offensive into India. This was stopped at Imphal and Kohima and, going over to the offensive, the British then liberated Burma in a lengthy campaign that, in its use of both operational maneuver and logistics, was one of the most astutely conducted of the conflict. Just as early modern conflict could be waged in remote areas that had acquired strategic value, late modern conflict in these areas was made possible, but only by substantial investments in logistics and adaptation of forces and tactics developed for Europe. The need to adapt to land warfare in Asia would confront all the world's major powers in the years after 1945. Few, if any, would do so as well as the forces that liberated Burma.

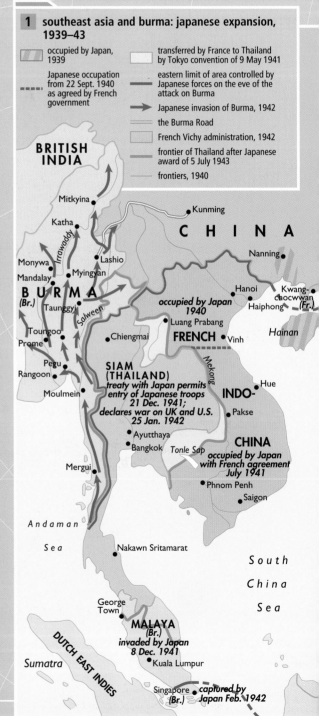

1 southeast asia and burma: japanese expansion, 1939–43

- occupied by Japan, 1939
- Japanese occupation from 22 Sept. 1940 as agreed by French government
- transferred by France to Thailand by Tokyo convention of 9 May 1941
- eastern limit of area controlled by Japanese forces on the eve of the attack on Burma
- Japanese invasion of Burma, 1942
- the Burma Road
- French Vichy administration, 1942
- frontier of Thailand after Japanese award of 5 July 1943
- frontiers, 1940

BRITISH INDIA

CHINA

Mitkyina
Katha
Kunming
Irrawaddy
Monywa
Lashio
Nanning
Mandalay
Myingyan
Hanoi
Kwang-chocwwan (Fr.)
BURMA (Br.)
Taunggyi
occupied by Japan 1940
Haiphong
Salween
Toungoo
Luang Prabang
FRENCH
Vinh
Hainan
Prome
Chiengmai
Pegu
Mekong
Rangoon
SIAM (THAILAND)
treaty with Japan permits entry of Japanese troops 21 Dec. 1941; declares war on UK and U.S. 25 Jan. 1942
INDO-
Hue
Moulmein
Pakse
Ayutthaya
Bangkok
Tonle Sap
CHINA
occupied by Japan with French agreement July 1941
Mergui
Phnom Penh
Saigon
Andaman Sea
Nakawn Sritamarat
South China Sea
George Town
MALAYA (Br.)
invaded by Japan 8 Dec. 1941
Sumatra
DUTCH EAST INDIES
Kuala Lumpur
Singapore (Br.)
captured by Japan Feb. 1942

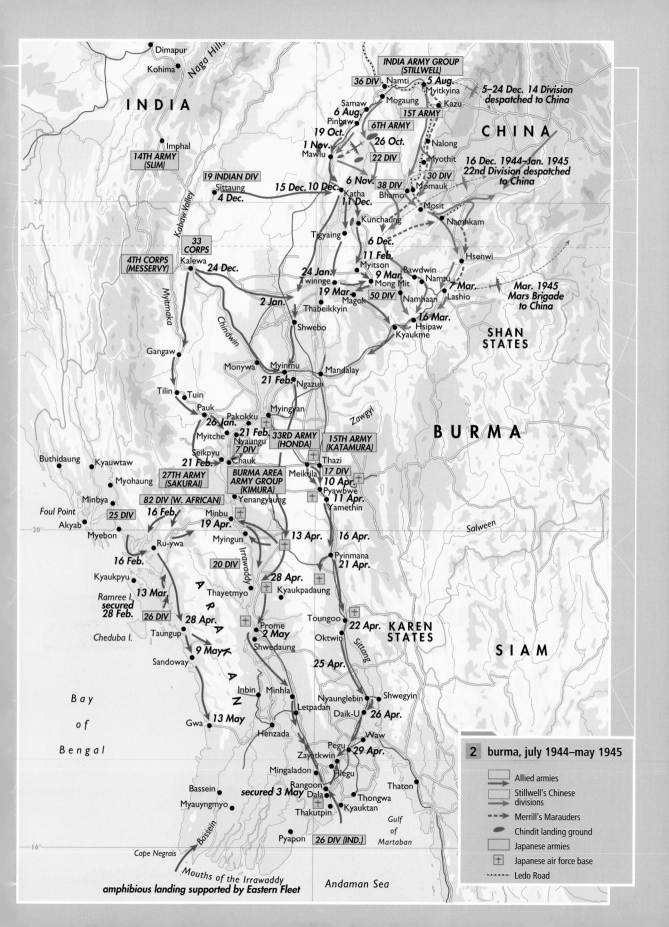

Dimapur

Kohima

Naga Hills

INDIA

Imphal

14TH ARMY
(SLIM)

19 INDIAN DIV

Sittaung

4 Dec.

Kabaw Valley

Kalewa

33
CORPS

4TH CORPS
(MESSERVY)

24 Dec.

Myittaka

Chindwin

Gangaw

Tilin   Tuin

Pauk

26 Jan.

Myitche

Seikpyu

21 Feb.

Buthidaung

Kyauwtaw

Myohaung

Minbya

Foul Point

Akyab

Myebon

16 Feb.

Kyaukpyu

13 Mar.

Ramree I.
secured
28 Feb.

26 DIV

Cheduba I.

Taungup

9 May

Sandoway

Bay

of

Bengal

Bassein

Myauyngmyo

Cape Negrais

Mouths of the Irrawaddy

INDIA ARMY GROUP
(STILLWELL)

36 DIV   Namti   5 Aug.

Samaw   Mogaung   Myitkyina   Kazu

6 Aug.   1ST ARMY

Pinbaw   6TH ARMY

19 Oct.   26 Oct.

1 Nov.   22 DIV

Mawlu

6 Nov.

38 DIV   30 DIV

15 Dec. 10 Dec.   Katha   Bhamo   Momauk

4 Dec.   11 Dec.   Mosit

Kunchaung

Tigyaing   6 Dec.   Namhkam

11 Feb.

24 Jan.   Myitson   Bawdwin   Hsenwi

Twinnge   9 Mar.   Namtu

2 Jan.   19 Mar.   Mong Mit   7 Mar.

Thabeikkyin   Magok   50 DIV   Namhaan   Lashio

Shwebo   Kyaukme   Hsipaw

16 Mar.

Monywa   Myinmu   SHAN
STATES

21 Feb.   Ngazun   Mandalay

Zawgyi

Myingyan

BURMA

Pakokku

21 Feb.   33RD ARMY
(HONDA)   15TH ARMY
(KATAMURA)

Nyaungu   7 DIV   Thazi

Chauk   17 DIV

27TH ARMY
(SAKURAI)   BURMA AREA
ARMY GROUP
(KIMURA)   Meiktila   10 Apr.
Pyawbwe

82 DIV (W. AFRICAN)   Yenangyaung   11 Apr.
Yamethin

25 DIV   Minbu

16 Feb.   19 Apr.

Ru-ywa   Myingun   13 Apr.   16 Apr.

20 DIV   Pyinmana
21 Apr.

Thayetmyo

28 Apr.

Kyaukpadaung

A   Toungoo   22 Apr.   KAREN
STATES

R   Prome   Oktwin

A   2 May
Shwedaung

K   25 Apr.

A

N   Inbin   Minhla

Z   Nyaunglebin   Shwegyin

13 May   Letpadan   Daik-U   26 Apr.

Henzada   Pegu   Waw

Zayatkwin   29 Apr.

Mingaladon   Hlegu

secured 3 May   Rangoon

Dala   Thongwa   Thaton

Thakutpin   Kyauktan

Pyapon   26 DIV (IND.)   Gulf
of
Martaban

amphibious landing supported by Eastern Fleet   Andaman Sea

CHINA

5–24 Dec. 14 Division
despatched to China

Nalong

Myothit

16 Dec. 1944–Jan. 1945
22nd Division despatched
to China

Mar. 1945
Mars Brigade
to China

Salween

SIAM

Bassein

2   burma, july 1944–may 1945

→   Allied armies

→   Stillwell's Chinese
divisions

⇢   Merrill's Marauders

⬭   Chindit landing ground

☐   Japanese armies

✠   Japanese air force base

⋯   Ledo Road

victory in the pacific

1942
Japanese driven back on Guadalcanal (21 August); Battle of Cape Esperance off Guadalcanal (11–12 October); Kokoda taken by Australians (2 November)

1943
Allies take Buna (2 January); Japanese evacuate Guadalcanal (1–19 February); Battle of Bismarck Sea (2–5 March); U.S. Marines land on Bougainville (1 November)

1944
U.S. Marines land on Saipan (15 June); Japanese wiped out on Saipan (7 July); Allies land on Guam (21 July); U.S. troops land in Leyte Gulf (20 October); First B-29 raid on Tokyo (24 November); Japanese resistance on Leyte ends (22 December)

1945
U.S. landings on Luzon (9 January); Battle of Iwo Jima (19 February–26 March); Corregidor captured (28 February); U.S. lands on Okinawa (1 April); end of resistance on Okinawa (22 June); Japanese agree to unconditional surrender terms (14 August)

The U.S. counter-offensive against Japan started with the invasion of Guadalcanal in August 1942. It came to its conclusion with the end of resistance on Okinawa almost three years later. The bitter fighting of the island-to-island advance, bypassing many major centers of resistance such as Truk and Rabaul, was made possible by massive naval battles: those of the Guadalcanal campaign, the Philippine Sea, and Leyte Gulf. The Japanese capability to wage war was directly attacked by the U.S. submarine offensive and, starting in 1944, strategic bombing.

2 Many armies talk about fighting to the last man and last cartridge, but only the Japanese army has done so consistently. Island garrisons often resorted to bayonet charges in the face of overwhelming U.S. firepower, survivors preferring suicide to surrender. On Iwo Jima they dug extensive tunnel networks, holding out inside Mount Suribachi long after the U.S. flag was famously planted on the summit (map right).

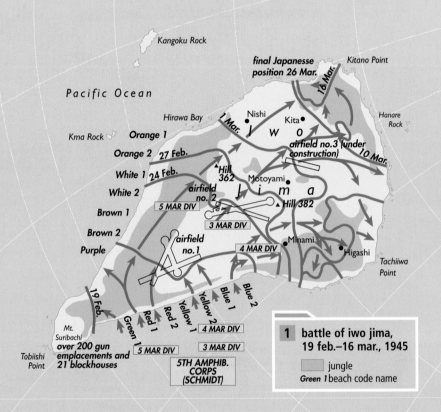

1 battle of iwo jima, 19 feb.–16 mar., 1945

jungle

Green 1 beach code name

The U.S. offensive required mastering modern amphibious operations, a type of warfare seen as obsolete after Gallipoli. It required unprecedented investment in logistics, to be able to sustain forces at sea or in distant jungles. All this was made possible by the U.S.'s industrial potential and the adaptability of its military and war-fighting institutions. The U.S. was able to overwhelm Japan with only a fraction of its total capability. From the carrier task forces to the base-building bulldozers, it was all an immense triumph of organization, and the levels of strategy, operations, and tactics were high enough to make sure it was effectively applied.

Savage resistance and the introduction of large-scale kamikaze suicide attacks marked the last battle of the Pacific war on Okinawa. It became obvious that, despite U.S. control of the air and sea, an invasion of Japan would likely require many months of intense close-quarters combat. The Soviet invasion of Manchuria and the U.S. use of the atomic bomb finally led to the Japanese surrender.

The bomb was certainly the most dramatic example of the technology and industrial strength that gained the victory in the Pacific. The fact that it had to be used at all also underlined the limits of that sort of strength, even against less well-equipped and -supplied but highly resolute enemies. War termination also was shown to be a key element of effective war-fighting. It is no longer enough to win, but necessary to do so without paying the cost associated with total victory.

The U.S. forces had a choice of routes to Japan. General MacArthur wished to liberate the Philippines, advancing via the Solomons and New Guinea; the U.S. Navy preferred an "island-hopping" strategy aimed directly across the Pacific. In the event, the U.S. had the resources to do both (map below). While these plans unfolded, Japan maintained a substantial field army in Manchuria. Some 750,000 troops remained there until 1945 when the Soviet army demolished the Japanese defenses in a week.

U S S R

Soviet army attacks 9 Aug. 1945

Bering Sea

Sea of Okhotsk

Kamchatka

Komandorski Is.

Attu Aleutian Is.
Kiska Amchitka

17 Aug. 1945

Kurile Is.

10 Oct. 1943

May–Aug. 1943

Japanese perimeter Mar. 1944

MANCHURIA (MANCHUKUO)

Khabarovsk

Hokkaido

INNER MONGOLIA
Peking

Tientsin Dairen

Seoul

KOREA

Fusan

Sea of Japan

JAPAN

Tokyo

Hiroshima
6 Aug. 1945

fighters sweep over Japan from May 1945

Pacific Ocean

Midway

ese advance into
a after Oct. 1943
ese offensive into
India Feb.–June 1944
h offensive into
a after Nov. 1944
oon retaken May 1945

C H I N A

East China Sea

Nanking
Shanghai

Nagasaki
9 Aug. 1945

Shikoku

Kyushu

Japanese perimeter Oct. 1944

1944 Japanese bombing raids from June 1944

Chinese counter-offensive Apr.– June 1945

Ichi-Go Offensive

Amoy

Okinawa

Formosa

direct air attack on Japan from Okinawa from May 1945

Bonin Is.

Volcano Is.

Iwo Jima
Feb.–Mar. 1945

20th Air Force begins direct air attack on Japan from 24 Nov. 1944–14 Aug. 1945

Hawaiin Is.

Oahu
Pearl Harbor

Kunming

Laokai
Hanoi

Canton

Hong Kong

Hainan

Gulf of Tongking

Luzon
landings Jan. 1945

Philippine Is.

Manila

Battle of Philippine Sea. Japanese carrier aviation annihilated June 1944

Wake I.

ndalay

FRENCH INDO-CHINA

SIAM

goon

Bangkok

om Penh

Saigon

Gulf of Siam

25 Oct. 1944
Battle of Leyte Gulf. Heavy Japanese naval losses

Leyte

Leyte landing 20 Oct. 1944

Mindanao
May 1945

Zamboanga

Sulu Sea

Palau
Sept. 1944

Marianas
Saipan
June 1944

Tinian

Guam
July 1944

Ulithi
Sept. 1944

Caroline Is.

Truk

Eniwetok
Feb. 1944

Marshall Is.

Kwajalein
Feb. 1944

Majuro
Jan. 1944

Pacific Ocean area forces

MALAY STATES

Kuala Lumpur

Singapore

BRUNEI
June 1945

SARAWAK

Tarakan
May 1945

Borneo

Sumatra

D U T C H   E A S T   I N D I E S
July 1945

Palembang

Bandjarmasin

Batavia
Java Surabaya

Macassar

Celebes

Amboina

Lombok

Sumba

Banda Sea

Timor

Morotai
Sept. 1944

Halmahera

Noemfoor
July 1944

Sansapur
July 1944 Sorong

Biak
May 1944

Ceram

Aru Is.

Tanimbar Is.

Flores

Timor Sea

Darwin

Manus
Feb. 1944

Admiralty Is.

Bismarck Arch.

Hollandia

Wewak

New Guinea

Saidor
Jan. 1944

Cape York

Buna

Port Moresby

New Ireland

Rabaul

Bougainville
Nov. 1943

Solomon Is.

Tulagi

Guadalcanal
7 Aug. 1942–
9 Feb. 1943

17–25 Sep. 1942
Japanese ground forces repulsed

Coral Sea

Makin

Gilbert Is.
Tarawa Nov. 1943

Abemama

Ellice Is.

Battle of Santa Cruz Oct. 1942
Eastern Solomons Aug. 1942
Japanese forces repulsed

South Pacific area forces

Espiritu Santo

Fiji Is.

New Hebrides

Japanese perimeter Aug. 1945

New Caledonia

A U S T R A L I A

1   the allied counter-offensive

→	Allied advance	●	Japanese base
✈	Allied air attack	◉	Japanese base bypassed or neutralized
■	Allied base		
✸	atomic bomb target	✕	battle

Japanese perimeters

········· March 1944

–·–·– October 1944

––––– August 1945

Sydney

Melbourne

the **chinese civil war**

1947 to 1949

1927
purge of Communists in Shanghai and other cities

1934
"The Long March" of the Communists to Shansi; Mao Tse-tung emerges as communist leader

1947
civil war between Communists and Nationalists erupts; Nationalists capture Yenan (1947); Communist offensive in Manchuria (summer)

1948
Communists capture Jinzhou (October), thereby controlling most of Manchuria; Huai-Huai battle in central China, 500,000 Nationalist troops defeated (November–December)

1949
Peking falls to Communists (January); Shanghai falls to Communists (May); Communists capture Guangzhou (October); People's Republic of China proclaimed (October); Chiang flees to Taiwan (December)

How wars are fought in a world with nuclear weapons was demonstrated in two Asian conflicts within five years of Hiroshima. Insurgencies (as exemplified by the Chinese Civil War) and limited wars (exemplified by Korea, set a pattern repeated many times—though seldom with such intensity—up to 1991.

The Chinese Civil War that erupted in the 1940s had its roots in the overthrow of the Manchu emperors in 1911. A period of turmoil ensued in which Chinese political forces struggled to found a post-imperial state that could command widespread allegiance. The task was almost impossible and China fragmented into a number of military dictatorships. Between 1925 and 1937 Chiang Kai-shek and his Kuomintang movement suppressed most of the warlords' power bases and brought the majority of China under one central control. In the early phases of this process the Kuomintang worked hand-in-hand with the fledgling Chinese Communist Party, but in 1927 the Communist cells in the major cities were destroyed. Mao Tse-tung kept resistance alive in the province of Kiangsi, and when Chiang's forces attacked there in 1934, the fragments of the Chinese Communist Party trekked 6,000 miles to the northern province of Shansi.

Following the Japanese establishment of the puppet state of Manchukuo in the north in 1932, the priority became resistance to the Japanese, whilst still consolidating local power bases. But after the war with Japan ended in 1945, a full-scale civil war broke out between the Communists and Nationalists. Initially successful, Chiang thought he could smash Mao's cadres. But the Communists could rely on a powerful reservoir of support amongst the peasantry and their army swelled in number. Communist tactics relied on holding off attacks by the larger Nationalist armies in the south, whilst picking off Kuomintang units in Manchuria and the north. Once this northern flank had fallen, by autumn 1948, the Communists pushed southwards, winning battle after battle and taking Peking itself in January 1949.

By September 1949 the Nationalist cause had all but collapsed. The loss of Guangzhou in October 1949 left only southwest China in Nationalist hands. The hopelessness of the situation precipitated the flight of Chiang to Taiwan, which the Nationalists succeeded in holding, and from where the Kuomintang continued to claim to be the legitimate government of China.

The Chinese Civil War represented the implementation of the Maoist paradigm of insurgency. Starting with a Leninist cadre in arms, it culminated (after 1945) with conventional warfare. It presented a way to challenge the West where it was weakest, where its colonial empires were either receding or struggling to hang on. Against insurgency, neither nuclear weapons, nor air power nor, the technological warfare evolved from the two world wars could present an effective barrier.

1 After the defeat of Japan, the Chinese Nationalists and the Chinese Communists competed for the administration of the liberated areas. The Communists dominated Manchuria and the north. In 1947 full-scale civil war broke out between the two sides. Nationalist armies were defeated in Manchuria in 1948, and at Suchow from November 1948 to January 1949. In October 1949 a Communist republic was proclaimed and in May 1950 the Nationalist remnants fled to Taiwan. The Maoist prescription for revolutionary warfare began with small-scale guerrilla action and culminated in full-scale conventional warfare. Communist movements would try to put this model into operation all over the world, but few would be as successful as Mao Tse-tung.

1 **communist victory in the civil war, 1946–49**

occupied by Communist armies at outbreak of civil war
occupied July 1946–June 1948
occupied July 1948–June 1949
occupied by 1950
Communist guerrilla operations 1945–49
→ Communist forces advance
Apr. 1946 date of capture by Communists
★ battles, with date

place names in brackets are Pinyin forms adopted after 1949

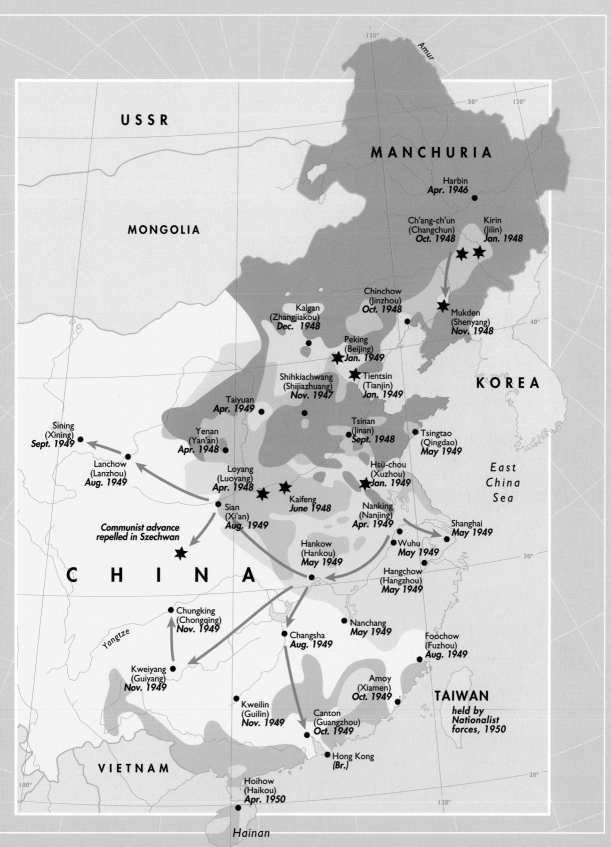

USSR

MONGOLIA

MANCHURIA

Harbin
Apr. 1946

Ch'ang-ch'un
(Changchun)
Oct. 1948

Kirin
(Jilin)
Jan. 1948

Chinchow
(Jinzhou)
Oct. 1948

Mukden
(Shenyang)
Nov. 1948

Kalgan
(Zhangjiakou)
Dec. 1948

Peking
(Beijing)
Jan. 1949

KOREA

Shihkiachwang
(Shijiazhuang)
Nov. 1947

Tientsin
(Tianjin)
Jan. 1949

Taiyuan
Apr. 1949

Tsinan
(Jinan)
Sept. 1948

Tsingtao
(Qingdao)
May 1949

Sining
(Xining)
Sept. 1949

Yenan
(Yan'an)
Apr. 1948

*East
China
Sea*

Lanchow
(Lanzhou)
Aug. 1949

Loyang
(Luoyang)
Apr. 1948

Kaifeng
June 1948

Hsü-chou
(Xuzhou)
Jan. 1949

Sian
(Xi'an)
Aug. 1949

Nanking
(Nanjing)
Apr. 1949

Shanghai
May 1949

**Communist advance
repelled in Szechwan**

Hankow
(Hankou)
May 1949

Wuhu
May 1949

Hangchow
(Hangzhou)
May 1949

C H I N A

Chungking
(Chongqing)
Nov. 1949

Changsha
Aug. 1949

Nanchang
May 1949

Foochow
(Fuzhou)
Aug. 1949

Yangtze

Kweiyang
(Guiyang)
Nov. 1949

Amoy
(Xiamen)
Oct. 1949

TAIWAN

*held by
Nationalist
forces, 1950*

Kweilin
(Guilin)
Nov. 1949

Canton
(Guangzhou)
Oct. 1949

VIETNAM

Hong Kong
(Br.)

Hoihow
(Haikou)
Apr. 1950

Hainan

Amur

1949 to **1953**

1945
Korea divided into U.S. and Soviet occupation zones, split along 38th parallel

1950
North Korean army invades South Korea (25 June); North Koreans capture Seoul (29 June); U.S. ground forces ordered into Korea (30 June); Battle of Taejon forces U.S. retreat (22 July); Pusan perimeter established (4 August); UN counterattack fails (13 August); UN forces land at Inchon (15 September); UN forces attack and capture Seoul (19–26 September); UN forces cross 38th parallel (1 October); Chinese forces cross into Korea (14 October); UN forces capture Pyongyang (20 October); Chinese attacks at Chosin force UN retreat (11 December)

1951
Chinese capture Seoul (4 January); renewed UN offensive (25 January); UN reaches point between 37th and 38th parallels (1 March); UN retakes Seoul (14 March); British 1st Battalion Gloucester Regiment annihalated at "Gloucester Hill" (23–25 April); UN forces take Heartbreak Ridge following 18-day battle (23 September); truce talks begin at Panmunjom (27 November)

1953
Battle of Pork Chop Hill (18 April); peace talks resume (26 April); renewed Communist offensive (14 June); cease-fire signed (27 July)

The war in Korea was made possible by the Communist victory in the Chinese Civil War. While its roots were in long-suppressed Korean nationalism, the lasting impact of the Korean War was to define the Communist threat to the West primarily in military terms, of tanks rolling across borders, rather than the internal penetration that had threatened Europe (and claimed Czechoslovakia) in 1945–48.

Korea was also a proxy war. It was how the two nuclear-armed superpowers fought. In addition to providing the majority of Communist air power, the Soviet Union provided the material support that allowed the Chinese and the North Koreans to be sustained on the battlefield.

Militarily, the initial North Korean invasion conquered most of the peninsula. Forced back to the Pusan perimeter, U.S. and UN reinforcements were able to counter-attack. They were aided by the Inchon landings, deep behind Communist lines, one of the few brilliant operational strokes of the war. The over-optimistic UN offensive had, within a few months, overrun most of North Korea until it too was defeated in a massive Chinese intervention. The Chinese pushed south until they, like the North Koreans before them, outran their logistics and were pushed back. Then, by mid-1951, static warfare and truce talks dominated the remainder of the conflict.

Militarily, Korea led to the United States emphasizing nuclear deterrence rather than conventional war-fighting capability. Most pronounced in the late 1950s, it still had not been undone when the next U.S. land war in Asia, in Vietnam, started in the 1960s.

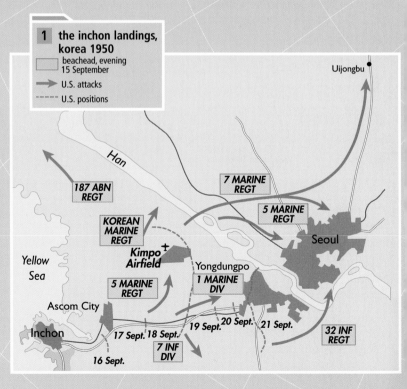

1 the inchon landings, korea 1950
- beachead, evening 15 September
- ➤ U.S. attacks
- - - U.S. positions

1 U.S. naval supremacy enabled General MacArthur to outflank the Communist forces by an amphibious landing at Inchon. The following month, airborne and amphibious assaults seized new bridgeheads in the north, compelling the enemy to withdraw towards the Chinese border (map above).

2 the korean war

2 The Korean War carried the Cold War to the Far East. Occupied in 1945 by Soviet and American forces, the country was already divided *de facto* by 1948 (map right). In 1950, after the withdrawal of the occupying armies, the North Koreans attacked the South. The United States and United Nations immediately intervened. After initial North Korean successes, the Americans under General MacArthur counter-attacked and advanced to the Chinese frontier. This resulted in Chinese intervention and stalemate, ended only by the armistice of Panmunjom and the partition of the country along the 38th parallel.

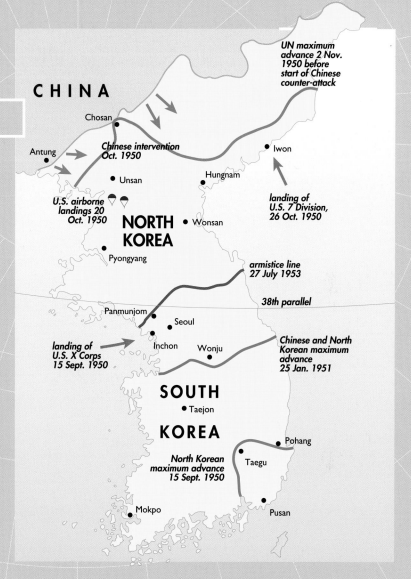

CHINA

UN maximum advance 2 Nov. 1950 before start of Chinese counter-attack

Chosan

Antung

Chinese intervention Oct. 1950

Iwon

Unsan

Hungnam

U.S. airborne landings 20 Oct. 1950

NORTH KOREA

Wonsan

landing of U.S. 7 Division, 26 Oct. 1950

Pyongyang

armistice line 27 July 1953

38th parallel

Panmunjom

Seoul

landing of U.S. X Corps 15 Sept. 1950

Inchon

Wonju

Chinese and North Korean maximum advance 25 Jan. 1951

SOUTH

Taejon

KOREA

Pohang

North Korean maximum advance 15 Sept. 1950

Taegu

Mokpo

Pusan

1948
Malayan Emergency begins with insurrection by Malayan Communist Party (MCP)

1949
France grants limited independence to Vietnam, Laos, and Cambodia

1950
China and USSR recognise Ho Chi Minh's Communists as legitimate government of Vietnam; Vietminh launch offensive against French (September); in Malaya, :Briggs Plan" resettles villagers away from Communist-controlled areas

1952
French operation near Nghia Lo fails to draw Vietminh into full-scale battle

1954
the Viet Minh decisively defeat the French at Battle of Dien Bien Phu; French surrender 7 May; Geneva accords divides Vietnam into North and South (July); last French troops leave Hanoi (October)

1957
Malaya becomes independent (31 August)

1960
Malayan government declares Emergency over

Just as the end of wars causes new wars, so does the end of empires. The British gave up India without a conflict, but the Netherlands' colonial empire ended only after a lengthy war of independence.

The course of post-imperial Asia was shown in the outcome of two insurgencies. In French Indo-china, in 1945–54, the Vietminh, with the benefits of extensive Chinese aid, were eventually able to implement the Maoist example, starting as guerrillas linking nationalism with Leninism. In 1953–54, they were able decisively to defeat the French in a conventional battle at Dien Bien Phu. In Malaya, in 1948–60, the British defeated an insurgency aiming at the same result. The

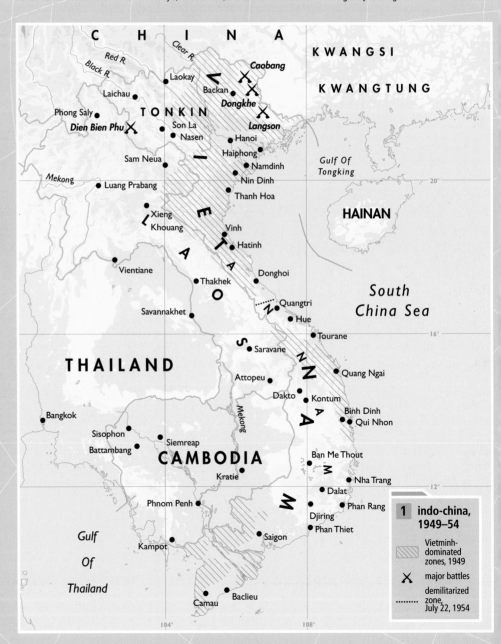

1 France clung to her colonial empire, but with Chinese military aid, the Communist revolutionaries dominated the north of the country and much of the Mekong Delta (map right). The French government shrank from sending conscripts to Indochina, relying mainly on her colonial regiments and the Foreign Legion.

1 indo-china, 1949–54

⬚ Vietminh-dominated zones, 1949

✕ major battles

⋯⋯ demilitarized zone, July 22, 1954

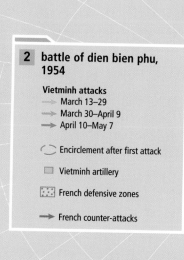

2 battle of dien bien phu, 1954

Vietminh attacks
⟶ March 13–29
⟶ March 30–April 9
⟶ April 10–May 7

◡ Encirclement after first attack

▢ Vietminh artillery

▨ French defensive zones

⟶ French counter-attacks

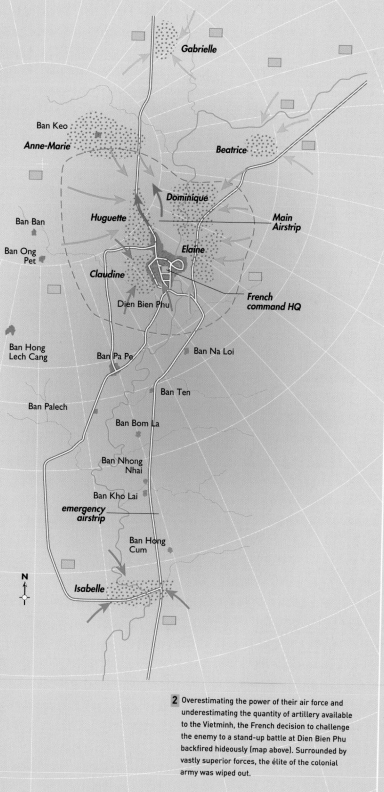

Gabrielle

Ban Keo

Anne-Marie

Beatrice

Dominique

Main Airstrip

Ban Ban

Huguette

Elaine

Ban Ong Pet

Claudine

French command HQ

Dien Bien Phu

Ban Hong Lech Cang

Ban Pa Pe

Ban Na Loi

Ban Ten

Ban Palech

Ban Bom La

Ban Nhong Nhai

Ban Kho Lai

emergency airstrip

Ban Hong Cum

N

Isabelle

British implemented what became the paradigm of effective counter-insurgency, a slow, primarily political process, with military action aimed principally at permitting the evolution of legitimate indigenous institutions. They were able to help defend these against a later, more conventional military challenge in the confrontation with Indonesia in Borneo in the early 1960s.

In Malaya, the guerrillas could claim neither foreign arms nor the banner of nationalism. Two Communist insurgencies in the Philippines were also defeated despite that country's political weakness.

The component countries of the British Indian Empire opened their independence with mass slaughter and "transfer of populations." India and Pakistan have clashed in three limited, conventional wars: in 1948 and 1965, over the disputed state of Kashmir; and in 1971, which led to the creation of Bangladesh. India lost a brief border conflict with China in 1962. India has also, in recent years, been involved in substantial internal security operations including, in the 1980s, one in the island nation of Sri Lanka, which, as in Burma, has ongoing ethnic insurgencies. Now, with India and Pakistan both nuclear-armed and the Kashmir issue unresolved, the future of conflict in Asia is likely to make all that has occurred since 1945 seem tame and safe.

2 Overestimating the power of their air force and underestimating the quantity of artillery available to the Vietminh, the French decision to challenge the enemy to a stand-up battle at Dien Bien Phu backfired hideously (map above). Surrounded by vastly superior forces, the élite of the colonial army was wiped out.

civil wars in africa

1954–62
War of Algerian Independence

1967–70
civil war in Nigeria against Biafran secession

1975–1992
civil war in Mozambique

1975–91, 1993–2002
Angolan civil wars

1977–78
Ethiopian–Somali War in Ogaden

1989
civil war begins in Liberia

1991
Ethiopian regime of Mengistu overthrown; civil war begins in Sierra Leone

1994
Rwandan genocide

1996–
civil war in Congo–Zaire draws in forces from Rwanda, Uganda, Zimbabwe, and Namibia

Conflict in Africa after 1945 was, at first, aimed at the apparently weakened French empire, leading to risings in Madagascar and Algeria. The French ability to suppress these, plus the counter-insurgency lessons from Indo-china, gave the French confidence that they could retain Algeria as a possession as well as a position of influence with other colonies and protectorates that achieved independence. The resulting war in Algeria, eclipsing the previous French colonial conflicts, led to Algerian independence. The French military was never defeated and was winning on the battlefield until the day it lost the war. Politically, the war brought down the Fourth Republic.

1 Savage civil wars have been fought throughout the Horn of Africa since the 1970s (map right). Military rule came to Somalia in 1970, to Ethiopia in 1974, and to the Sudan in 1969. In Ethiopia the Marxist–Leninist regime of Mengistu Haile Mariam fought a long war against the Eritrean and Tigrean independence movements until his overthrow in 1991, as well as a war with Somalia over the Ogaden region. In 1998–99 Ethiopia fought a war against the newly independent state of Eritrea for control of disputed border areas. By 1999 the central Somali state had effectively ceased to exist, with the northwest breaking away as "Somaliland" and the south divided between competing warlords. Civil war between the Islamic north and Christian south has been endemic in the Sudan since independence.

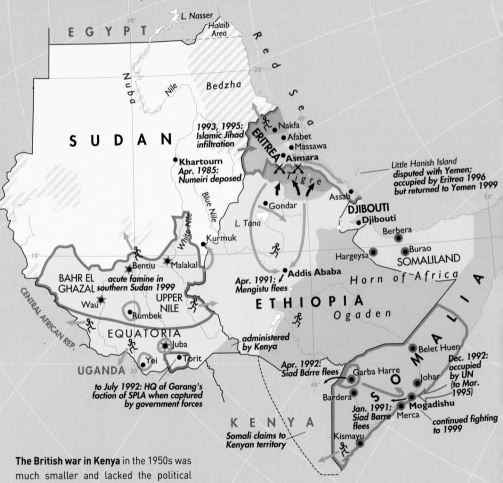

The British war in Kenya in the 1950s was much smaller and lacked the political costs of Algeria. The British successfully applied their counter-insurgency tactics developed in Malaya, helped by the insurgents being a tribal minority and lacking external support. But the war still brought home the need for colonial possessions to achieve independence to prevent future conflicts.

Portuguese efforts to hold on to their three colonies of Guinea, Angola, and Mozambique, starting in the late 1950s, lasted until after the government in Lisbon fell in a left-wing revolution in 1974. The Portuguese had also militarily kept the upper hand, fighting effectively despite their limited resources. The end of these conflicts led to civil wars

2 In 1954, disappointed at failing to win independence for Algeria after the war, Algerian Nationalists set up the Front de Libération Nationale (FLN) and launched a guerrilla war that lasted until 1962 (map right). The French settler community fought back through their own organization, the OAS, which perpetrated atrocities against both Algerians and the French administration. High losses and high costs forced the French hand and independence came on 3 July 1962. The French Army and Algerian rebels had drawn different lessons from the war in Indo-china. Militarily the French succeeded in containing the rebels and even clearing out their urban strongholds, but the political cost was prohibitive.

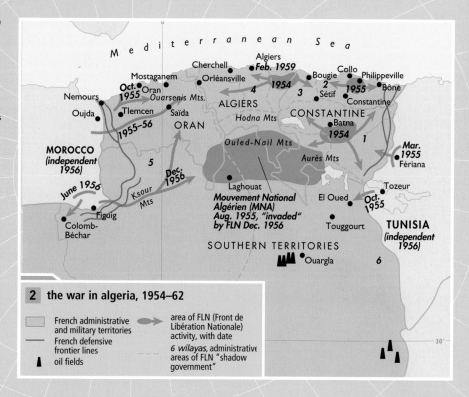

2 the war in algeria, 1954–62

- French administrative and military territories
- French defensive frontier lines
- ▲ oil fields
- ➡ area of FLN (Front de Libération Nationale) activity, with date
- *6 wilayas*, administrative areas of FLN "shadow government"

1 ethiopia, somalia, and sudan, 1985–2003

Ethiopia
- provinces claimed by Somalia, 1977–88
- held by Eritrean People's Liberation Front, 1986
- captured by EPLF by Mar. 1988
- secured by Tigre People's Liberation Front, Apr. 1988
- ➡ government counter-attacks, June 1988
- captured by TPLF, early 1989
- captured by EPLF, Feb. 1990
- ➡ advance of anti-government forces, Apr. 1991
- de facto independent Apr. 1991, independence declared May 1993

Somalia
- controlled by competing tribes, clans and factions from 1989
- Siad Barre's base, Feb. 1991–Apr. 1992
- de facto independent, Mar. 1991
- ➡ Siad Barre's last attempt to regain power, Apr. 1992
- controlled by Aidid, June 1992
- ● areas of most intense fighting

Sudan
- southern Sudan (non-Muslim, non-Arab), limited autonomy from 1972
- non-Arab populations in northern Sudan
- main areas of operation of South Sudan People's Liberation Army from 1984
- ★ under SPLA attack, Aug. 1986
- ➡ SPLA attacks, Nov. 1987 and May 1989
- ◯ areas of intense fighting, 1990
- ---- frontier claimed by Egypt

others
- ✕ Eritrean war, 1998–2000
- 🏃 refugees and refugee movements

between the participants in the liberation struggle (that in Angola was finally ended in 2002; that in Mozambique halted in the early 1990s). They also increased the pressure on Rhodesia and South Africa.

The white governments of Rhodesia (now Zimbabwe) and South Africa, with tactically excellent armed forces, were militarily undefeated but succumbed to inter-national pressure that led to both countries being governed by representatives of their black majority populations.

In the 1990s, Africans have been fighting Africans in much of the continent. These conflicts include the civil conflicts in the former Belgian Congo (leading to an early UN intervention) and Nigeria in the 1960s. Other civil conflicts have been long-running and bloody, often with foreign intervention: Chad, Sierra Leone, Rwanda, Burundi, and Sudan, among many others. More recently, there has been an increasing tendency towards inter-state and well as intrastate conflict in Africa. This is not a new development, but the end of Cold War has led to an increasing willingness on the part of neighboring states to intervene in intrastate conflicts.

the **middle east** from **suez** to **yom kippur**

Arab–Israeli conflict started with the waning of the British mandate in Palestine. The Israeli War of Independence that followed demonstrated that the improvised Israeli Defense Force (IDF) was capable of overcoming the post-imperial armies of its Arab opponents in a low-technology conflict.

The Cold War inevitably invested the Arab–Israeli conflict with a proxy war element. Soviet involvement increased after the 1955 arms deal with Egypt. Israel's pro-western orientation was sealed by its covert alliance with France and Britain to invade Egypt in the 1956 Suez crisis. After the 1967 war, Israel turned increasingly to the U.S. for arms, economic aid and diplomatic support.

By 1967, the IDF was no longer a third-world military force, and U.S. arms increased its already high level of technology. The Israelis seriously studied operations and tactics, resulting in original approaches to low-cost, high-technology warfare.

Starting with the 1967 war, Arab–Israeli confrontations brought about increasing interest in how emerging technologies performed in combat. In 1967, it was the conventional pre-emptive strike, stressing air attacks and armored forces, by Israel that influenced both Soviet and NATO military thinking. In the 1967–73 war of attrition, it was the evolution of an integrated air defense system by Egypt and Syria to counter Israeli air power, a trend also seen in the 1973 war. At that time, the emergence of the anti-tank guided missile seemed to threaten the superiority of Israel's tanks.

2   the yom kippur war, 1973: the golan heights and the suez canal

Golan Heights

— de facto frontiers before the war

— occupied by Israel at the end of the Six Day War, 1967

➤ Arab advances

➤ furthest Arab advance into Israeli territory

➤ Israeli counter-offensives

— Syrian territory held by Israel at cease-fire, 24 October

Suez Canal

occupied by Israel at the end of the Six Day War, 1967

— de facto frontier before the war

➤ Egyptian advances

➤ furthest Egyptian advance into Israeli-held territory

➤ Israeli counter-offensives

Israeli territory held by Egypt at cease-fire, 24 October

Egyptian territory held by Israel at cease-fire, 24 October

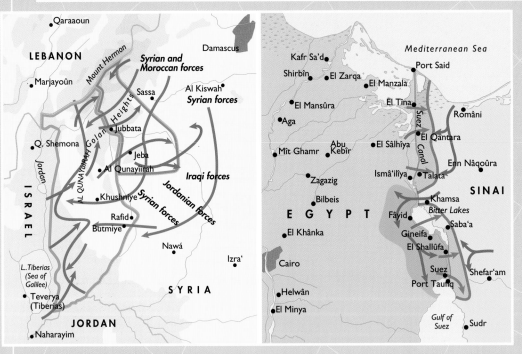

2 In October 1973, Egypt and Syria launched on surprise attack on Israeli-held territory. After initial success, Egyptian forces were surrounded by an Israeli counter-attack. Syria's attempt to recapture the Golan Heights ended in bloody defeat, its masses of Soviet tanks proving no match for the better-trained and more determined Israeli mechanized units (maps left).

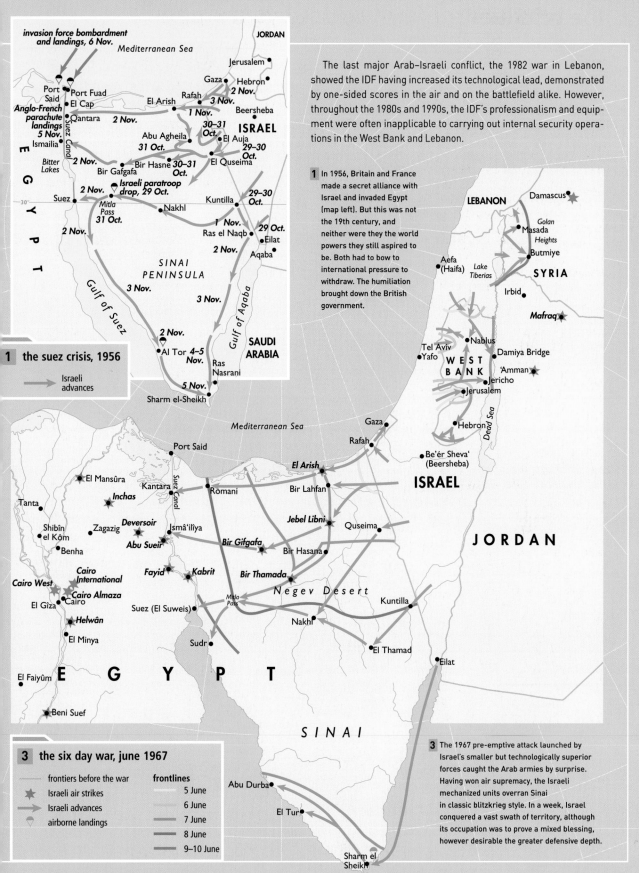

The last major Arab–Israeli conflict, the 1982 war in Lebanon, showed the IDF having increased its technological lead, demonstrated by one-sided scores in the air and on the battlefield alike. However, throughout the 1980s and 1990s, the IDF's professionalism and equipment were often inapplicable to carrying out internal security operations in the West Bank and Lebanon.

1 In 1956, Britain and France made a secret alliance with Israel and invaded Egypt (map left). But this was not the 19th century, and neither were they the world powers they still aspired to be. Both had to bow to international pressure to withdraw. The humiliation brought down the British government.

1 the suez crisis, 1956

→ Israeli advances

invasion force bombardment and landings, 6 Nov.

Mediterranean Sea

JORDAN

Jerusalem
Gaza · Hebron
2 Nov.
Rafah *3 Nov.*
El Arish *1 Nov.*
Beersheba
Port Said · Port Fuad
El Cap
Qantara *2 Nov.*
Anglo-French parachute landings 5 Nov.
Ismailia
Abu Agheila *31 Oct.* · *30–31 Oct.*
ISRAEL
El Auja
Bitter Lakes
2 Nov.
Bir Gafgafa · Bir Hasne *30–31 Oct.*
El Quseima *29–30 Oct.*
2 Nov. **Israeli paratroop drop, 29 Oct.**
Suez *2 Nov.*
Nakhl
Kuntilla *29–30 Oct.*
Mitla Pass *31 Oct.*
1 Nov.
Ras el Naqb *29 Oct.*
2 Nov. Eilat
2 Nov. Aqaba

S I N A I P E N I N S U L A

Gulf of Suez
3 Nov.
3 Nov.
Gulf of Aqaba

SAUDI ARABIA

2 Nov.
Al Tor *4–5 Nov.*
Ras Nasrani
5 Nov.
Sharm el-Sheikh

E G Y P T
30°

---

3 the six day war, june 1967

— frontiers before the war
★ Israeli air strikes
→ Israeli advances
◉ airborne landings

frontlines
5 June
6 June
7 June
8 June
9–10 June

LEBANON · Damascus ★
Golan Masada *Heights*
Butmiye
Aefa (Haifa) · *Lake Tiberias*
S Y R I A
Irbid
Mafraq ★
Tel Aviv Yafo · Nablus
W E S T B A N K
Damiya Bridge
'Amman ★
Jericho
Jerusalem
Hebron
Dead Sea
Gaza
Rafah
Be'ér Sheva' (Beersheba)
ISRAEL

Mediterranean Sea
Port Said
El Mansûra · Kantara
Inchas
Tanta
Deversoir
Shibîn el Kôm · Zagazig · Ismâ'ilîya
Abu Sueir
Benha
Cairo West · Cairo International
Cairo Almaza
El Gîza · Cairo
Helwân
El Minya
El Faiyûm
Beni Suef

Romani
El Arish
Bir Lahfan
Jebel Libni
Quseima
Bir Gifgafa
Bir Hasana
Fayid · Kabrit
Bir Thamada
N e g e v D e s e r t
Suez (El Suweis)
Mitla Pass
Nakhl
Sudr
Kuntilla
El Thamad
Eilat

J O R D A N

E G Y P T
S I N A I

Abu Durba
El Tur
Sharm el Sheikh

3 The 1967 pre-emptive attack launched by Israel's smaller but technologically superior forces caught the Arab armies by surprise. Having won air supremacy, the Israeli mechanized units overran Sinai in classic blitzkrieg style. In a week, Israel conquered a vast swath of territory, although its occupation was to prove a mixed blessing, however desirable the greater defensive depth.

169

the **cold war**

1945 to 1991

1947
the Greek Civil War; Truman Doctrine announced

1948–49
Berlin airlift

1949
NATO formed

1949
Soviet Union detonates first nuclear bomb

1950–53
Korean War

1955
Warsaw Pact formed

1962
Cuban Missile Crisis

1964–75
Vietnam War

1979
Soviet Union invades Afghanistan

1987
INF Treaty; phased elimination of intermediate range nuclear weapons

1991
collapse of USSR

The way the Cold War was waged—without direct military confrontation but always in readiness—put a great emphasis on the balance of forces between the opposing sides. While competition in peacetime between military forces was hardly a new thing, the Cold War placed an unprecedented emphasis on the balance sheet of overall capability of the two principal powers.

The strategic nuclear balance compared the number of nuclear weapons systems that the United States and the Soviet Union could deliver against each other. The U.S. nuclear monopoly ended in 1948, but despite fears first of a "bomber gap," then a "missile gap," the Soviets were outnumbered in both categories well into the 1960s. The emergence of Soviet nuclear parity and then a potential first-strike capability in the SS-18 ICBM (intercontinental ballistic missile) force in the 1970s was one of the reasons the Soviets then thought the "correlation of forces" had shifted in their favor, only to see it swing back in the 1980s.

Crises and confrontations were what marked the course of the Cold War. Events gained importance because of the role of the opposing sides in them. The fears were that "backing down" would cost prestige and position both internationally and domestically, while the danger was, if both sides escalated, some spark could initiate a conflict.

The Berlin airlift of 1948 (when the U.S. and Britain supplied Berlin by air after the Soviets imposed a ground blockade) set the pattern. The willingness of the Western allies to take risks to support the Germans, their enemies of a few years before, paved the way for the integration of West Germany into Western Europe in the following decade and, as the Cold War ended, for German unification.

The Greek Civil War evolved from an internal Greek conflict to a Cold War proxy conflict, the other form for the use of military force in an era of nuclear weapons. First Britain, then, after the 1947 Truman declaration, the U.S., supported the Greek government against Communist guerrillas. The war ended only when Tito's

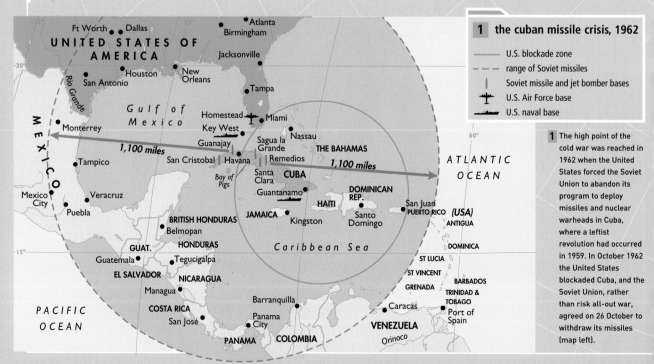

1   the cuban missile crisis, 1962

— U.S. blockade zone
-- range of Soviet missiles
| Soviet missile and jet bomber bases
✈ U.S. Air Force base
⚓ U.S. naval base

1 The high point of the cold war was reached in 1962 when the United States forced the Soviet Union to abandon its program to deploy missiles and nuclear warheads in Cuba, where a leftist revolution had occurred in 1959. In October 1962 the United States blockaded Cuba, and the Soviet Union, rather than risk all-out war, agreed on 26 October to withdraw its missiles (map left).

2 In the decade following the Second World War, much of the world was divided into two armed camps, one based around the Soviet Union and China, as the leading Communist states, the other centered around the United States, the most powerful and economically successful of the Western democracies (map above). Both sides built up military alliance blocs and engaged in a long-term arms race.

2 the cold war

- members of Rio Pact, 1948
- founding members of NATO, 1949
- later NATO members (with date)
- dependencies occupied by NATO members, 1954
- non-NATO members of Baghdad Pact and/or SEATO, 1955
- principal overseas U.S. military bases, (1962)
- principal foreign Soviet military bases
- states and dependencies with defence treaties with, and/or offering military facilities to, NATO, 1962
- Soviet-led Communist camp, 1954
- Warsaw Pact members and allies, 1985
- members of the conference of non-aligned states, 1987
- frontiers, 1987

Yugoslavia split from Moscow and stopped aiding the guerrillas.

The Cuban Missile Crisis of 1962 was generally considered the closest the Cold War came to open hostilities. A Soviet move to deploy intermediate-range missiles to Cuba was reversed when the U.S. imposed a naval "quarantine" and threatened an invasion.

The 1973 crisis was less serious, stemming from the heightened alert status of first the Soviet Union and then, in response, the United States arising from fears of Soviet intervention on behalf of Egypt in the closing stages of the 1973 Arab–Israeli War. Compounding the situation was the U.S. political weakness as the Nixon administration was engulfed in the Watergate scandal, and there was concern that a weak government could not afford to be seen to be "backing down."

1954
Geneva Conference: Laos, Cambodia, and Vietnam become independent states

1957
Communist insurgency in South Vietnam begins

1959–75
War between North and South Vietnam

1964
Gulf of Tonkin incident

1965
Operation Rolling Thunder; first U.S. ground forces arrive in Vietnam

1968
The Tet Offensive

China was not the only area to come under Communist control following the collapse of the Japanese empire in 1945. In Southeast Asia, Vietnam became the focus of communist activity.

In 1946 Vietnamese communists under Ho Chi Minh (the Vietminh) declared a Democratic Republic of Vietnam, but the French were determined to re-impose colonial control. In November 1946, French forces bombarded Ho's capital at Hanoi, killing 6,000 people. The Vietminh launched a guerrilla war against the French, which ended in May 1954 in a spectacular French defeat at Dien Bien Phu. Under agreements reached at Geneva in July 1954, a Communist state was established north of the 17th parallel, and a pro-American regime under Ngo Dinh Diem set up in the south with its capital at Saigon. Diem ignored the Geneva agreement and refused to hold elections in 1956. The North then launched a guerrilla war in 1957, and in 1960, in reaction to the excesses of the Diem dictatorship, the NLF (or Vietcong) was established in the South to work for his overthrow. The Vietcong came to control most of the countryside, and were supplied with arms from the North.

Direct U.S. involvement to shore up the South came in 1964 after North Vietnamese gunboats allegedly fired at U.S. destroyers in the Gulf of Tonkin. The U.S. Congress then passed a resolution that virtually amounted to a declaration of war. The Vietnam War, in which the United States now found itself embroiled, was not the "classic" counter-insurgency of Malaya. Once U.S. land and air forces started to deploy as combat units in 1964, rather than as "advisors" as in the previous decade, their opponents always included the Peoples' Army of Vietnam (PAVN) regulars and the Vietcong main force.

North Vietnam could put and sustain large forces in the field because, as this was a proxy conflict, they were being supported by the Soviet Union and, especially prior to 1970, China. It takes nothing away from the North Vietnamese achievement in providing a logistics system that was able to translate this support into combat power on the ground to see that the North Vietnamese "war economy" was located in the Soviet Union and China. The U.S. bombing campaigns against North Vietnam represented a large percentage of the total U.S. war effort, but it was far from hitting the enemy's Clausewitzian "center of gravity."

The U.S. was able to defeat every North Vietnamese challenge to the pro-Western Republic of Vietnam government in Saigon. The most serious challenge to the southern regime in the early days of U.S. involvement came with the large-scale Tet Offensive at the 1968 lunar new year. Whilst the offensive was crushed and the Vietcong suffered severe losses that left its ranks ever more dependent on reinforcements from North Vietnam, the southern government's internal stability and legitimacy was shown to remain limited and in its turn dependent, if not on U.S. troops, then on air support and aid.

1 indochina, 1966–68

areas of control, early 1966

controlled by the Vietcong

controlled by the government

under Vietcong influence

under government influence

heavily contested area

Tet Offensive, 1968

1 The Vietcong was the indigenous guerrilla movement that threatened to storm South Vietnam before the U.S. Army intervened (map left). It sustained fearsome losses in conventional battles with the U.S. forces and was all but destroyed in the 1968 Tet Offensive. After that, most Vietcong formations were filled out with North Vietnamese soldiers.

2 U.S. intervention in South Vietnam prevented a Communist take-over in the early 1960s, but the guerrilla war that followed remains controversial (map right). The U.S. forces never lost a major battle, but vocal internal opposition to the war persuaded successive presidents to end U.S. involvement. The impact of daily TV coverage, often graphic images not seen in World War II, had a profound influence on public opinion.

CHINA

Nanning

Lao Cai

NORTH VIETNAM

6A
(USAF)

5
(USAF)   Yen Bai   Lang Son

Kep

Dien Bien Phu   Phuc Yen

NORTH   Na San   Hoa Loc   6B
(USN)

Bac Mai   Hanoi   Gia Lam

Hon Gai

LS 85   Dong Song   Kien An   Haiphong

Na Khang   Cat Bi
(LS 36)   **EAST**   4
(USN)   Quang Te

LS 6

LS 32   Bai Thuong   Thanh Hoa Bridge

Luang Prabang   LS 201   Thanh Hoa

Mekong   Quang Lang   3
(USN)

LS 2

Long Tien   **Gulf
of
Tonkin**
(LS 20A)

WEST

Orange AP

Hainan
Island

Red AP

White AP   Vinh
2
(USN)

Vientiane   Lemon   **STEEL TIGER**   Do Khe

Peach   Chanh Hoa   B-52s from Guam
and Okinawa

Udorn
(1965–76)   Nakhon
Phanom   Khe Phat   Dong Hoi

Cherry   (1965–75)   Phu Qui   **YANKEE STATION**
(USAF)   Coral Sea

Blue   Savannakhet   **Demilitarized
Zone**   first air strikes   Hancock
February 1965   Ranger
plus escorts

Hue

THAILAND   STEEL TIGER
(after 1969)   TIGER HOUND   Da Nang
(1962–72)

Takhli
(1964–69)   Ubon
(1965–74)   Pakse

Korat
(1964–76)   Amber   Pleiku
(1962–70)   **SOUTH**

Phu Cat
(1967–71)

Don Muang
Airport
(1964–70)   **VIETNAM**

Bangkok   Tuy Hoa
(1966–70)

Battambang   **CAMBODIA**   Nha Trang
(1962–69)
Cam Ranh Bay
(1965–72)

U Tapao
(1966–76)   Tonle Sap   Phan Rang
(1966–72)

Bien Hoa
(1961–71)

Phnom
Penh   Tan Son Nhut Airport (1961–72)
U.S. Seventh Air Force HQ   **DIXIE STATION**

Saigon

Bin Thuy
(1965–70)   Vung Tau
(1967–70)   **South**

**Mekong
Delta**   **China**

Sea

Black
Green
Orange
Red
White
Green AP
Red
Mekong
Purple
Tan
Yellow
Mango
Grey

20°
16°
12°

2 **the vietnam air war, 1965–72**

U.S. 7th Fleet (Task Force 77)

U.S. air base (jet serviceable)

U.S. air base (non jet serviceable)

U.S. air tanker base

U.S. B-52 base

aerial refuelling tracks and anchor points (AP)

WEST air combat zones (route packages)

North Vietnamese airfield

SAM cover

major Lima site

Chinese buffer zone
(prohibited area)

Operation Rolling Thunder, 2 Mar.–1 Nov. 1968
main targets:;airfields, SAM sites, bridges, and
supply routes
targeting restrictions 1965–68:

Hanoi: prohibited zone: 10 nautical miles
restricted zone: 30 nautical miles
Haiphong: prohibited zone: 4 nautical miles
restricted zone: 10 nautical miles

Operation Linebaker 1, 8 May–23 Oct. 1972
strikes
fewer target restrictions than Rolling Thunder

Operation Linebaker 2, 19–30 Dec. 1972
strikes
unrestricted bombing; all targets of importance
in Hanoi and Haiphong hit

173

1968 to 1975

1968
Tet Offensive (January); battle for Hue (February); Paris peace talks begin (10 May)

1969
U.S. troop withdrawals from Vietnam begin (25 June); bombing of Cambodia begins

1970
Prince Sihanouk overthrown in Cambodia; number of U.S. troops in Vietnam falls to 280,000

1971
South Vietnamese troops in failed thrust into Laos

1972
Nixon cuts troop levels by 70,000; B-52s bomb Hanoi (April)

1973
bombing of North Vietnam halts (15 January); cease-fire signed in Paris (27 January); last U.S. troops leave Vietnam (29 March)

1974
Communists capture much of Mekong Delta

1975
Communists capture Phuoc Long; Hue falls to Communists; Saigon falls (30 April)

Following the Tet Offensive of 1968, the United States sought to disengage from Vietnam and pursued a policy of "Vietnamization," handing increasing responsibility to its local allies. As U.S. troop numbers fell, Vietcong strength increased, leading in 1975 to the inevitable fall of the regime.

The Tet Offensive and the subsequent battle for Hue had significantly undermined the political stability of the southern regime. Not long thereafter, peace talks began in Paris aimed at finding a peaceful settlement for Vietnam. Yet the war was destined finally to be settled on the battlefield: the United States gradually withdrew more and more of its troops, with numbers falling from over 450,000 in 1969, to 280,000 in 1970, and to barely 25,000 at the time of the final U.S. pullout in 1975. The Vietnamese army, increasingly demoralized by its failure to contain the Vietcong and significant territorial losses, began to crumble. U.S. domestic political opposition had started to greatly increase after three years' hard fighting showed no end in sight and the cut-off of aid to South Vietnam set the stage for the eventual North Vietnamese conquest of the south in 1975. Saigon itself fell on 30 April. The war had cost the lives of over 50,000 American troops, more than 200,000 South Vietnamese soldiers, and possibly more than a million on the North Vietnamese side.

Further wars in Indo-china followed. For a while it seemed that prophecies of a "domino effect" whereby pro-Western regimes would fall one-by-one to Communist insurgencies were proving to be accurate. The governments of Cambodia and Laos, with similar profiles to Vietnam of reliance on U.S. military aid, rule by military strongmen, and dissolving legitimacy in rural areas, were simply unable to resist the pressure of peasant-based Communist up-risings. In Laos, the Pathet Lao seized power in 1975, whilst in Cambodia the Khmer Rouge toppled the regime of Lon Nol. Renaming their country Kampuchea, the Khmer Rouge commenced a revolutionary remaking of society through auto-genocide, with up to one-third of the population being slaughtered in three-and-a-half years. Destabilization, ethnic tensions, and ideological rivalry with the Vietnamese led to their invasion of Kampuchea in 1978 to overthrow the genocidal Pol Pot regime. The Chinese, allies of the Khmer Rouge, responded by invading Vietnam, but the Sino-Vietnamese War resulted in a costly repulse at the hands of an outnumbered Vietnamese force.

The Vietnamese waged a counter-guerrilla war in Cambodia against the Khmer Rouge and non-Communist guerrillas through-out the 1980s, trying to keep a friendly government in power in Phnom Penh, but as the Cold War was ending, the Soviet Union could no longer support these operations. The Vietnamese with-drew and a United Nations force moved in and held elections. Despite this, conflict still continued in Cambodia into the 1990s. The last Khmer Rouge elements surrendered in 1999 and stability grad-ually returned, with further elections in 2003.

1 Left to its own devices, the military junta in Saigon had neither the political foundations nor military strength to resist the North Vietnamese invasion in 1975. Retreat became rout: within a month the scramble began to escape to the U.S. fleet offshore.

1   **vietnam, 1975**

Communist-controlled areas (approx.), mid-January 1975

and by 25 March

PAVN advances

frontline, 3 April 1975

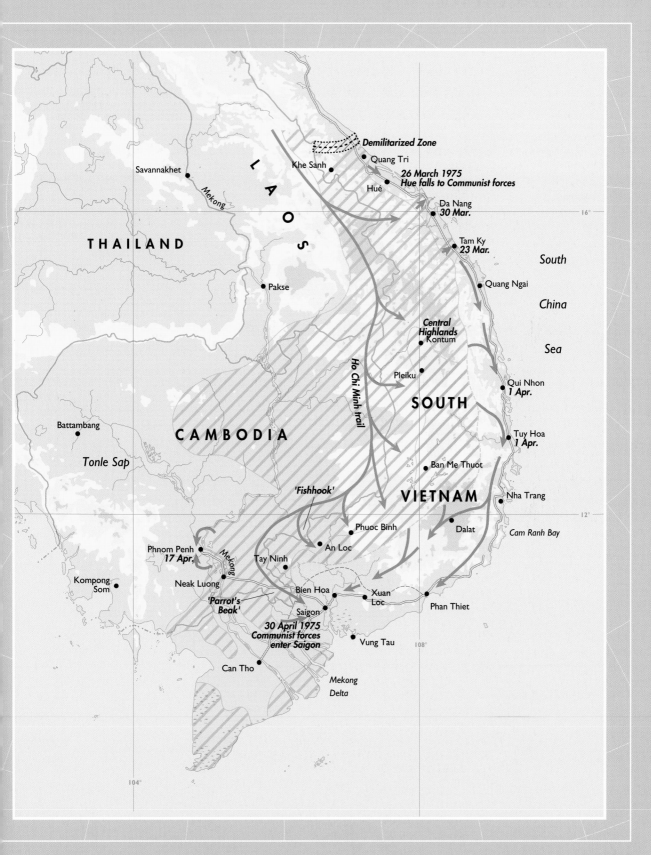

Demilitarized Zone

Quang Tri

26 March 1975
Hue falls to Communist forces

Khe Sanh

Hué

Savannakhet

Mekong

L A O S

Da Nang
30 Mar.

Tam Ky
23 Mar.

THAILAND

Quang Ngai

South

Pakse

China

*Central
Highlands*
Kontum

Sea

Pleiku

Ho Chi Minh trail

SOUTH

Qui Nhon
1 Apr.

Battambang

Tuy Hoa
1 Apr.

Tonle Sap

CAMBODIA

Ban Me Thuot

Nha Trang

VIETNAM

'Fishhook'

Phuoc Binh

Dalat

Cam Ranh Bay

Phnom Penh
17 Apr.

Mekong

Tay Ninh

An Loc

Xuan
Loc

Kompong
Som

Neak Luong

Bien Hoa

Phan Thiet

**'Parrot's
Beak'**

Saigon

30 April 1975
**Communist forces
enter Saigon**

Vung Tau

Can Tho

*Mekong
Delta*

the **soviet war** in **afghanistan**

The Soviet Union waged the Cold War through a number of invasions—including those of Hungary in 1956, Czechoslovakia in 1968, and Afghanistan in 1979—and the threat of potential ones, most notably that of Western Europe.

The three actual invasions were all aimed at replacing nominally pro-Soviet governments that were not following the course set by Moscow. All three invasions demonstrated the Soviet operational thinking that would also have been seen in an invasion of Europe: pre-empt resistance wherever possible; move to decapitate enemy centres of resistance; stress speed and shock of advance.

In Hungary (after considerable fighting) and Czechoslovakia, the invasions succeeded, after a fashion, but in the long run the political damage caused by the military action outweighed this success. When Moscow's East European empire came apart in 1989, no one was willing to take up arms in its defense. The fall of the Soviet empire itself was to follow in two years. It was economics rather than the clash of arms that decided the Cold War.

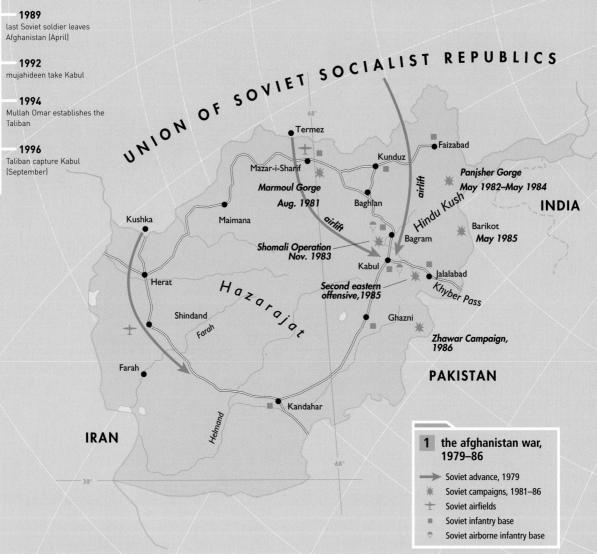

1 the afghanistan war, 1979–86

→ Soviet advance, 1979
✳ Soviet campaigns, 1981–86
✈ Soviet airfields
▪ Soviet infantry base
◇ Soviet airborne infantry base

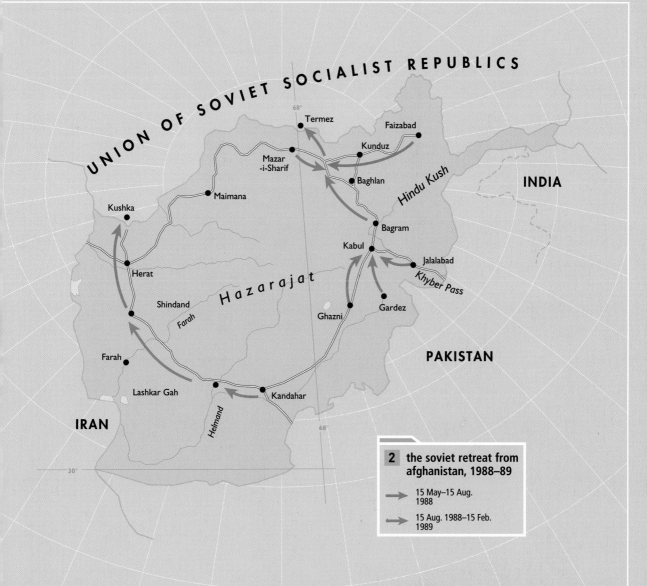

UNION OF SOVIET SOCIALIST REPUBLICS

68°

Termez

Faizabad

Kunduz

Mazar
-i-Sharif

Baghlan

INDIA

Maimana

Hindu Kush

Kushka

Bagram

Kabul

Herat

Jalalabad

Khyber Pass

Shindand

H a z a r a j a t

Farah

Ghazni

Gardez

PAKISTAN

Farah

Lashkar Gah

Kandahar

Helmand

IRAN

68°

30°

| 2 | the soviet retreat from afghanistan, 1988–89 |

→ 15 May–15 Aug. 1988

→ 15 Aug. 1988–15 Feb. 1989

The invasion of Afghanistan in December 1979 was intended as a short, surgical operation to restore a pro-Soviet regime in Kabul. It degenerated into a protracted guerrilla war that the Soviet army was never able to win.

After the withdrawal of Soviet forces, the guerrilla armies fought among themselves for control of the country, until the mujahideen government was overthrown by the Taliban in 1996.

Afghanistan was to the Soviet Union what the Boer War was to the British Empire or Vietnam was to the United States. Unlike those, however, the Soviet Union did not survive its frustrating, costly war. Afghanistan has been described as the "fatal pebble" that finally tripped up the stumbling Soviet colossus. Afghan resistance represented the largest national rising of the century. While the Afghan guerrillas lacked organization and training throughout the war—they did not aim to create their own Dien Bien Phu—they had the advantage of large-scale support from the Soviet Union's Cold War opponents, becoming another proxy war, and strong Islamic faith to provide motivation.

Wars of national liberation have often been followed by civil wars that can prove even more costly, and Afghanistan has been no exception. The Soviets invaded in 1979, waged a frustrating firepower-intensive war for many years, and started to withdraw in 1987, completing that withdrawal in 1989. Afghan civil wars followed from 1989 to 2001. Then, the U.S. intervened to oust the Taliban regime (holding Kabul since 1996) and their Al-Qaeda terrorist allies, leading to the first (relative) peace since 1978.

1982 to 1989

2 April 1982
Argentine navy lands thousands of troops on Falklands; British Royal Marine detachment surrenders

3 April 1982
Argentines seize South Georgia

25 April 1982
British commando force recaptures South Georgia

2 May 1982
Argentine cruiser *General Belgrano* sunk

25 May 1982
HMS *Coventry* sunk off the Falklands

28 May 1982
Battle of Goose Green: 200 Argentine soldiers killed

14 June 1982
Argentine garrison in Port Stanley surrenders (nearly 10,000 troops)

1983
U.S. invasion of Grenada

1989
U.S. intervention in Panama to overthrow General Noriega

Western interventions of the 1980s were not directly connected with conflict with the Soviet Union in the last decade of the Cold War but made a contribution to its outcome. Most notable was the British war to reclaim the Falkland Islands after their invasion by Argentina in 1982.

The Falklands was not the war on the north German plain or the streets of Ulster for which British forces had trained. As so often throughout history, the war that had to be fought was not the war that had been planned. The result put a premium on improvisation and the logistics capability that, far from being mere "tail," made victory possible thousands of miles from any base in the South Atlantic. It also underlined the continued importance of quality of military forces, especially when not undercut by technological weakness.

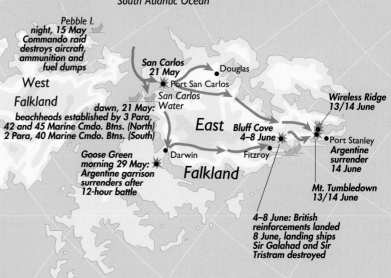

1 the falklands war, 1982

- – – British maritime exclusion zone
- British ships sunk
- Argentine ship sunk
- → main British advance
- ✳ principal engagement, with date

1 "The empire strikes back," as more than one serviceman observed when British forces splashed ashore to liberate the Falklands. The Argentine junta gambled that it would not come to a shooting war, so failed to extend the Port Stanley runway for fast jets, leaving their garrison to rely on air support from the distant mainland. In the naval war, the Argentine fleet withdrew to harbor after the British submarine *Conqueror* sank the cruiser *General Belgrano*.

In many ways, the Falklands was a low-technology conflict. The British infantry had to fight their way into Port Stanley in a series of hill battles, relying on finely honed tactics rather than firepower or technological advantage. Infantry patrols carried out reconnaissance that today would be carried out by electronic means of pilotless aircraft. Yet the Argentine air force failed in its attempt to defeat the British invasion force, despite inflicting painful casualties. Brave men in low-technology aircraft lacked the supporting infrastructure of modern air war: the tankers, jamming planes, anti-radiation missiles, and the like. Argentina's greatest successes came from the use of Exocet air-launched anti-ship guided missiles.

The U.S., overcoming the aftermath of its defeat in Vietnam, increased its capability to carry out unilateral actions, including the failed Iranian hostage rescue of 1979, the landing on Grenada in 1983, clashes with Libya in 1981 and 1986, and the intervention in Panama in 1989. There was also the abortive multinational force in Beirut in 1982–83, withdrawn after the U.S. and French contingents suffered heavy losses to suicide terrorist bombings.

2 Advancing across terrain remarkably similar to the training areas in Wales used by the British forces, the British Army broke the Argentine defenses outside Stanley on the eve of the Antarctic winter. Both sides used similar weapons, but Britain's long-service professionals made short work of inexperienced conscripts. The trend since the 1980s has been towards smaller, professional armies instead of the conscript armies once favored by Western industrialized nations.

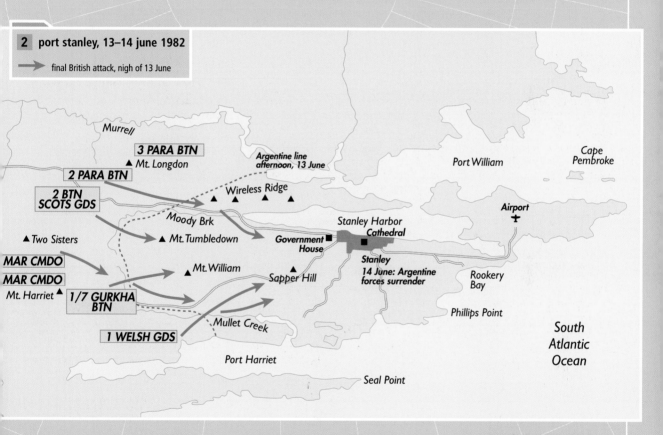

2 port stanley, 13–14 june 1982

final British attack, nigh of 13 June

These interventions had implications for the course of the Cold War beyond their limited military significance. Along with the policy of supporting those indigenous groups resisting the Soviet Union and its allies—most notably in Afghanistan—these actions demonstrated that the West was not permanently put on the defensive. The Soviets had hoped to achieve this by the shift in the "correlation of forces" emerging with the attainment of nuclear parity, by Vietnam, and by the potential erosion of support for the military implementation of the strategy of containment the West had tried to implement since the early 1950s. These interventions also showed the way to later "out of area" actions such as the Gulf War in 1990–91 and Kosovo in 1999.

the **iran–iraq war** and the **gulf war**

1979
Iranian revolution: brings Ayatollah Khomeini to power

1980
Iraq invades Iran

1982
Iranian counter-offensive pushes Iraqis back to their borders

1988
cease fire brings end to war

1990
Iraq invades Kuwait (August)

1991
coalition air attacks on Iraq; ground offensive starts (24 Feb.); Iraq accepts cease fire (3 Apr.)

The regions bordering the Persian Gulf increased in strategic importance with the first oil shortage of 1973–74. Iran, then under the shah, increased its armed forces, looking to assure its regional dominance, but the Iranian revolution of 1979 brought a radical Islamic government to power. The hostage crisis of 1979–81 brought U.S. forces to the region and, after the war in Afghanistan started in 1979, superpower tensions. The "Carter Doctrine" and the organization of the Rapid Deployment Force, later Central Command, put then-weakened U.S. credibility on the line for Gulf stability.

With Iran in disorder, the weaker but aggressive regime of Saddam Hussein in Iraq saw a chance for a military victory and, in 1980, invaded, starting the Iran–Iraq War. In years of bitter fighting and battles of attrition, the Iran–Iraq War included the first mutual use of chemical weapons since 1918 and mutual use of ballistic missiles in the "war of the cities" until Iran, finally exhausted, sued for peace.

Saddam's goal of regional domination was still unrealized when, in August 1990, he invaded and occupied Kuwait, to which Iraq had long-standing claims. Saudi Arabia and the Gulf States, now threatened by their former protector, asked for foreign help. The bulk of the foreign troops were from the U.S., but support came also from Britain, France, Egypt, and Syria. Aircraft arrived from even more allies.

1 the iran–iraq war, 1980–88

- non-belligerent countries supporting Iraq
- non-belligerent countries supporting Iran
- Iraqi penetration, Dec. 1980–June 1982
- southern limit of maritime exclusion zone declared by Iraq, Aug. 1982
- Iranian penetration, with dates
- ✳ bombed or attacked by missiles
- Ⓐ centers of oil industry
- frontline at cease-fire, July 1988
- Kurdish ethnic areas
- Arab ethnic areas in Iran
- Shia-inhabited territory in Iraq

1 Saddam Hussein took advantage of the Iranian revolution, invading the oil fields in the hope that the weakened Iranian forces would be no match for his well-equipped army. But Iraqi reluctance to take casualties and the fanaticism of the Iranian Revolutionary Guards led the offensive to break down. A 10-year war of attrition followed, with both sides attacking foreign oil tankers plying the gulf. The destruction of an Iranian airliner by the USS *Vincennes* inspired a wave of terrorist attacks against the West.

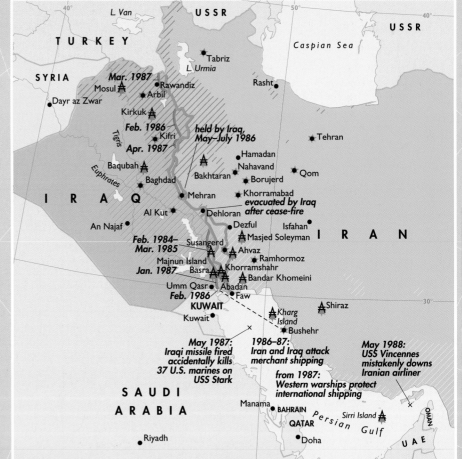

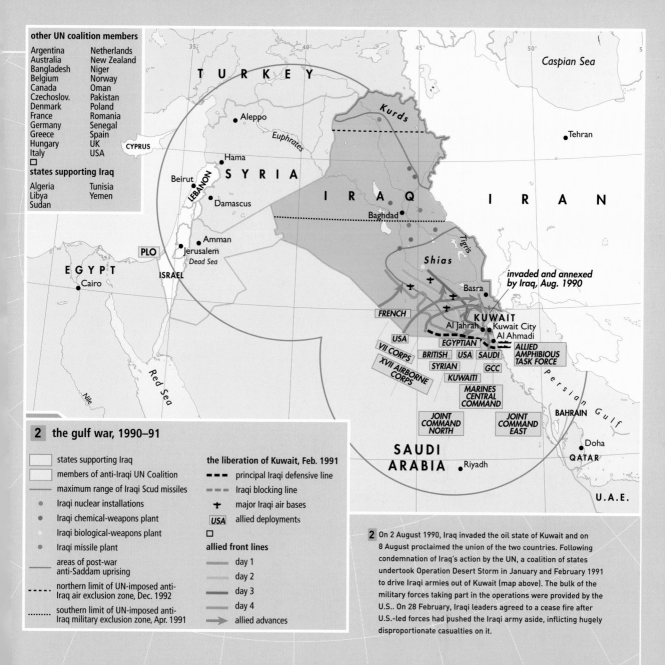

other UN coalition members

Argentina	Netherlands
Australia	New Zealand
Bangladesh	Niger
Belgium	Norway
Canada	Oman
Czechoslov.	Pakistan
Denmark	Poland
France	Romania
Germany	Senegal
Greece	Spain
Hungary	UK
Italy	USA
☐	

states supporting Iraq

Algeria	Tunisia
Libya	Yemen
Sudan	

2 the gulf war, 1990–91

☐	states supporting Iraq
☐	members of anti-Iraqi UN Coalition
——	maximum range of Iraqi Scud missiles
●	Iraqi nuclear installations
●	Iraqi chemical-weapons plant
○	Iraqi biological-weapons plant
●	Iraqi missile plant
——	areas of post-war anti-Saddam uprising
- - - -	northern limit of UN-imposed anti-Iraq air exclusion zone, Dec. 1992
··········	southern limit of UN-imposed anti-Iraq military exclusion zone, Apr. 1991

the liberation of Kuwait, Feb. 1991

- - - principal Iraqi defensive line
- - - Iraqi blocking line
✛ major Iraqi air bases
USA allied deployments
☐

allied front lines

—— day 1
—— day 2
—— day 3
—— day 4
➜ allied advances

2 On 2 August 1990, Iraq invaded the oil state of Kuwait and on 8 August proclaimed the union of the two countries. Following condemnation of Iraq's action by the UN, a coalition of states undertook Operation Desert Storm in January and February 1991 to drive Iraqi armies out of Kuwait (map above). The bulk of the military forces taking part in the operations were provided by the U.S.. On 28 February, Iraqi leaders agreed to a cease fire after U.S.-led forces had pushed the Iraqi army aside, inflicting hugely disproportionate casualties on it.

A lengthy build-up and diplomatic efforts were followed by a 40-day air bombardment and a ground offensive that swiftly evicted Iraq from Kuwait. The Gulf War of 1991 was a unique event. It represented a coalition effort not seen since the Second World War. The movement of large-scale mechanized forces from the U.S., Europe, and the Middle East to the Gulf was possible due to the in-place infrastructure and the six months between the invasion of Kuwait and the opening of the land war. While it featured many elements of the digital revolution incorporated in operational and tactical war-fighting, it probably represented at best a transitional stage, with the armed forces of the Cold War and the modern eras fighting their last large-scale conventional battle.

The military situation became less clear-cut after the cease-fire. Allied forces intervened to support Kurds in the north of Iraq, but not when Saddam slaughtered Shia opponents in the south. No-fly zones were imposed in both the north and the south of Iraq, and the country's skies were patrolled for over a decade by allied air forces. International alarm at Iraq's massive stocks of chemical and biological weapons, the Scud missiles fired during the war, and how close Iraq had come to a nuclear weapon led to the imposition of an intrusive arms-control verification regime. Limited attacks since 1991, largely by U.S. and British forces, were provoked by continued Iraqi non-compliance with UN resolutions, especially as to their weapons of mass destruction, and action against the Kurds. Saddam's alleged continued efforts at acquiring weapons of mass destruction and supposed links to terrorism were to prompt a U.S.–UK-led coalition to invade Iraq and oust Saddam in 2003.

the **civil wars** in **yugoslavia**

1990 to 1999

1987
Slobodan Milosevic comes to power in Serbia

25 June 1991
Slovenia and Croatia declare independence

July 1991
war between Croatia and Serbia

April 1992
Bosnia declares independence; civil war breaks out

August 1995
NATO warplanes attack Serb positions in Bosnia; Croats retake the Krajina

1995
Dayton Peace Accord

1998–99
Serb massacres of Albanians in Kosovo prompt international outcry

March 1999
NATO launches air strikes on Yugoslavia

June 1999
Yugoslav forces evacuate Kosovo

Peacekeeping and peacemaking are largely about what comes after failure. When wars themselves fail in their aim of achieving political goals by Clausewitz's "other means," the underlying conflicts remain.

Peacekeeping was a product of the end of the Cold War. During the Cold War, the realities of the global balance meant that the use of the military in peacekeeping would either be purely domestic (such as in the British commitment of forces to Northern Ireland, starting in 1969) or in peripheral conflicts when neither superpower had heavy investments in one side (the Congo, Cyprus, south Lebanon). In these years, the use of military observers to assure impartial application of disengagement provisions was also used.

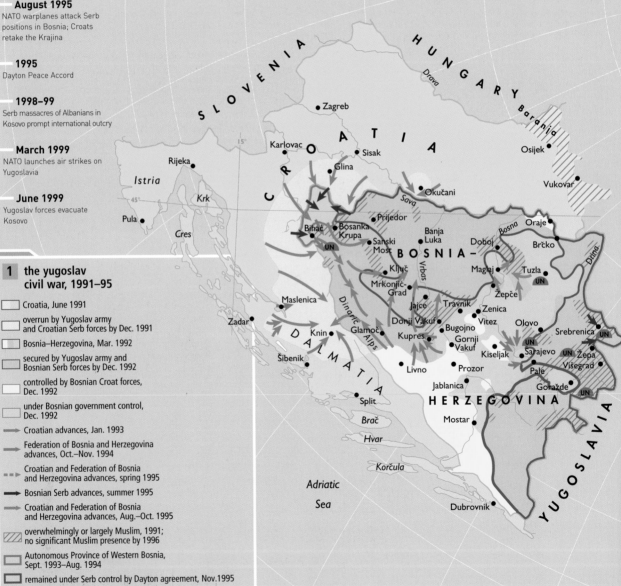

1 the yugoslav civil war, 1991–95

- Croatia, June 1991
- overrun by Yugoslav army and Croatian Serb forces by Dec. 1991
- Bosnia–Herzegovina, Mar. 1992
- secured by Yugoslav army and Bosnian Serb forces by Dec. 1992
- controlled by Bosnian Croat forces, Dec. 1992
- under Bosnian government control, Dec. 1992
- → Croatian advances, Jan. 1993
- → Federation of Bosnia and Herzegovina advances, Oct.–Nov. 1994
- ⇢ Croatian and Federation of Bosnia and Herzegovina advances, spring 1995
- → Bosnian Serb advances, summer 1995
- → Croatian and Federation of Bosnia and Herzegovina advances, Aug.–Oct. 1995
- ⬚ overwhelmingly or largely Muslim, 1991; no significant Muslim presence by 1996
- Autonomous Province of Western Bosnia, Sept. 1993–Aug. 1994
- remained under Serb control by Dayton agreement, Nov.1995
- ⬚ returned to Croatian control 1997 under Zagreb agreement
- **UN** UN-designated "safe areas"

1 The former Yugoslav federal republic of Bosnia and Herzegovina declared its independence in March 1992. There followed three-and-a-half years of civil war between the Muslim, Serb, and Croat populations, with interventions from Croatia and Serbia (map below left). In 1992 the United Nations sent peacekeeping forces, and in November 1995 NATO intervened to keep the warring peoples apart and impose a peace settlement.

2 In 1990 the government of Slobodan Milosevic canceled the autonomy that Kosovo had enjoyed within Serbia. Pressure for its restoration grew. In 1998 a low-level guerrilla war between the Albanian KLA and Serb security forces escalated sharply (map below). At peace talks in France in 1998–99 the Albanian side accepted and the Serbs repudiated peace terms. As massacres of Albanians continued, pressure for NATO action mounted. On 24 March, NATO bombers attacked Serbia, beginning an 11-week campaign. Yugoslav security forces responded by forcing Albanians from their homes, looting, and killing. In early June, Milosevic capitulated: his forces left Kosovo, and 40,000 NATO peacekeeping troops took over.

Post–Cold War peacekeeping and peacemaking covers a broad spectrum. Of the interventions into failed states, the multinational force in Somalia stands out as both an example of the potential for humanitarian relief—preventing imminent starvation when internal fighting interfered with food distribution—and of the inevitability that the peacekeepers would become involved in the local fighting, most notably in a bloody battle in Mogadishu with U.S. Army Rangers that prompted the U.S. withdrawal.

Russia's peacekeeping and peacemaking interventions in the former Soviet Union have never been impartial. In Moldova, Georgia, and Tajikistan, however, safeguarding Moscow's interests coincided with reducing the level of violence. In Chechnya, attempted secession from Russia was met with an inept attempt to use massed force and intense firepower to defeat resilient and hard-fighting guerrillas. The Russians were forced to grant the Chechens de facto independence, though they have never received international recognition. A resumption of Russia's war in Chechnya remains unresolved.

The most intensive use of international peacekeeping and peacekeeping forces after the Cold War has been in the former Yugoslavia. International forces have operated in Croatia, Bosnia–Herzegovina, Macedonia, and Kosovo. In Bosnia, the initial commitment of peace-keepers under UN auspices proved ineffective in halting the conflict; the UN was never set up to be an effective military decision maker. After the military defeat of Serb forces in Croatia and Bosnia, a NATO bombing campaign led to the Dayton Accord, UN peacekeepers were replaced by a NATO-led stabilization force. In Kosovo, peacemaking, in the form of a 78-day bombing campaign (notable for its lack of aircrew casualties and use of precision weapons), was followed by peacekeeping in the form of a multinational NATO-led force.

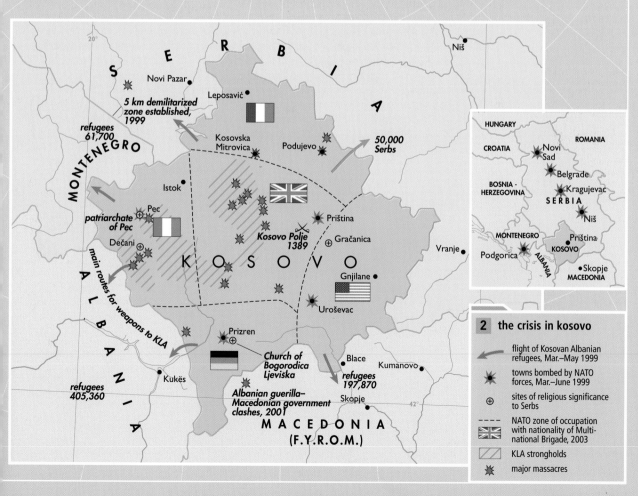

2 the crisis in kosovo

↖ flight of Kosovan Albanian refugees, Mar.–May 1999

✴ towns bombed by NATO forces, Mar.–June 1999

⊕ sites of religious significance to Serbs

- - - - NATO zone of occupation with nationality of Multi-national Brigade, 2003

⧅ KLA strongholds

✴ major massacres

chechnya, afghanistan, and iraq

1991 to 2003

1991
Chechen leader Dzhokar Dudayev declares Chechnya independent

1994
first Russian invasion of Chechnya

1995
Russian troops take Grozny

1996
Khasavyurt agreement ends First Chechen War

1998
Iraq withdraws cooperation with UN weapons inspectors (January); Operation Desert Fox, intensive air strikes on Iraq (16–19 December)

1999
Chechen attack on Dagestan; Russia launches second invasion of Chechnya

2001
terrorist attacks on U.S. (11 September); U.S. air attacks on Afghanistan begin (7 October); Northern Alliance take Mazar-e-Sharif (9 November), Kabul (12th), Herat (12th), and Jalalabad (14th); Kunduz falls to Northern Alliance (25 November); last Taliban stronghold at Kandahar falls (6 December)

2002
UN weapons inspectors arrive back in Baghdad (18 November); U.S. accuses Baghdad of being in "material breach" of UN resolution on weapons inspections (19 December)

March 2003
U.S. air strikes on Baghdad begin, Coalition ground forces enter Iraq at Faw Peninsula (20th); port of Umm Qasr seized by U.S. troops; heavy fighting around Nasiriya and Basra (24th); U.S. forces reach Euphrates at Samarra (27th)

April 2003
U.S. troops surround Karbala (2nd); U.S. troops reach Baghdad airport (3rd); British forces enter Basra (6th); Baghdad falls to U.S. forces (9th); Kirkuk falls to Kurdish fighters (10th); Mosul falls (11th); last major town in control of Iraqi Army,Tikrit, falls to U.S. Marines (15th)

The increasingly disparate and diffuse challenges faced by military planners since the Cold War ended is amply demonstrated by the range and scope of the conflicts that have erupted in the early 21st century.

The violent nationalist tensions that had emerged in the wake of the break-up of the Soviet empire continued to engage Russian forces in a bitter guerrilla war in Chechnya. In Afghanistan, following the 11 September 2001 attacks on the U.S., the American government was forced into action to oust the Taliban and Al-Qaeda in a mixture of a post-imperialist policing expedition and a very modern intelligence war to exterminate the multi-headed threat of religiously inspired international terrorism. Meanwhile, in 2003, the U.S. fought a more conventional war in Iraq, ostensibly to prevent that country gaining unconventional weapons of mass destruction.

The Chechen conflict had its origins in the collapse of the Soviet Union in 1991. Chechen Nationalists under Dzhokar Dudeyev declared the Caucasus republic's independence. A stand-off ensued, ended only by a massive Russian invasion in 1994. The assault on the Chechen capital of Grozny underlined the limitations of poorly trained conscripts with little real intelligence and an over-reliance on heavy armor. In the urban landscape of Grozny, the Russian tanks turned into deathtraps. Eventually the Chechen resistance was pushed out, but continued vigorous resistance in the mountainous south of the republic ultimately forced a cease fire and Russian withdrawal in 1996. Impatient at cross-border terrorist attacks, Russia again invaded in 1999. Lighter, more maneuverable columns and long-range artillery bombardments sapped Chechen resistance in the urban areas but, once more, the Russians failed to subdue the southern mountain regions and guerrilla attacks have caused a constant stream of Russian casualties.

In Afghanistan in 2001, the U.S. seemed to have learnt the lesson of previous foreign forays into south Asia. Unable to rely on the full spectrum of its high-tech weaponry or to bring massive force to bear in difficult terrain, the U.S. relied on local proxies (the Northern Alliance) with knowledge of the battlefield and everything to gain by overthrowing the Taliban regime. Sustained air strikes against which the Taliban had no defense or reply, and the targeted use of Special Forces to bolster the patchy tactical abilities of U.S. allies, meant that the Taliban regime folded like a pack of cards. Just, however, as past imperial powers have found in the region, victory has not brought stability and Osama bin Laden and other leading lights of the Al-Qaeda terrorist movement against which the assault had been aimed slipped away to menace U.S. interests from even more impenetrable or inscrutable hideouts.

In Iraq, too, in 2003, the U.S. found that, in 21st-century terms, winning the war can potentially mean losing the battle. Saddam Hussein's refusal to cooperate with UN inspectors gave rise to the belief that his regime was hiding weapons of mass destruction, and the Iraqi dictator did nothing to dispel this impression. By March 2003, the momentum for war was unstoppable. This time the coalition was much smaller in terms of member countries and number of

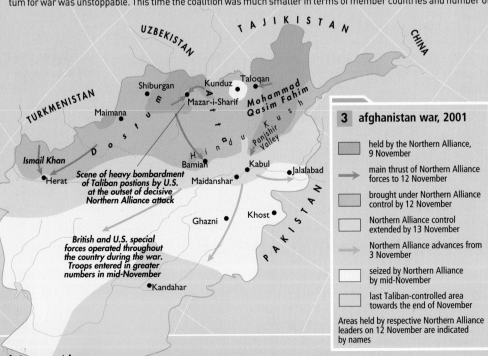

Scene of heavy bombardment of Taliban postions by U.S. at the outset of decisive Northern Alliance attack

British and U.S. special forces operated throughout the country during the war. Troops entered in greater numbers in mid-November

3 afghanistan war, 2001

- held by the Northern Alliance, 9 November
- main thrust of Northern Alliance forces to 12 November
- brought under Northern Alliance control by 12 November
- Northern Alliance control extended by 13 November
- Northern Alliance advances from 3 November
- seized by Northern Alliance by mid-November
- last Taliban-controlled area towards the end of November

Areas held by respective Northern Alliance leaders on 12 November are indicated by names

2 war in chechnya

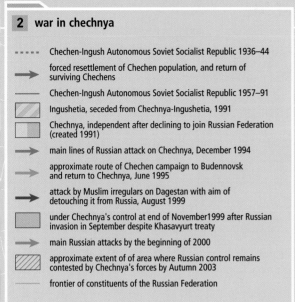

- - - - Chechen-Ingush Autonomous Soviet Socialist Republic 1936–44

⟶ forced resettlement of Chechen population, and return of surviving Chechens

——— Chechen-Ingush Autonomous Soviet Socialist Republic 1957–91

▨ Ingushetia, seceded from Chechnya-Ingushetia, 1991

▧ Chechnya, independent after declining to join Russian Federation (created 1991)

⟶ main lines of Russian attack on Chechnya, December 1994

⟶ approximate route of Chechen campaign to Budennovsk and return to Chechnya, June 1995

⟶ attack by Muslim irregulars on Dagestan with aim of detouching it from Russia, August 1999

▨ under Chechnya's control at end of November1999 after Russian invasion in September despite Khasavyurt treaty

⟶ main Russian attacks by the beginning of 2000

▨ approximate extent of of area where Russian control remains contested by Chechnya's forces by Autumn 2003

——— frontier of constituents of the Russian Federation

3 The United States began air attacks on Afghanistan in October 2001. By early November, America's Northern Alliance partners had begun advancing in earnest and the Taliban regime crumbled. Within a month its last stronghold at Kandahar had fallen (map below left).

2 In the aftermath of the collapse of the Soviet Union in 1991, Nationalist leaders in Chechnya took advantage of the chaos to declare independence. A Russian invasion in 1994 to reassert control ended with bitter street fighting for the capital Grozny and the withdrawal of the Russian Army (map above right). A further invasion in 1999 succeeded in establishing a more lasting Russian presence, but large areas of the republic eluded Moscow's control, while continuing Chechen guerrilla and terrorist campaigns claimed large numbers of Russian lives both inside and outside Chechnya.

forces than in 1991. After some initial stiff resistance in the south, the Iraqi Army's élite formations simply evaporated rather than fight street-by-street for Baghdad. All the U.S. Army's smart weaponry, and ruthlessly effective war-fighting tactics which delivered victory at the cost of little over 100 American losses, could not staunch a growing Iraqi resistance, which seemed united in little save its distaste for the foreign occupiers. The U.S. Army had become unrivaled in its capacity to fight and to win wars, but its ability to win the battle for hearts and minds was far less developed. The U.S. military machine was left feeling unchallenged but unloved.

1 Saddam Hussein was allowed to survive the 1991 Gulf War, but without international consensus on further action against his regime. He was finally overthrown in 2003 (map right).

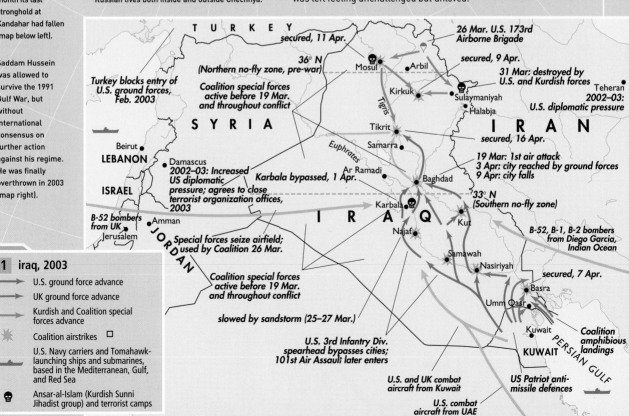

1 iraq, 2003

⟶ U.S. ground force advance

⟶ UK ground force advance

⟶ Kurdish and Coalition special forces advance

✳ Coalition airstrikes ☐

⛴ U.S. Navy carriers and Tomahawk-launching ships and submarines, based in the Mediterranean, Gulf, and Red Sea

☠ Ansar-al-Islam (Kurdish Sunni Jihadist group) and terrorist camps

future war

Future war will be shaped by a range of postmodern changes in politics, culture, and society, as well as by technology. Non-state actors have become as powerful on the world stage today as they were in the pre-industrial age. Transnational threats include international crime, narcotics, and even population flow. Organized crime and terrorism have demonstrated their ability to shake even developed governments. They have the capability to affect the quality of life of the citizens of even the most comfortable developed countries. In the developing world, they can bring down governments and fuel insurgencies. A war against terrorism has dominated U.S. policy since the September 2001 attacks.

Subnational threats had been submerged in the larger conflicts of 1914–91, but were seldom resolved by them. The nationalism and violence of Northern Ireland, Serbia and Bosnia–Herzegovina, and elsewhere showed that violence within states was more likely to have an impact on those outside once the damping effects of the Cold War and the firewalls of superpower patronage had been removed.

State threats, however, may well return, more potentially deadly for having access to new weapons technology. The superpowers used the deterrent combination of missiles and weapons of mass destruction to wage a war without mass violence. It is uncertain whether these weapons will have the same effect when interjected in regional rivalries.

Other proliferation is less easy to project. In addition to the widespread information-age technologies now in the world's armed forces—the U.S. Air Force has more computers than personnel—a range of spin-offs is emerging. Intelligence—vital ever since the radio was introduced—has now grown into "information warfare," seeking to use these new technologies while denying their benefits to an opponent.

2 Intermediate-range ballistic missiles are becoming cheaper and more plentiful, and the technology to add a nuclear tip to them is available on the Internet. The end of the cold war has ushered in a new age of anxiety (map below).

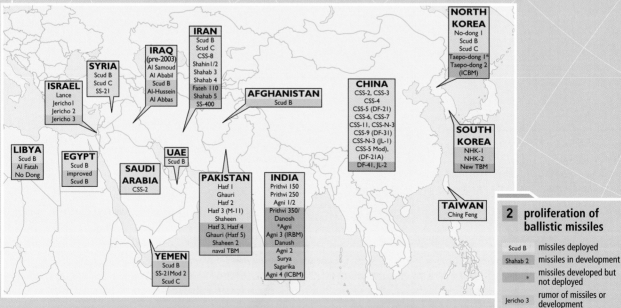

2 proliferation of ballistic missiles

Scud B	missiles deployed
Shahab 2	missiles in development
*	missiles developed but not deployed
Jericho 3	rumor of missiles or development

1 Guerrilla wars followed the withdrawal of European powers from their empires and the cold war tendency to fight wars by proxy. At the same time, established states in South America and Europe have faced internal threats from terrorist organizations (map below). Of course, one man's terrorist is another man's freedom fighter, and many such groups have been sustained by foreign money. In South America and Germany, robust action against the terrorists did not produce the populist revolt anticipated by the Marxists: it led to their extinction.

Technological change will affect war in the post-industrial age. The major weapon systems themselves may reflect the more mature technologies of the late industrial age. The U.S. Air Force currently plans to fly its B-52 bombers until they reach 80 years of age.

But even if it is believed that the bombers of the future will look much like those of today, other more dynamic areas will be making fundamental changes in the way wars are fought. Smaller and cheaper micro-circuitry, nanotechnology, and biotechnology advances are already finding their way to the battlefield.

The spread of ballistic missiles and weapons of mass destruction—nuclear, biological and chemical—beyond developed nations will likely soon allow even poor, weak countries (such as North Korea) to threaten rich, strong ones and has motivated the United States to start the development of missile defenses.

Since the Cold War ended, war has ranged from the highly technological and practically bloodless (for the practitioner) conflict waged in aid of sophisticated statecraft (as in the NATO operations against Kosovo), to religiously motivated terrorism (as in Al-Qaeda's strikes).

1 terrorist challenges, 1945–2003

- successful Marxist revolutions involving terrorism, with date
- unsuccessful Marxist terrorist challenges, with date and name of group
- Nationalist, Communist, and religious terrorist challenges, with date and name of group
- detected terrorist biological weapons facility

Index